TO GAVIN
you are doing a great job.
keep up the good work.
I hope this book Answer
some questions.
love
Sistah
Maria
Beginner SS Teacher

THE ONE YEAR
BOOK OF

Fun & Active
Devotions for Kids

The ONE YEAR®
BOOK OF

Fun & Active
Devotions for

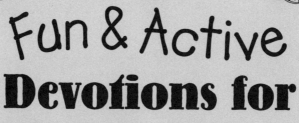

Kids

by
Betsy Elliot

TYNDALE KIDS

Tyndale House Publishers, Inc.
Wheaton Illinois

Visit Tyndale's exciting Web site at www.tyndale.com

Edited by Betty Free

Designed by Jackie Noe

Produced for Tyndale by Lightwave Publishing and The Livingstone Corporation. David R. Veerman, Livingstone project editor; Ed Strauss, Lightwave project editor

Adapted from the 101 Questions Children Ask series. Livingstone writers and contributors: David R. Veerman, M.Div., James C. Galvin, Ed.D., James C. Wilhoit, Ph.D., Bruce B. Barton, D.Min., Daryl J. Lucas, Jonathan Farrar, J. Alan Sharrer. Lightwave writers and contributors: Richard Osborne, Ed Strauss

---

Library of Congress Cataloging-in-Publication Data

Elliot, Betsy Rossen.
   One year book of fun and active devotions for kids / activity writer, Betsy Elliot ; illustrator, Lillian Crump.
      p. cm
   ISBN 0-8423-1976-X
      1. Christian children—Prayer-books and devotions—English. 2. Devotional calendars—Juvenile literature.
   [1. Prayer books and devotions. 2. Devotional calendars.] I. Crump, Lil, ill. II. Title.

   BV8470 .E44 2000
   242'.62—dc21   00-028677

Printed in the United States of America

06   05   04   03   02   01
 7   6   5   4   3

CONTENTS

25 Why do people put garbage in their heads by watching bad movies?

26 Why can't we put new books in the Bible?

27 Why do people worship idols instead of God?

28 Why do people pray to idols?

29 Why do countries fight wars with each other?

30 Is God happy for one country and sad for the other at the end of a war?

31 What's a parable?

June

1 Why do we have marriage?

2 If Jesus doesn't want us to get hurt, why did he tell us to chop our hands off and poke our eyes out?

3 My parents want me to play a certain sport, but I hate it. What should I do?

4 Why does my coach care so much about winning? It's not fun anymore.

5 Do we have to pray to be forgiven?

6 What are some good things to do when you're not in school?

7 Will God be with me all the time in heaven?

8 Why does eternity last for a long, long, long, long time?

9 Why do people kill animals to eat when they could just buy food at the store?

10 Why doesn't God just give us money when we need it?

11 How do poor people get poor?

12 Why did the Israelites who left Egypt have to wander in the wilderness until they died?

13 Is it OK to keep a toy that belongs to someone else if they don't ask for it back?

14 Who invented vegetables?

15 Do I really have to eat my vegetables or are my parents just making sure I clean my plate?

16 If we prayed to find something we lost, would we really find it?

17 I want to be with my friends. Why do we have to go to church so much?

18 Do angels get tired?

19 What should I say if someone makes fun of the Bible?

20 What mean things does Satan do to people?

21 Are demons red with horns and long tails?

22 Why did Jesus appear to Saul?

23 If I put money in a savings account, can I get it back?

24 How is God always there?

25 How will the world end?

26 Why doesn't God give us some things we pray for?

27 What happens to people who don't go to church?

28 Is it all right to throw rocks at someone who threw rocks at you?

29 How much do investments cost?

30 What if the waiter gives me a kid's meal free because he thinks I'm younger than I really am?

July

1 Does God have a sense of humor?

2 Why do my friends break their promises to me?

3 If the law says something is right but God says it's wrong, who's right?

4 It's a free country—why do we pay tolls?

5 Why are some kids so big and other kids so small?

6 What if I don't like the music that everyone else listens to?

7 In heaven, we don't just sing and worship all day, do we?

8 Why do I feel afraid if Jesus is with me?

9 Was Samson a good guy or a bad guy?

10 Why did Samson tell Delilah his secret?

11 If I break something that belongs to someone else but fix it, do I have to tell what I did?

12 Why can't I have everyone as a friend?

13 Why do I have to give money to church?

14 Where does the money I give to church go?

15 Why do some people die before they are old?

16 Why hasn't God told us when Jesus is coming back?

17 How will I know what I want to do when I grow up?

18 Should people stay at a good paying job that they don't like?

19 Why is there a universe?

20 Why do people want to fly to other planets?

21 Why is it wrong to be bad?

22 Is God sad when I do something wrong?

23 What does God want me to do when I do what's wrong?

24 Why are some people different from others?

25 Is it OK to tell people to shut up if they are being jerks?

26 Why are some countries rich and others poor?

27 My friend's parents are getting a divorce. What can I do?

28 Doesn't God ever get tired of answering prayers?

29 Does it matter how much faith we have?

30 Is it selfish to save money?

31 Why do some people spend every cent they get right away?

August

1 What's so bad about wanting to wear clothes that are in style?

2 If you don't like something a person wears and they ask you if you like it, are you supposed to tell them the truth?

3 How was God created?

4 How can God be three persons and one person at the same time?

5 How did God make Adam and Eve?

6 Why did Eve disobey God when she knew she would die?

7 Are Satan and Jesus still at war?

8 How did computers get so smart?

9 Is it wrong to copy computer games?

10 How did Noah build a boat that was so big?

11 Why did God flood the whole earth?

12 Why did God put a rainbow in the sky?

13 Why doesn't God take rich people's money and give it to the poor people?

14 Do angels watch television?

15 Why is there so much fighting on TV?

16 Does God only give us things that we need?

17 Do children have to pray with an adult?

18 How does God answer our prayers?

19 When we're bad, can we still pray?

20 Why do some kids say bad things about others?

21 Is it wrong to spread rumors?

22 Is it all right to pray to God for money?

23 Is money one of the most important things in life?

24 How should I treat kids who are different?

25 Why was it against the law to make friends with a Gentile?

26 What happens if a person doesn't pay a credit card bill?

27 What do prayer warriors do?

28 Will there be a Bible "hall of fame" in heaven?

29 Why do people litter?

30 Why is it wrong to do something if all the other kids do it?

31 If I swear, will I go to hell when I die?

September

1 Why do we have to pray when God already knows what we are going to pray?

2 Why did people kill animals for church?

3 Why did Cain kill his brother?

4 Can I ask God to help me pass a test?

5 Why are grades so important?

6 I want to get A's, but my friends say getting good grades is dumb. What should I do?

7 Does God listen to any prayer, big or small?

8 Why do we pray for our enemies?

9 Why do my parents want me to be involved in so many things?

10 Why do teachers give so much homework?

11 Why do people cheat?

12 How can I do better in spelling?

13 Why did Hannah leave her son at the church?

14 Why do some kids act tough?

15 What if I don't have enough money to pay my bills?

16 Does Jesus live with God in heaven or does he live by himself?

17 Are all people nice in heaven?

18 How does God concentrate on millions of people all praying at once?

19 Why do you have to be good and obey in school?

20 Why is it so hard to find things in my desk?

21 Why do movie companies make scary movies if they know people will have nightmares?

22 Why does God let animals suffer from dangers in nature?

23 Do we have to give money to poor people?

24 Why do some people believe that humans came from monkeys?

25 Why doesn't God want us to have fun?

26 If we've prayed all through the day, do we still need to pray at night?

27 Are your daytime prayers as effective as your night ones?

28 What did Goliath eat that made him so big?

29 How did David fight Goliath if he was so small?

30 When will the world end?

October

1 If Jesus has already won, why is everyone still fighting?

2 What are politics?

3 Why do governments do wrong things?

4 Does God have things to do at night time?

5 If someone isn't popular, how come others think less of him or her as a person?

6 Why do some kids dress so weird?

7 How do you get someone to like you if you aren't as popular as everyone else?

8 Should I hang out with popular people to become popular?

9 How can I get better at art?

10 Why didn't God give us money right away when my dad lost his job?

11 Why does God sometimes wait until the last minute to supply our needs?

12 Do you need to learn math only if you want to be a pilot or a construction worker?

13 Why do people believe that trees and plants and animals have spirits?

14 What will I do in heaven with no friends?

15 Does God have friends or is he alone?

16 Why do they put horoscopes in the newspaper?

17 Why do people commit crimes?

18 Why did Jesus talk about money when he didn't have very much?

19 Does money make people bad?

20 Why do people like different kinds of music?

21 Why are musicians treated like idols?

22 What should I do if other kids laugh at me for going to church?

23 How can I love my enemies?

24 Can an angel be a person to us like a real person?

25 Why do we have to respect teachers?

26 Why was Saul jealous of David?

27 Is it OK to use Canadian coins in U.S. vending machines?

28 Why does God kill nature with forest fires?

29 When kids tease me, should I tease them back?

30 How come some people are asking for sunshine while other people are asking for rain?

31 Why are there spooky things like skeletons and monsters?

November

1 Does God know about people who are hungry?

2 Why did the people (of Israel) want to have a king?

3 Why do some kids always try to be first?

4 Why does God let us get sick?

5 How does medicine make someone better?

6 Why do doctors and nurses give some shots that are long and some that are short?

7 If I die when I'm a kid, will I miss out on doing fun things on earth?

8 Why did Elijah go up to heaven before dying?

9 Do you pray in heaven or just talk to God face-to-face?

10 How can we think of something good to pray about if we've had a bad day?

11 Why do countries have armies, navies, and air forces?

12 Why are nuclear weapons even around?

13 Why does God let wars happen?

14 Why did people used to have so many kids?

15 Does God get angry when I spend my money foolishly?

16 Why can't I have all the things I want?

17 How fast is technology changing?

18 How do people think of things like the Hubble telescope?

19 Why do people have to speak different languages?

January 1

Who created God?

[Moses is speaking:] Lord, through all the generations you have been our home! Before the mountains were created, before you made the earth and the world, you are God, without beginning or end. Psalm 90:1-2

N o one created God—he has always existed. It's hard to understand this because everything that we know has a beginning and an end. Each day has a morning and night; basketball games have an opening tip-off and a final buzzer; people are born and they die. But God has no beginning or end. He always was and always will be.

When something new starts in our lives—no matter how big or how small—we can know that God is already there. An actress in a play might not enter the stage until Act Two, even if she has a very important role. But God is there when the curtain opens at the very beginning of all of our real-life roles. And he is there at the end.

It sure feels good to know that God will always be there for us!

ACTIVITY
Take your Bible and look up the first few verses of Genesis—the first verses of the whole Bible. Now put a bookmark there and look up the first four verses of the Gospel of John. What words are the same in both places? What do they tell you about who created God?

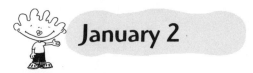

January 2

Why did God create the world?

In the beginning God created the heavens and the earth. . . . Then God looked over all he had made, and he saw that it was excellent in every way.   Genesis 1:1, 31

JASON'S IMAGINATION

God created the world and everything in it because he enjoys making things and because he wanted to be with us. God created people because he wanted to have friends—men and women, boys and girls with whom he could share his love. He created the world for them to live in and enjoy.

When we enjoy nature, look for the best in other people, or do an art project, we are saying thank you to God. We thank him for what a creative God he is and for giving us such a wonderful world. God wants us to keep our eyes open to his creation—the people, animals, places, and things on earth with us.

ACTIVITY
Look closely at the tips of your fingers. Do you see your finger-prints? Every person on the earth has his or her own fingerprints. No two people have the same ones. Next, look closely at a leaf (on a plant in the house or on a tree outside if you live in a warm climate). As you look at the leaf and your hand, thank God for making all of his amazing creation.

January 3

What is prayer?

[David is speaking:] O God, listen to my prayer. Pay attention to my plea.   Psalm 54:2

Prayer is the way we talk with God, just as conversation is the way we talk with our friends and parents. It is the way God has given us to thank him and to ask him to be involved in our lives. Prayer is an important part of a friendship with God. Friends talk with each other a lot. It is the same with God and his friends. They talk. They communicate. They pray.

Prayer does not have to be very formal or serious. Prayer can be casual, like having a talk with a friend. Whenever you have a need, you can just talk to God. You can tell him what you are excited about, tell him what worries you, or ask him for help. So when you pray, you are just having a conversation with God. You are talking to your best friend.

ACTIVITY

Usually, when people in the Bible prayed, they spoke to God in a normal voice. But sometimes they shouted, wept, or whispered. One woman named Hannah only moved her lips when she prayed. She was even quieter than a whisper. Yet God heard her and gave her baby Samuel, a miraculous answer to prayer! So try whispering a prayer to God. Then, after a few minutes, just move your lips when you "talk" to him. God will hear you!

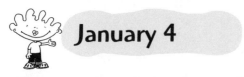

January 4

How do I make friends?

Love each other with genuine affection, and take delight in honoring each other.

Romans 12:10

The first step to making friends is thinking of places where you could find potential friends. Actually, they can be found almost anywhere—in your neighborhood, at school, on your sports team, and at church. You probably already know a lot of kids who could become very good friends.

The best way to make friends is to be friendly. In other words, you should be the kind of person whom others would like to have as a friend. Think about what you like in a friend, and be that kind of person to others. This probably will mean showing interest in other people and being a good listener—all of us want friends who will listen carefully to what we say and take us seriously. The Bible has many good examples of people whom God brought together as friends. To have a friend, be a friend!

ACTIVITY

Do a role play with your parents or an older brother or sister. Practice introducing yourself to another student at school. Then switch roles. Have someone play the part of a shy new kid who just moved near you. What questions could you ask to get him or her talking?

Why do we have to study subjects that we might not need to know when we grow up?

Teach the wise, and they will be wiser. Teach the righteous, and they will learn more.

Proverbs 9:9

People may think that the only reason to take a class in school is to learn something that they may need to know in a future job. But that's wrong. Some classes teach information and skills that students can build on. Some classes teach students how to think.

Most of what you learn in the early grades of school, such as reading and math, will help you in many areas of your life. Also, you never know when God will use you and what you have learned to help others. It will be exciting to see how God will someday use what you're learning now. What do you think your loving heavenly Father has in mind for you?

ACTIVITY

Many public libraries have a summer reading program. Why not make a winter reading program for yourself? Reading is always something to get better and better at. Talk with your mom or dad about how many library books will be realistic for you to read, given schoolwork and other activities. Then set a goal for yourself and try to read at least one type of book you don't usually read, such as poetry or a biography.

What is a Bible?

Your word is a lamp for my
feet and a light for my path.
Psalm 119:105

The Bible is God's message to people. Actually, the Bible is not just one book, but a collection of many books that have been put together. It is often called *the* Book because it is so important—the Bible is *God's* book. (The word *Bible* means *book*.)

The Bible is our instruction manual for living God's way. It tells what's right and what's wrong. The Bible has many stories and lessons that God wants us to know. But most important, the Bible tells about God and his Son, Jesus, and it tells how we are supposed to live.

So when you read the Bible, you should see it as God's special message to you!

ACTIVITY
Look at the Table of Contents in your Bible. You will see that the Bible is divided into two parts. The Old Testament tells how God created the world. It also is filled with stories about God's people and tells how God wants people to live. Take a few minutes to find these stories: Noah (Genesis 7–9) and David and Goliath (1 Samuel 17). In the New Testament, look for Jesus' healing of ten lepers (Luke 17), the Resurrection (John 20), and Paul's letter to the church at Philippi (Philippians 1–4). The Bible has many great stories that are fun to read.

January 7

How come people get the flu when God is watching over them?

Our bodies now disappoint us, but when they are raised, they will be full of glory. They are weak now, but when they are raised, they will be full of power.
1 Corinthians 15:43

Sickness was not part of God's original plan for his creation. We have sickness in the world because sin brought it in. As long as we live in this world, we will have sickness. God does not promise that he will keep us safe from all pain and sickness. But he promises to always be with us.

The next time you are sick, take comfort from God. That way, when others are sick, you can comfort them the way God comforted you. And don't forget to pray. We can trust God to listen and care for us no matter what we are going through, for he loves us. Ecclesiastes 7:14 says, "Enjoy prosperity while you can. But when hard times strike, realize that both come from God." Someday God will end all sickness. This life is not all there is—don't forget heaven!

ACTIVITY

The next time you hear that somebody is sick, plan to bring over a gift basket. Get a small basket ready that you can fill with things the person would like. Your mom or dad can help you. Grown-ups may like baked goods, special tea, flowers, bath goodies, and candles. Kids might enjoy neat pencils, trading cards, a small stuffed animal, and hair things (for girls). Any age would like your own artwork, handmade stationery, and fruit.

What are bacteria and viruses?

[David is speaking:] Thank you for making me so wonderfully complex! Your workmanship is marvelous—and how well I know it.

Psalm 139:14

B acteria are one-celled living things; viruses are parasites. Both are so small that you need a microscope to see them. Harmful bacteria and viruses are often called "germs." Germs make you sick by reproducing inside your body. Bacteria are not always harmful. E. coli bacteria live in your intestines and help your body break down food. Several kinds of bacteria live in the ground and break up dead leaves, sticks, grass, and other organic matter to make compost. These bacteria could make you sick if they got on your food, but they serve a good purpose. Other bacteria are very harmful: Streptococcus bacteria, for example, cause strep throat, a sickness that children and adults sometimes get. Doctors treat it with antibiotics—medicines that kill bacteria.

Bacteria and viruses are everywhere, but God made your body to fight them off. He gave you white blood cells and antibodies. These are your body's way of staying well and curing itself of sickness. Isn't God's work amazing?

ACTIVITY

Look up and read Psalm 139:13-16, the song that includes today's verse. One of King David's most famous psalms, it celebrates what an amazing job God did in making our bodies! Try putting the words to music—they should make a great song (especially verse 14).

How did God make people?

The Lord God formed a man's body from the dust of the ground and breathed into it the breath of life. And the man became a living person. Genesis 2:7

SCULPTURE
(not the way God did it)

The Bible says that God made Adam from the "dust of the ground." In other words, God took something he had already made—dust—and formed a man's body out of it. Then God gave life to that body. God made Adam, the first man, just the way he wanted him. Then God made Eve just the way he wanted her. God made her from part of Adam so that she would match the man perfectly.

You are made by God. And he has made you just right. Do you wish you were taller? shorter? Would you have liked a different hair color? Please know that God made you just how he wanted you to be—inside and out. He is a creative God, and he is loving, too.

ACTIVITY

If you have an extra copy of a school photo, paste it to the top of a piece of paper. Otherwise, draw a self-portrait. Below your picture, write some things you like about yourself—your personality, your talents, and your skills. Then hang the picture in a place where you can see it often. When you look at it, remember to thank God for making you special. Also, ask him to help you learn and grow and be the best that you can be.

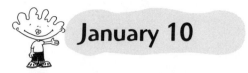

January 10

What is evil?

Keep away from every kind of evil.   1 Thessalonians 5:22

E*vil* is another word for what is bad or sinful. Anything that goes against God and displeases him is evil. This includes a selfish attitude, bad actions, and ignoring God. Evil entered the world when Adam and Eve sinned in the Garden of Eden. Ever since then, humans have been born wanting to do what is wrong. That's called our "sinful nature." So evil in the world comes from sinful human beings doing what comes naturally.

Evil also comes directly from Satan. He is the enemy of God. Satan, also known as the devil, tries to get people to turn against God and disobey him. The good news is that we can overcome evil in ourselves and in the world by giving our lives to Jesus. God is far greater than Satan!

ACTIVITY
You can read how evil came into the world in the book of Genesis in the Bible. The story is found in chapters 2 and 3. Read it to a grown-up, or have a grown-up read it to you.

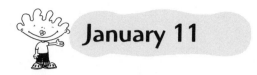

January 11

Why did God make Satan if God knew Satan would make sin?

[Jesus is speaking:] "Yes," he told them, "I saw Satan falling from heaven as a flash of lightning!"

Luke 10:18

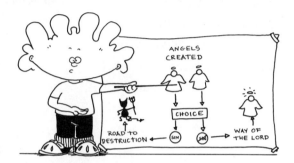

God created all people and all angels with the ability to choose whether to obey him. God knew that some would choose to obey and some would choose to disobey. Still he created them because he knew it was good to do that. God makes everything good, and this includes people and angels who have the choice of whether to serve God. God has allowed Satan to have freedom now, but in the end God will defeat Satan and punish him.

Satan did not invent sin, but he tries to get people to choose it. You have the choice every day to choose God's way or Satan's way. Actually, you have the choice many times a day! Choose God!

ACTIVITY

Make a light-switch cover that will remind you to choose God. Take an index card or a piece of construction paper four inches by six inches. Cut a slot in the middle, going the long way down the paper, for the light switch to poke through. Use markers to write above the slot: "I choose God." Below the slot, write: "God is with me." Then decorate the rest of the paper. Put two loops of masking tape on each side of the hole and attach your reminder card to the light-switch plate. (Be careful to tape it to the plate and not to the wall.)

Why do we have the Bible?

The word of God is full of living power. It is sharper than the sharpest knife, cutting deep into our innermost thoughts and desires. It exposes us for what we really are. Hebrews 4:12

G od gave us the Bible because he wanted to talk to us in a way that we would understand. The Bible is a book, and we can read a book over and over. We can also share a book with a friend.

The Bible is like a map because it shows us the direction to go in life. The Bible is like a love letter because it tells us about God's love for us. The Bible is like food because it gives us strength to live. To find out what God is like and how he wants us to live, read the Bible. It's a great book!

ACTIVITY

Explain to a friend how to go from your home to the library or some other place that you know how to find. Use no words or pictures. Just point and try other hand motions. Is your friend confused yet? Now draw a map. Your friend probably understands these directions much more quickly. You can understand God's direction for you by reading his excellent map, the Bible.

January 13

How can people find out what is right and wrong?

[God is speaking:] "Be careful to obey all my commands so that all will go well with you and your children, because you will be doing what pleases the Lord your God." Deuteronomy 12:28

We can know what is right by knowing God. God is perfect and always right, so everything good matches what God is like. For example, we know it is right to be loving and kind because God is love. On the other hand, everything that is wrong goes against what God is like. So it is wrong to hold grudges and not forgive people because we know that God forgives.

You can learn what God is like by reading his Word, the Bible. Because God loves you, he has given you rules and guidance for how to live. Those are also in the Bible. When you read rules such as the Ten Commandments, you can know for sure how God wants you to act. What a great feeling to know that God loves you enough to give you guidance!

ACTIVITY

Find the Ten Commandments in the Bible. They are listed in Exodus 20:3-17. On a piece of drawing paper or small poster board, write out the commandments as a list. You can make each one stand out by using a different colored marker or pencil for each commandment. Put the list on a wall or bulletin board.

Does God see everything that we do?

[Elihu is speaking:] "God carefully watches the way people live; he sees everything they do. No darkness is thick enough to hide the wicked from his eyes."

Job 34:21-22

God sees everything we do, both good and bad. We can't hide from him. God is happy when we do what is right and sad when we do what is wrong.

Some people think that if they do something bad and don't get caught, it's OK. Maybe you've disobeyed your parents, and you think that nobody saw you. But somebody *did* see you: God. The good news is that he also sees the good things you do that nobody else knows about. He can reward his people for doing what's right even when no one else knows about it.

ACTIVITY

Think of two good deeds that you can do for family members today without being asked and without anyone seeing you. For example, you could help clean up the house, fix something that is broken, or get some flowers and put them in a vase on the kitchen table. As you do your kind deeds, remember that God sees you and knows your heart.

January 15

Why did God make people red and yellow, black and white?

In this new life, it doesn't matter if you are a Jew or a Gentile, circumcised or uncircumcised, barbaric, uncivilized, slave, or free. Christ is all that matters, and he lives in all of us.

Colossians 3:11

JESUS LOVES THE LITTLE CHILDREN, ALL THE CHILDREN OF THE WORLD...

Imagine a world in which everyone looked the same—height, weight, color of hair, length of nose, color of eyes, size of ears, and color of skin. That would be boring! But that's not how it is. God created all kinds and colors of people. Some are tall; some are short; some are brown; some are pink; some have straight black hair; some have curly red hair. All people are special to God.

Don't you just love the differences, including those that make you special? God does! You can also notice and be glad for the things about people that are alike. Each person is made in the image of God. We each communicate something about his love, his interests, his power. What matters most is this: Have we let Jesus Christ come to live in us?

ACTIVITY
Write down the names of four kids in your class at school or in Sunday school. Include yourself! Next to each name, write something about how the person looks or acts that is special to him or her. One may have wonderful red hair. Another may always have a smile ready. Now write down what you have in common. Each person is special, but we're not all by ourselves in life either. Thank God that both things are true.

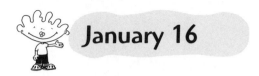

January 16

I don't get it—why are people prejudiced?

God does not show favoritism.
Romans 2:11

JASON'S IMAGINATION

BABIES	COLORS	TODAY'S SPECIAL
singles	red	7lbs. 9ozs.
twins	yellow	
triplets	black	
	white	

The biggest reason for prejudice is fear of people who are different. People tend to fear or think badly of what they don't know or understand, including other people or their customs. People become prejudiced when they believe false ideas about what others are like. We do not need to be afraid of such differences as the way people cook, dress, or talk. We need to appreciate these differences instead of judging or criticizing people for not doing things our way.

Some people also believe—wrongly—that certain kinds of people are better or more important than others. This is called *racism*. People who have this perspective don't realize that God created *all* people in his image. Every person who has ever been born is equally important and valuable. No one is better or deserving of superior treatment.

God wants you to love and respect others even if you don't know or understand them. He will help you get to know other people if you ask him.

ACTIVITY

Today is the birthday of Dr. Martin Luther King Jr. Find information about this African-American leader on the web or in an encyclopedia. You'll discover that he did a lot to try to break down prejudice between blacks and whites in the United States.

Is it OK to hit my brother back if he hit me first?

Never pay back evil for evil to anyone. Do things in such a way that everyone can see you are honorable.

Romans 12:17

Hitting back would be revenge. In the Bible, God says that vengeance belongs to him. And he has given police, teachers, and parents the authority to settle fights. It's not our place to hit back or to hate. If we say we love God but hate people, then we don't really love him. If we can't love someone in our own family whom we can see, how can we possibly love God whom we cannot see? That's why Jesus told his followers to be kind and to respond with love, even when someone hits them.

So if your brother (or sister) hits you, be nice back to him or her. If he or she continues to be mean, let one of your parents take care of it. God wants you to learn how to get along with everyone. If you can learn to love and to be kind to your family members, you probably will be able to get along with almost anyone else.

ACTIVITY

Suggest to your parents that you have a family mini-theater night. Act out scenes from life in your family, but switch roles. In other words, take turns being other family members—your brother, your sister, even a parent or grandparent. Just don't play yourself. Act out ways to end arguments without hitting back.

Do God and Jesus cry?

Jesus wept.   John 11:35

A s a man, Jesus cried real tears when he was sad. He was especially sad when his friend Lazarus died. (You can read the whole story in John 11.) We can be sure that God knows how we feel when we're sad because we know that his Son, Jesus, was a person with emotions, too.

God does not shed tears today, but he feels sad when people are hurting, when they disobey him, and when they don't believe in him. We can bring God joy by living as we should, showing love to others, and telling people about Christ. Think of how you can make God smile.

ACTIVITY

Draw a picture of Jesus with Mary and Martha. Use crayons and poster board or some other strong paper. With your mom's permission, make tears out of clear nail polish to show the three of them crying.

Why is it good to exercise?

Physical exercise has some value, but spiritual exercise is much more important, for it promises a reward in both this life and the next.
1 Timothy 4:8

Your body needs exercise just as it needs food, air, and water. Muscles need to be stretched and strengthened. Lungs need to breathe fresh, clean air. Joints need to be moved around. Blood needs to get moving.

Exercise also helps people lose weight by using the calories from food, building muscle, and burning fat. Some people today don't get enough exercise—they sit around watching TV, playing video games, or surfing the Internet for a long time. Sitting around all the time is not good for a person's health. You can get good exercise from working around the house, working in the yard, riding your bike, running, walking, and playing sports.

God gave us wonderful bodies, and he wants us to take care of them. Ready, get set, exercise!

ACTIVITY

Take a big poster board, and draw lines to divide it into four equal blocks. Label each block with one of the seasons: Winter, Spring, Summer, Fall. How do you get exercise in each of the seasons? Team sports? Walking or biking with your family? Physical education class at school? Write down the activities for each block. Is there a season when you don't get much exercise? What else can you do to keep healthy during that time of year?

Why did God choose Abraham to go to the Promised Land instead of someone else?

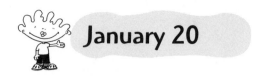

The Lord told Abram, "Leave your country, your relatives, and your father's house, and go to the land that I will show you. I will cause you to become the father of a great nation. I will bless you and make you famous, and I will make you a blessing to others." Genesis 12:1-2

God chose Abram, later known as Abraham, to become the father of a great nation, not because he was especially good, but simply because God wanted to—the Bible doesn't give us God's reasons. God doesn't always tell us why he does what he does. He knows everything and can do anything he wants. God knew that Abraham would obey.

God knows what's best for you. He also has his reasons for letting things happen in your life and family as they do. Do things seem wrong or unfair right now? God still loves you and has the big picture in mind.

ACTIVITY

Imagine that you are the radio or TV announcer for a ball game where the umpire or referee calls plays however he or she wants, ignoring the rules. Describe the teams' and the crowd's reactions as the official calls a safe runner out, never blows the whistle when the ball goes out of bounds, or refuses to give a penalty, even when a player commits a foul. Talk about chaos! A good referee may not call everything just right, but he or she is a lot better than one who doesn't follow any rules at all. Abraham wasn't perfect, but God knew that he would try his best to follow God.

January 21

What is tithing?

"Should people cheat God? Yet you have cheated me! But you ask, 'What do you mean? When did we ever cheat you?'

"You have cheated me of the tithes and offerings due to me."

Malachi 3:8

BIBLE EXPERIMENT #563 FRUIT TITHE

Tithe is a word used in the Bible. It means "a tenth." In Old Testament times, God commanded the Israelites to give to the priests a tithe of all they produced. They gave sheep, grain, cows, and so forth. These tithes were like income for the priests, making it possible for them to work full-time at leading the people in worship and taking care of God's house. Sometimes people gave even more to say thank you to God for all the good things he provided. Their giving showed that they trusted God to supply their needs. Many Christians use the word *tithe* to describe their giving. Usually they mean that they give back to God part of their income. Sometimes they give 10 percent; sometimes they give less or more.

When you give gladly, you show that you trust God to take care of you. You have a trustworthy God, so why not show it in your giving?

ACTIVITY

Make a tithe bank by taking a small jar and labeling it "God's Money." Place it on your desk so that it will remind you to put at least 10 percent of your money in there. You can put the money in the church offering or give it to some other organization that promotes a Christian cause.

January 22

Why do people smoke?

I really want to do what is right, but I don't do it. Instead, I do the very thing I hate. I know perfectly well that what I am doing is wrong. . . . But I can't help myself, because it is sin inside me that makes me do these evil things.

Romans 7:15-17

People smoke because they are addicted to nicotine, a chemical in tobacco. Once you start putting nicotine into your body, your body starts to crave it, making it hard to stop. People also get addicted to the experience. Smoking becomes a habit.

Most people who smoke started when they were very young. They may have thought that smoking would make them look cool or tough, or maybe they liked the taste. After a while, it's not cool anymore, but they have become addicted to the nicotine. Try not to be too hard on people who smoke. Quitting is very difficult.

Smoking damages many parts of the body. God didn't make our lungs to breathe in smoke. God wants you to take good care of your body, which he made for you.

ACTIVITY
Do you know somebody who smokes whom you wish would quit? Pray for that person every day for a week. Tell God how much you wish the person would stay healthy because you love him or her. Then, ask God to give you the courage and love to say to the person, "I love you and want you to be healthy. I wish you would quit smoking." This does not guarantee that the person will quit—at least not right away. But you have planted the idea. Keep praying!

Where does God live?

Will God really live on earth?
Why, even the highest heavens
cannot contain you. How much
less this Temple I have built!
Listen to my prayer and my
request, O Lord my God. . . .
Yes, hear us from heaven where
you live."   1 Kings 8:27-30

Sometimes we think of God as though he were another person like us. We can be in only one place at a time, and we need a place to live. So we think that God is the same way. But God isn't limited to a physical body. He lives everywhere, especially inside people who love him. We call a church building "God's house" because that's where people who love God gather to worship him. He doesn't have a bedroom in that house; but he is always there, accepting the praises of his people.

Church is not the only place where God lives. No matter where we are, God is with us. God also lives in heaven—eventually we will live there, too. Wherever you go today, remember that God is with you and will never leave you.

ACTIVITY

Draw a picture of people worshiping God inside your church. Perhaps your church has a fancy style, or perhaps it is more plain. That's not important. What's important is that the people are singing praises to God and praying together, as well as learning about God and how to live for him all week. What are the people in your picture doing?

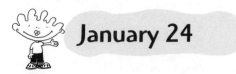
What is heaven like?

[Jesus is speaking:] "There are many rooms in my Father's home, and I am going to prepare a place for you. If this were not so, I would tell you plainly. When everything is ready, I will come and get you, so that you will always be with me where I am."

John 14:2-3

The Bible uses wonderful pictures to tell us what heaven is like. In our world we think that gold is important because it's so valuable. But in heaven, the streets will be gold—we'll *walk* on it. The best way to picture heaven is to imagine the most exciting and fun place that you've ever been to. Heaven will be like that— only much, much better. Jesus told his followers that he was leaving earth and going to heaven to prepare a place for them. Have you chosen to follow Jesus? Then he has a special place for you, too. The book of Revelation tells us there will be no crying or sadness, and we will be filled with joy.

ACTIVITY

Make a jeweled decoration. Start with a small Styrofoam egg or ball (available at craft stores). Use straight pins to attach multi-colored sequins in rows, with the sequins overlapping each other a bit. Cover the whole surface. Pin a few fake jewels or extra-large sequins at different places on the egg or ball. Glue a gold cord around the middle of your decoration. Pin a separate loop of the cord at the top, so you can hang up your decoration. Let it remind you how beautiful heaven is.

Why can't we go to heaven and just see it and then come back?

I saw a door standing open in heaven, and the . . . voice said, "Come up here. . . ." And instantly I was in the Spirit, and I saw a throne in heaven and someone sitting on it! The one sitting on the throne was as brilliant as gemstones. . . . And the glow of an emerald circled his throne like a rainbow. Revelation 4:1-3

Try to imagine a teenager asking, "Can I grow up and then come back to be a kid again?" Not only would it be impossible to do that, but after someone grows up, that person probably would not want to be a kid again. In the same way, anyone who goes to heaven will never, ever want to leave! Heaven is more than a place that you can visit. It's a very special place reserved for the end of our life on this earth. And God uses our time here to help us change and get ready to go there.

We know that heaven exists because God has told us so in his Word, the Bible. Living with Jesus in heaven will be so wonderful that you will never even think about coming back!

ACTIVITY

Take a quick survey about heaven. Choose five people of varying ages, and ask them these two questions:

What are you looking forward to most in heaven?
Do you think you'll want to stay there? Why?

Jesus is preparing a place in heaven for those who believe in him. We know it will be a very special place because he loves us so much!

Why do we worship God?

Jesus replied, "Believe me, the time is coming when it will no longer matter whether you worship the Father here or in Jerusalem. You Samaritans know so little about the one you worship, while we Jews know all about him, for salvation comes through the Jews. But the time is coming and is already here when true worshipers will worship the Father in spirit and in truth. The Father is looking for anyone who will worship him that way. For God is Spirit, so those who worship him must worship in spirit and in truth."

John 4:21-24

Worship means praising and thanking God for who he is and for what he has done. People worship in many different ways. Worship can involve group singing, group reading, special music, giving money, prayer, Communion, Bible reading, teaching, preaching, and other activities. God has given us everything good that we have. He loves us and wants the very best for us. Shouldn't we spend time with him and tell him how grateful we are? We play with our friends because we enjoy them. We worship God because we enjoy him.

ACTIVITY
Borrow a songbook or hymn book and find some praise and worship songs. Go through two or three songs and count how many times words like *thanks, praise, thank, thanksgiving,* and *worship* appear. What's the grand total? Aren't you glad we have a God who is worth worshiping?

Is it OK to think that you are better than somebody else if you really are better?

As God's messenger, I give each of you this warning: Be honest in your estimate of yourselves, measuring your value by how much faith God has given you. Just as our bodies have many parts and each part has a special function, so it is with Christ's body. Romans 12:3-5

Be careful not to fall into the trap of thinking of yourself as better than others. Who says you are better? If we believe that we are better than we are, we become filled with pride. Be realistic about yourself and humble, too. Remember that all your abilities and talents are gifts from God. All people, even those who are good at what they do, need to depend on God.

There is nothing wrong about being glad that you did a good job at something (singing a solo, scoring points in a game, getting good grades, being honest). It's OK to feel good about yourself and to have confidence in what you do. You don't have to pretend that you aren't good or apologize for being good. When someone pays you a compliment, say thank you. But don't compare yourself to others or think of yourself as better than they are. You may be a better basketball player than someone else, but that doesn't make you a better person. Just remember that your relationship with God is most important.

ACTIVITY

Long ago the storyteller Aesop wrote the fable of "The Tortoise and the Hare." Read the story and think about the big mistake the hare made. What was his opinion of himself before the race? after the race?

Did the Bible stories really happen, or are they like fairy tales?

All these events happened to them as examples for us. They were written down to warn us, who live at the time when this age is drawing to a close.
1 Corinthians 10:11

The stories in the Bible really happened. Some of the events seem amazing because they're miracles, but they still happened. We know that the stories are true because the Bible is God's Word, and God wouldn't lie to us or fool us. The Bible also says that every word in it is true. Some people don't believe the Bible because they haven't read it. Some don't believe it because they don't think miracles can happen. Others don't believe because they don't want to—they don't want to learn about God and do what he tells them to do.

God made us, so he's the best one to tell us how to live. Just think—God is your heavenly Father, and he gave you the Bible to tell you about himself and how to live. Do you want God to help you believe his Word and understand it? You can tell him so, and he will!

ACTIVITY
Ask your mom, dad, Sunday school teacher, or another older Christian to show you some of the books and other resources they use for Bible study. Some of the resources might include a devotional book like this one, a concordance, a study Bible, a journal, and others. Ask this person why the Bible is so important to him or her.

January 29

Why did Jacob trick his dad?

Jacob carried the platter of food to his father and said, "My father?" "Yes, my son," he answered. "Who is it—Esau or Jacob?" Jacob replied, "It's Esau, your older son. I've done as you told me. Here is the wild game, cooked the way you like it. Sit up and eat it so you can give me your blessing."

Genesis 27:18-19

Isaac had two sons, Jacob and Esau. Jacob tricked his father because he wanted the inheritance that should have gone to his brother. Jacob was selfish and greedy. Although he received the inheritance, his actions broke up the family and caused everyone a lot of trouble and sadness.

Do you remember a time when you tried to trick your brother or sister or maybe even your mom or dad? Perhaps you got away with it. But really, you didn't get away with it because God knows what happened. And the person you tricked may have a hard time trusting you in the future. Families get along best when each person is honest and kind. Isn't that how you want the rest of your family to treat you?

ACTIVITY

What are your chores? Perhaps you have been tempted to say you did one of them when you didn't. Or maybe you've tried to trick somebody else into doing one of your jobs for you. Choose one of your chores—making your bed, feeding your pet, cleaning your room, or whatever. Now, do your absolute best to do it very well, before being asked and without complaining. It will feel much better than being a trickster!

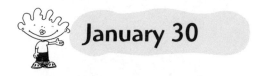

January 30

Why did Adam and Eve eat the forbidden fruit if God said not to?

The serpent was the shrewdest of all the creatures the Lord God had made. . . . "Did God really say you must not eat any of the fruit in the garden?" "Of course we may eat it," the woman told him. "It's only the fruit from the tree at the center of the garden that we are not allowed to eat. God says we must not eat it or even touch it, or we will die." "You won't die!" the serpent hissed. . . "You will become just like God." Genesis 3:1-5

Adam and Eve were sinless and perfect when God created them. But they still could choose to do what was wrong (just like you can choose to do what you aren't supposed to). When the devil tempted them to eat the forbidden fruit, they chose to do it.

Adam and Eve ate the fruit because the devil started them thinking about what it would be like. Then he lied about God's rule to make them think that God was keeping something good from them. Pretty soon they wanted to eat the fruit more than they wanted to obey God's rule. That was a big mistake, wasn't it?

ACTIVITY

Think of something that is a "forbidden fruit" for you. Maybe your parents don't want you to watch a certain TV program or eat a lot of junk food before dinner. Draw a picture of a new kind of "fruit" to represent that temptation, and hang it where you'll see it when you're tempted. You may also want to draw a picture showing how you'll look if you give in to the temptation.

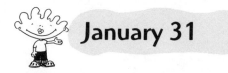

January 31

Why was there an angel with a fiery sword guarding the entrance to the Garden of Eden?

After banishing them from the garden, the Lord God stationed mighty angelic beings to the east of Eden. And a flaming sword flashed back and forth, guarding the way to the tree of life.

Genesis 3:24

JASON'S IMAGINATION

GARDEN of EDEN

An angel stood at the entrance to the Garden of Eden to keep Adam and Eve from going back in. God had sent them out of the garden after they sinned. Because they disobeyed God, they would never be allowed to live in Eden again.

God is still serious about punishments. He wants you to know that he is your heavenly Father. This means that he loves you, so he will punish you for your own good if you disobey him. But he also sent his Son, Jesus, to die for your sins. When you disobey God, you can tell Jesus you're sorry, and he'll forgive you. God promises punishment, but he also promises that he'll always be ready to forgive.

God keeps his promises. You can trust him.

ACTIVITY

With a grown-up's permission or help, light a candle. Set it on a table and quietly watch the flame. See how brightly the flame burns. Think about the flaming sword that guarded the entrance to the Garden of Eden after Adam and Eve sinned. Pray with thanks to God that he keeps his promises—to punish when necessary to bring us back to him, and to forgive when we're ready to come back.

February 1

What is prayer for?

[Jesus is speaking:] "You haven't done this before. Ask, using my name, and you will receive, and you will have abundant joy."

John 16:24

The purpose of prayer is for people to get closer to God. When we tell God that we are sorry for our sins, thank him for all he has done, and ask for his help, God begins to change us so that we love him more and see things from his point of view. Through prayer we can work with God to change the world.

God, your loving Father, wants to meet your needs, to teach you how to live, and to be your friend. When you pray, you invite your Father in heaven into your life and into your world.

ACTIVITY

Make an invitation to God, asking him to be part of your life each day. Use construction paper, markers, stickers, or whatever other supplies you have on hand. Fold the paper, and draw a morning picture on the front of your card. (The sun shining through a window, an unmade bed, or perhaps you stretching.) Here are some sample words for the inside of your card. Feel free to change them.

What? God, you're invited to visit and celebrate with me.
When? Every morning after I wake up.
Where? Next to my bed.
Why? Because I love you, Lord!

February 2

What does my angel do?

[Jesus is speaking:] "Beware that you don't despise a single one of these little ones. For I tell you that in heaven their angels are always in the presence of my heavenly Father." Matthew 18:10

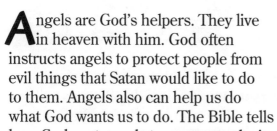

Angels are God's helpers. They live in heaven with him. God often instructs angels to protect people from evil things that Satan would like to do to them. Angels also can help us do what God wants us to do. The Bible tells how God sent angels to many people, including Abraham, Moses, Hagar, David, Mary, Peter, and Paul.

So, even if you never actually see an angel, you can be sure that angels are watching over you!

ACTIVITY

Spread some newspapers onto a table. Place a piece of waxed paper about twelve inches square on the newspaper. Put one of your hands on the waxed paper, spreading your fingers. Now trace around your hand and draw a line where your wrist would be. Squirt a thick but even line of white glue on the outline of your hand. Next, cut a two-foot piece of string, and tie the ends together to make a circle. Put the knotted end at the tip of your gluey pointer finger. Squirt more glue there to cover the knot. Let the glue dry completely—it could take several hours. When the hand is dry, use colored markers to decorate it. Then hang it up and think about how your angel is "giving you a hand" all the time.

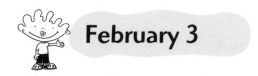

February 3

When you're making friends, how do you know what to say?

Kind words are like honey—sweet to the soul and healthy for the body. Proverbs 16:24

SO THIS THING-A-MA-BOB MAKES THIS DOO-HICKEY MOVE SO THAT SLIMY GOO STUFF CAN BOIL IN THAT WEIRD LOOKING BOTTLE...

The best way to start a conversation with someone is to ask questions about that person. You can look for clues on the person to help you know what to ask. For example, if the person is wearing a hat or shirt of a professional sports team, you could ask about the team. If someone is holding a book, you could ask what the book is about. It's important to ask people questions about themselves. Talk about them, not just about yourself.

Also, look for ways to give compliments. If you hear about a good grade or honor that someone received, you could say, "Good going!" or "Great job!" If someone did well in a concert, you could say something like, "I really enjoyed your solo." Try to make others feel good about themselves. When you do this, you will be pleasing God and making friends for yourself, too!

ACTIVITY

It's fun to learn words in different languages. Pick three languages other than English and find out how to say "Hello, how are you?" Use the Internet or foreign language dictionaries at the library to find out what the phrases are. Use them at school for a new conversation starter—and to make new friends.

February 4

Do angels stay in the car or fly beside?

He orders his angels to protect you
wherever you go.   Psalm 91:11

God watches over us, using angels as his servants. Angels go wherever God tells them to go. If God wants an angel to be with us in a train or a bus, that is where the angel will be. If God wants the angel to be outside a car and moving along at the speed of the car, that's where the angel will be. Angels can be anywhere—inside or outside the car.

This doesn't mean that Christians never get into car accidents. Some bad things will happen as long as we live on this earth. That's because of the sin that's in the world. But you can be certain that God's care is very personal. He loves you and will always be beside you. His angels will be with you wherever you travel!

ACTIVITY
With your parent's permission, put a sticker (like a star or a heart) on your seat belt. Or tie a ribbon on around it, making sure you put it in a place that doesn't interfere with how the seat belt works. The next time you ride in the car, slowly pull the seat belt over you. Let the sticker or ribbon be a symbol of how angels are around you to protect and comfort you. God's care really is everywhere!

February 5

What if one parent says you can watch a certain movie, and then the other one says you can't?

My son, obey your father's commands, and don't neglect your mother's teaching. Keep their words always in your heart. Tie them around your neck. Proverbs 6:20-21

JASON'S IMAGINATION

If one parent tells you no, then accept that as your answer and don't go looking for permission from another parent. Some kids go back and forth between parents until one gives in and says OK. That's wrong, because it dishonors what the first parent said.

If Mom or Dad says you can't do something (like watch a certain movie), you can nicely ask why. But don't argue, complain, or whine about it. God wants us to honor and obey our parents. He told us that in his Word.

Why does God want you to obey your parents? Because that's how God keeps you safe and helps you learn the things you need to know. Then you can live a happy and productive life.

ACTIVITY

When your mom and dad were kids, they had to learn to be obedient and to respect their parents, too. As you think about your whole family, now would be a great time to make a family tree. Try to put as many people as you can on it—parents, brothers and sisters, grandparents, great-grandparents, aunts, uncles, and cousins. Remember that each one of those people was a kid at some time and had to learn the lesson that you are studying.

February 6

Why did Joseph's brothers sell him?

"Here comes that dreamer!" they exclaimed. "Come on, let's kill him and throw him into a deep pit. We can tell our father that a wild animal has eaten him. Then we'll see what becomes of all his dreams!"

Genesis 37:19-20

Joseph was Jacob's favorite son because Joseph was born when Jacob was an old man. Joseph's older brothers were jealous of him when their father gave him a beautiful coat. The brothers also became angry when Joseph told them he dreamed that they bowed down before him. Eventually the brothers became so upset with Joseph that they decided to kill him. But Reuben talked the others into just putting Joseph in a well. Reuben planned to set his brother free later. While Reuben was gone, however, the other brothers sold Joseph as a slave to some traders.

If you have brothers or sisters, perhaps it seems that your parents have a favorite. But the truth is that all good parents—especially God, your heavenly Father—love all their children. Families are special. Don't waste your time fighting and being upset with one another.

ACTIVITY

Think about one of your brothers or sisters. (If you don't have a brother or a sister, pick a cousin or a friend.) What special treat, such as candy or bubble gum, does he or she like? (Choose one that is OK with your parents.) The next time you go to the store, buy that treat and share it. Enjoy the good feeling of giving and getting along. And don't spoil this experience by expecting something in return!

February 7

Why didn't Joseph go back home?

[Joseph is speaking to his brothers:] "Yes, it was God who sent me here, not you! And he has made me a counselor to Pharaoh— manager of his entire household and ruler over all Egypt."

Genesis 45:8

Joseph couldn't go home—first because he was a slave, then because he was in prison, and finally because he was in government service. He also was a long way from home, and there were no buses, trains, or airplanes. Also, Joseph may have been afraid of facing his older brothers again. It's good that Joseph stayed in Egypt because God used him to save his family (and thousands of others) from starvation. Eventually God brought the whole family back together again.

If you're in the middle of a bad time, you may wonder why God doesn't immediately make things better. No one knows all of God's reasons or his timing, but you can be sure that he will turn bad things into good. God does always have a plan!

ACTIVITY

Think about all the kids you know. Right now, at least one of them is probably sad—dealing with a pet or a loved one who is sick or dying, having to move, listening to parents fight, or something similar. Make a card with a nice drawing or painting. Write a short message to say that you care, and promise to pray for your friend. Mail it to your friend. And keep your promise to pray for him or her.

One Year Book of Fun & Active Devotions for Kids

When did all this Bible stuff happen?

When we were utterly helpless,
Christ came at just the right time
and died for us sinners.

Romans 5:6

GRANDPA, WERE YOU ALIVE WHEN JESUS WAS HERE?

Everything in the Bible happened hundreds and hundreds of years before your grandparents were born. In fact, when you say what year it is right now, that tells about how many years have passed since Jesus lived on earth, and that's about when the New Testament was written. The Old Testament came to an end four hundred years before that. The events described in the Old Testament took place over thousands of years.

God has all the times and events of history under control. He knows the best time and place for the big events. But he also knows and cares about the little details of your life. God guides you, always working "at just the right time."

ACTIVITY
Make a timeline of the big events of the Bible. Use a long, horizontal piece of paper or several pieces taped together. Put the creation of the world at the far left-hand corner. Ask a grown-up to help you with the research—many study Bibles have charts, or you could use a reference book or encyclopedia from your church library. Add events such as the Flood, the Exodus from Egypt, King David's life, and Jesus' birth, death, and resurrection.

February 9

Why did people go to wells instead of using the water at home?

[The Samaritan woman is speaking to Jesus:] "But sir, you don't have a rope or a bucket," she said, "and this is a very deep well. Where would you get this living water?"   John 4:11

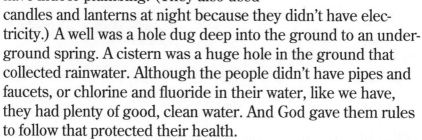

JASON'S IMAGINATION

PLEASE DON'T USE! (not invented yet)

In Bible times, people went to rivers, streams, wells, and cisterns for their water because they didn't have indoor plumbing. (They also used candles and lanterns at night because they didn't have electricity.) A well was a hole dug deep into the ground to an underground spring. A cistern was a huge hole in the ground that collected rainwater. Although the people didn't have pipes and faucets, or chlorine and fluoride in their water, like we have, they had plenty of good, clean water. And God gave them rules to follow that protected their health.

As he talked to this woman at the well, Jesus used a discussion about water to tell her about eternal life. Water gives life, and "living water" gives eternal life! Whenever you take a drink today, remember God's living water.

ACTIVITY

Ask your mom or dad to tell you where the water in your house and your city comes from. (It could be from wells or from a river or lake.) Ask how the city water department makes sure that the water is pure. If your parent doesn't know, look it up in an encyclopedia and talk about it together later. Also, look up the words *well, cistern,* and *spring* to find out how people in ancient times got their water.

How come when I pray to God he doesn't always answer?

[David is speaking:] The Lord hears his people when they call to him for help. He rescues them from all their troubles. The Lord is close to the brokenhearted; he rescues those who are crushed in spirit. The righteous face many troubles, but the Lord rescues them from each and every one.

Psalm 34:17-19

Hello - you've reached heaven's 1-800 number. There isn't anyone here to take your call right now, but if you leave a long message at the sound of the choir, we will return your call. This is a recording...

There's a difference between hearing and answering. And there are many ways for God to answer. God hears and answers all our prayers, but he doesn't always give us what we ask for. And he doesn't always answer us right away. When we ask God for something, sometimes he has a reason for saying "no" or "wait." A "yes" answer is not always the best one. God has the big picture of the whole world, so he knows what the best answer is for every one of your prayers. So keep praying and keep trusting him to give the answer that's right for you, right now!

ACTIVITY

Start a prayer journal. In a spiral notebook, draw a line down the middle of the page to make two columns. Label the first column "Prayers" and the second column "God's Answers." Write down what you pray for; then write down how and when God answers. Keep looking back at earlier requests—he *will* answer, even though for some it may be days, weeks, or even months later!

February 11

Why do I have to obey my parents?

Children, obey your parents because you belong to the Lord, for this is the right thing to do. "Honor your father and mother." This is the first of the Ten Commandments that ends with a promise. And this is the promise: If you honor your father and mother, "you will live a long life, full of blessing." Ephesians 6:1-3

The most important reason for children to obey their parents is because God said to. God knows that children need protection and guidance, and parents are the best ones to do that. Parents take care of their children, give them food and other things they need, and teach them to know right from wrong.

Living God's way means listening to him and doing what he says, and that includes obeying Mom and Dad. Obeying your parents is the best way for you to learn and grow now, and to have a better life in the future. After all, God is your heavenly *Father,* so he wouldn't steer you wrong about how things work best in families.

ACTIVITY

Use photo corners or glue to attach a photo of your parents to a piece of paper. If you don't have a photo, draw a picture. With your best lettering, or stencil letters if you like, write "Honor your father and mother" around the picture. Hang it on your mirror or bulletin board.

February 12

Can I do whatever I want when I'm older?

Don't let anyone think less of you because you are young. Be an example to all believers in what you teach, in the way you live, in your love, your faith, and your purity.   1 Timothy 4:12

JASON'S IMAGINATION

Some kids think that when they grow up they will be able to do anything they want. And some adults still act as if they think it's OK to live that way. But it's <u>not</u> OK. All our lives we will have rules and laws to obey. When God gave the Ten Commandments, he gave them to all people of all ages for all time. No one outgrows the need to follow God's ways.

Doing what your parents tell you now helps you learn to obey those who will be in authority over you later in life. It also helps you want to do what's right. Someday you'll find out that it's great to be a grown-up other people can look up to—and not just because you're taller!

ACTIVITY

Write down the names of three grown-ups whom you want to be like. They could be famous or just people you know. They could be alive today, or maybe they lived long ago. They could be teachers, parents, other relatives, scientists, athletes, pastors, missionaries, writers, performers, or people from other walks of life. What do you like about them? What were they like as children? Are there any books or articles you can read about them? Make a collage or start a scrapbook of your heroines and heroes.

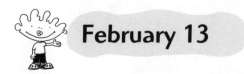

Why is it so hard to love your enemies?

[Jesus is speaking:] "But I say, love your enemies! Pray for those who persecute you!"

Matthew 5:44

It is very difficult to love enemies because it's not natural. And it's the opposite of how everyone around us seems to be behaving. When people hurt us, we want to get back at them. When people don't like us or act mean toward us, it's natural not to like them.

But Jesus tells us to love our enemies, and he promises to give us the strength to do it. "Loving" enemies doesn't necessarily mean being best friends with them. It means acting in a loving way toward them—praying for them, being kind to them, and so forth. Jesus knows just how hard this can be, and he will help you.

ACTIVITY

Think of someone at school or in the neighborhood who seems not to like you or is mean to you. Write this person a card, wishing him or her a nice day, but don't sign your name. In other words, do something nice in secret. You could even make a batch of cookies for this person and leave them at his or her door with a nice note. This way you will learn how it feels to return good for evil.

February 14

I want to have nice friends, but how do I know if kids are nice?

Many will say they are loyal friends, but who can find one who is really faithful?
Proverbs 20:6

You can get an idea of what a person is like by his or her reputation, especially if the reputation is good. For example, if you hear from a lot of people that someone is nice, that's probably a good sign that the person really *is* nice. Sometimes, however, a person's reputation is not always accurate. For example, someone may say that a boy is stuck-up when, instead, he is only shy. Be careful not to judge kids before you know them—give them a chance.

The best way to learn what kids are like is to get to know them yourself. Start by talking with them. The Bible teaches that a person's words show what is in that person's heart. If a person talks about bad things, swears, or tells dirty jokes, that is a sign of what he or she is really like. Also, you can watch kids in action with others. The Holy Spirit will help you decide if they're nice or not.

ACTIVITY
After dinner some night soon, place a bunch of magazines on a table and look through them with your family. Choose a picture of someone in a story or an advertisement and discuss what you think the person is like. Can you really tell what's inside the person by looking at the outside?

Does God sleep or does he just rest?

*He will not let you stumble
and fall; the one who watches
over you will not sleep. Indeed,
he who watches over Israel
never tires and never sleeps.*

Psalm 121:3-4

God does not have a physical body like us, so he doesn't need to sleep or eat. When the Bible says that God "rests," it means he has stopped doing something. To us, that is like rest. In the Creation story from the book of Genesis in the Bible, it says that God rested on the seventh day. He did this after he had created the whole world.

But God doesn't get tired or worn out, so he doesn't need to rest the way people do. And at night, when people sleep, God never closes his eyes—he continues to watch over everyone. So when you go to bed, don't worry—God is awake and watching over you.

ACTIVITY

Pretend that you are a little mouse. (Actually, a big mouse!) Very quietly, watch someone in your family who is sleeping. Be extra careful not to wake him or her. Notice the breathing, the peaceful dreaming, perhaps even the snoring! The person does not even know you're in the room. Remember that God is *not* like this sleeping person. God never sleeps. He is always caring for you and never gets tired.

Did God know Adam and Eve were going to sin?

Long ago, even before he made the world, God loved us and chose us in Christ to be holy and without fault in his eyes. His unchanging plan has always been to adopt us into his own family by bringing us to himself through Jesus Christ. And this gave him great pleasure. Ephesians 1:4-5

God knows everything, even before it happens, so he knew that Adam and Eve were going to sin. But it was their choice—they chose to disobey God. While God was very disappointed with what Adam and Eve did, God still loved them. Because he loved them (and because he loves us), he made a way for the sin to be forgiven. God's plan was to send Jesus to die on the cross for Adam's, Eve's, and our sins. By trusting in Jesus Christ, we can have eternal life—we can live with Jesus forever in heaven.

When Jesus came to earth as a person, he started the "adoption" work that today's verse talks about. The word *adopt* means to choose someone and make that person a member of the family. Jesus' death on the cross for us made our adoption into God's family possible.

ACTIVITY

Many children today have been adopted. Some were even born in faraway countries. Were you adopted? Do you know someone who has been adopted, perhaps in your own family, church, or school? Talk with your mom or dad about how these adoptions are like God's adoption of us. How are they different?

February 17

If Adam and Eve hadn't sinned, would people sin today?

Because one person disobeyed God, many people became sinners. But because one other person obeyed God, many people will be made right in God's sight.

Romans 5:19

We really don't know what would have happened if Adam and Eve hadn't sinned in the Garden of Eden, but their temptation was a very important test. Unfortunately, they failed the test, and sin entered the world—the perfect world became damaged, broken, and dirty.

Because of Adam and Eve's sin, every person who has ever lived has been born a sinner. That includes you. Sin has been passed on from your parents to you. You do wrong things because you are a sinner. But you can get back into friendship with God because of Jesus. He is God's Son and the only person who always obeyed God.

ACTIVITY

To sin means "to miss the mark" or fall short—every person has sinned and failed to live up to God's expectations. Think of the areas in your life where you often fall short. Then turn them into a challenge. Write at the top of a piece of paper, "With God's help . . ." Then write all the good things you want to do and the good ways you want to act. For example: "With God's help . . . I want to do my chores more cheerfully." And "I want to be patient with my baby brother."

One Year Book of Fun & Active Devotions for Kids

February 18

Does God want us to pray for our friends?

I urge you, first of all, to pray for all people. As you make your requests, plead for God's mercy upon them, and give thanks.

1 Timothy 2:1

... AND GOD, PLEASE HELP TOMMY FEEL BETTER IN TIME FOR THE BIG SPELLING TEST TOMORROW.

God definitely wants us to pray for our friends. John 17 tells about Jesus praying for his disciples. He prayed that they would be filled with joy, made holy, unified, and protected from Satan. Jesus thought that it was important to pray for his friends in this way. We can also pray for our friends' problems and for their attitudes. We can pray that they learn to know Jesus and that they discover how to be better friends. Praying for them is one way we keep them as friends.

You can pray for all kinds of things for your friends. In fact, you are being a good friend by thinking of them! God welcomes such prayers. He cares about your friends, too.

ACTIVITY

Time to write something in your prayer journal! Ask God to help you think of two friends who are in special need of your prayers this week. Perhaps they're facing a hard week at school or they have some sad things going on in their families. Write down each name in the left-hand column along with a few words describing your prayer for each one of them. Try to pray for each friend at least once a day. In the coming days and weeks, watch how God chooses to answer your prayers.

February 19

Should I tell the truth to someone even if they won't like it?

We will hold to the truth in love, becoming more and more in every way like Christ, who is the head of his body, the church. Ephesians 4:15

Sometimes the truth hurts, but we still need to say it. If a friend asks you to a party that you know you can't go to, should you say you will be there? No! It will be much better to tell the truth right away.

Another friend might start hanging around with a bad crowd. Being a good friend means telling your friend the truth about what he or she is doing. That friend needs to hear it from you.

Being truthful, however, does *not* give you permission to be cruel. Remember, God is loving and kind. So don't tell people things that will unnecessarily hurt their feelings. For example, it would be cruel to say: "You have a long nose." "You don't play basketball very well." "Your clothes are old and worn out." Ask God to help you be kind *and* truthful.

ACTIVITY

Make a "Hard Love" list, and write down the hard things in your life that make you better. For example, think of certain foods you have to eat, chores you do, schoolwork, bedtime, and even discipline. Now think of a time when someone said a hard thing to you out of love and you could later be thankful about it. A little hard love goes a long way!

February 20

Does how we pray matter?

[King David is speaking:] You would not be pleased with sacrifices, or I would bring them. If I brought you a burnt offering, you would not accept it. The sacrifice you want is a broken spirit. A broken and repentant heart, O God, you will not despise.

Psalm 51:16-17

DEAR DADDY IN HEAVEN...

We should pray sincerely, secretly, and respectfully. To pray *sincerely* means to use words that say just what we're trying to say. It means we do not use fake language or fancy words. We're honest with God and tell him whatever is on our mind because we know he loves us and wants to hear from us.

To pray *secretly* means to make a habit of praying alone. Some people call it "quiet time." We do not limit our prayers to church, meals, or bedtime with Mom or Dad. To pray *respectfully* means to treat God as the great God he is. It means we do not make light of prayer or act silly. It's important to show respect to God, the maker of all creation, the Lord of the universe, and the King of kings.

How you pray matters to God. And because you want him to be your best friend, it matters to you.

ACTIVITY

Make a sign to remind you of the three attitudes of prayer you learned about today. Fold a piece of black construction paper in half. Then use a silver or gold gel marker to write in your best handwriting: *Pray sincerely, secretly, and respectfully.* Place the paper by your bed or some other place near where you often pray.

Why do people pray on their knees?

[Jesus] walked away, about a stone's throw, and knelt down and prayed, "Father, if you are willing, please take this cup of suffering away from me. Yet I want your will, not mine."

Luke 22:41-42

humble happy tired

The Bible tells of people praying in all sorts of positions. Some stood and raised their hands. Some lay down on the ground. Some put their heads between their knees. Some sat down. Some stood but bowed their heads and beat on their chests. We can pray in almost any position. But some people kneel in prayer to show respect for God. It is their way of saying that they want to do things God's way.

How you act with your body can affect your relationship with God. It's true. It's not a magical thing—it's just the way God made you. Kneeling can make you feel humble and submissive to God, which is the right attitude to have in prayer. But whether or not you kneel, remember that it's your attitude that matters most.

ACTIVITY

As you pray today, do it kneeling. If you usually kneel, then go to a different place than your usual place to pray. For example, if you usually kneel next to your bed and rest your elbows on it, you could pray over by your closet or by the bathtub. Are your shoulders relaxed? Are you quiet before God? Tell God that you're ready to pray and talk with him.

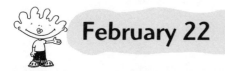

February 22

Where does money come from, God or people?

It is a good thing to receive wealth from God and the good health to enjoy it. To enjoy your work and accept your lot in life—that is indeed a gift from God.

Ecclesiastes 5:19

The Bible says that everything was made by God (John 1:3). So everything came from God. The sun, moon, oceans, trees, animals, sky, and land all came from him. The Bible also says, "Whatever is good and perfect comes to us from God above" (James 1:17). But this doesn't mean that God makes every little thing in the world himself. Instead, he expects people to use the materials he has given them to make things like bread, cars, toys, medicine, houses, clothes, and money. God made the world and people, and he makes it all work right. You might say that money comes from God through people. But God doesn't make money—people print money and mint coins.

God does make it possible for people to earn money. He made you and gave you skills. And he will be pleased to see you grow up, work hard, and earn money. If you ask him, God will show you how to use your money to take care of yourself and help others.

ACTIVITY
What are the ways that your family, relatives, and friends earn money? On a piece of paper, list all the jobs that are done—from your brother's lawn-mowing service to your aunt's career as a doctor. Isn't it interesting to see all the ways that God helps people earn money?

February 23

Why do I have to brush my teeth?

Don't you know that your body is the temple of the Holy Spirit, who lives in you and was given to you by God? You do not belong to yourself. 1 Corinthians 6:19

If your parents tell you to brush your teeth, then you should do what they say. God wants children to obey their parents. But there's another reason for brushing. You see, each person is a very special creation of our loving God. He has given us bodies to live in and to use for serving him. It is our job to take care of our bodies and to use them well. This means eating the right food, getting enough sleep, watching our weight, exercising, dressing warm in cold weather, and not hurting ourselves with drugs or alcohol or tobacco. It also means brushing our teeth and keeping ourselves clean.

It wouldn't be a sin if you didn't brush your teeth one day. It *would* be a sin, however, if you didn't take care of your teeth and let them get decayed. It's not a sin to eat candy. But it would be sinful if you ate so much candy that you destroyed your health. God wants you to take care of your body.

ACTIVITY

Ask a parent to help you buy a new toothbrush. Shop for one that does the job, is easy to use, and looks good. Promise yourself now that you will brush every day.

I feel so stupid in some subjects. What can I do?

If you need wisdom—if you want to know what God wants you to do—ask him, and he will gladly tell you.

James 1:5

Some subjects are difficult to understand at first—not everyone gets everything right away. God made each person different, each with special gifts. It's normal that some subjects will be easier for you than others. But you can still conquer the ones that seem very difficult. In those classes you can ask the teacher for help. Most teachers want their students to ask questions and to ask for help when they need it.

Your parents will also be happy to help you. They will remind you that difficult subjects can help you learn to think and figure things out.

God wants to teach you many things as you grow up. Ask him to help you do your best. Then study and be patient with yourself. Remember that all students are better at some subjects than others. So you'll need to spend a little more time on the subjects that are hardest for you.

ACTIVITY

Talk with a parent about what school was like for him or her. What was the most difficult subject for your mom or dad? What helped him or her learn?

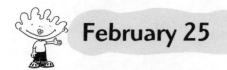

Why did God make people?

*God said, "Let us make people in our
image, to be like ourselves. They will
be masters over all life—the fish in the
sea, the birds in the sky, and all the
livestock, wild animals, and small
animals." So God created people in
his own image; God patterned them
after himself; male and female he
created them.*   Genesis 1:26-27

People are special creations, not just different animals. God
created people to be his friends and to take care of the world.
Unlike animals, human beings can talk to each other and to God.
People are the only part of God's marvelous creation that can be
friends with God. And he created them perfect—that's why Adam
and Eve were not ashamed of being naked.

People are also the only ones who can sin, however. They can
choose not to follow God's ways. They can ignore what he said
about taking care of the earth and the animals. Many people live
like that. But God's Word shows us a better way to live.

So today, remember that God made you like himself, in his image.
Isn't that great? Then think about the special jobs that you can do
for God. What are they? How can you do them better?

ACTIVITY
What kinds of animals do you and your friends have for pets?
Write down what is necessary for taking good care of a pet.
What things about people make them able to care for animals?

Why do so many people keep translating the Bible?

[Jesus is speaking:] "Go and make disciples of all the nations, baptizing them in the name of the Father and the Son and the Holy Spirit. Teach these new disciples to obey all the commands I have given you."

Matthew 28:19-20

The Old Testament first was written in the Hebrew language, and the New Testament was written in Greek. If no one had ever translated the Bible, only people who read ancient Hebrew and Greek would be able to understand the Bible today. Fortunately, over the years men and women have put the Bible into other languages, including English, so that speakers of many different languages can read it. But some people still don't have the Bible in their own language. Some don't even have a written language. That means a translator has to put their language into written words so they can read. Then someone has to translate the Bible into their new language.

God wants people to take the message about Jesus to everyone all over the world, and that means translating the Bible into every language there is. Thank God for giving you a Bible you can read. And pray for the people who work hard to translate God's Word into other languages.

ACTIVITY

Look in an encyclopedia to learn about John Wycliffe. He lived in the 1300s. He and his followers were the first people to translate the Bible into English. Their work inspired the translation work that is still going on all over the world today. Be thankful for God's work through translators.

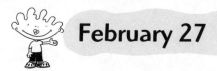

Why do we study the Bible?

Work hard so God can approve you. Be a good worker, one who does not need to be ashamed and who correctly explains the word of truth.   2 Timothy 2:15

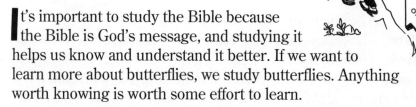

It's important to study the Bible because the Bible is God's message, and studying it helps us know and understand it better. If we want to learn more about butterflies, we study butterflies. Anything worth knowing is worth some effort to learn.

Studying the Bible helps you find out how to live and how to know what God wants. When you only read the Bible (without studying it), you may not see the meaning right away. Studying helps you learn lessons for life—you learn God's will so you can obey him. Studying the Bible is like reading a story many, many times—each time you read it you see something different and learn more.

ACTIVITY

Look at the opening part of the Gospel of Mark. Read Mark 1:1-8. Then answer these questions:

> Who are the characters?
> What happened to Jesus?
> Where did the action happen?
> Why do you think Mark started his Gospel this way?
> What do you learn from this story?

Why do we memorize verses?

I have hidden your word in my heart, that I might not sin against you. Psalm 119:11

We memorize Bible verses because we want to remember what God has told us. When we have the Bible in our head, God's Word will be with us when we're playing, studying, shopping, or doing anything—it will be with us wherever we go.

If you know God's Word, when you face a problem or a tough situation, you will be able to remember what God has told you to do. Memorizing verses can be fun, too. Then you can always think about the verses and what they mean.

ACTIVITY

Pick one of these verses to memorize: Deuteronomy 6:5, Psalm 121:7, or John 3:16. Write it out on an index card. Don't forget to write the Bible book, chapter number, and verse number after the verse. Read the verse aloud and memorize it. Put the card in your backpack or coat pocket so that you can pull it out and work on memorizing it. Add another verse next week.

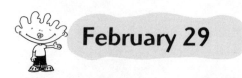

February 29

Is thinking something bad the same as doing it or saying it?

O Jerusalem, cleanse your hearts that you may be saved. How long will you harbor your evil thoughts?   Jeremiah 4:14

CLEANSING POOL

Hating someone or wishing that the person were dead is terrible, but hating only affects the person who is thinking the bad thoughts. He or she would make the situation much worse by actually killing the other person. The same is true with stealing, lusting, lying, and bad thoughts. As wrong as it is to think bad thoughts, it's even worse to do the bad action or say the bad words.

However, thoughts are very important, because we often end up doing what we keep thinking about. Suppose your mother told you not to eat any cookies before dinner. But you see the cookies on the counter and keep thinking about how good they would taste, especially with a glass of cold milk. If you keep thinking about this, the desire to eat those cookies probably will grow and grow until, eventually, you disobey your mom and take one. God knows what you are thinking, and he wants you to fill your mind with good thoughts, not bad ones. He wants this because he loves you.

ACTIVITY
Read Philippians 4:8. Now read it again, like a prayer. Ask God to help you think only about things that are honorable and right, pure, lovely, admirable, excellent, and worthy of praise.

March 1

Why shouldn't we take drugs?

Don't be drunk with wine,
because that will ruin your life.
Instead, let the Holy Spirit fill and
control you. Ephesians 5:18

Prescription drugs (medicines) are OK to take. In fact, doctors prescribe them to help make people well when they're sick. But other drugs are bad for us. That's why they are against the law. Illegal drugs hurt and even kill. They affect our brains so that we can't think very well. Some people use these drugs because they make them feel good for a little while. But often, people get hooked, and the drugs take over their lives.

Don't let anything you put into your body control you, whether it's food, drink, drugs, alcohol, or any other chemical. Only God should be in control of your life. And God wants you to take care of your body. He doesn't want you to use bad drugs, which destroy it. Stay far away from all illegal drugs. Stay close to your loving God.

ACTIVITY
Write out today's verse, Ephesians 5:18, on an index card. Memorize the words, including the Bible reference. Pray that the Holy Spirit will fill and control you.

March 2

Are Beatitudes short for bad attitudes?

One day as the crowds were gathering, Jesus went up the mountainside with his disciples and sat down to teach them.

Matthew 5:1

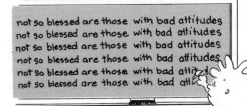

esus taught a short sermon called the Beatitudes to describe good attitudes, the attitudes that God wants us to have. The word *beatitude* means "blessed." Jesus said that whoever followed him should be poor in spirit, merciful, and so forth, and should expect rejection from others for being his follower. Jesus' disciples may have been thinking that they would become rich, famous, and powerful by following him. But Jesus was telling them that they should expect their rewards in heaven, not here on earth.

The same is true for us today. Those who follow Jesus will be blessed in many ways, even if bad things happen to them. In all situations, as Jesus' follower you will have his joy and peace, knowing that he will never leave you.

ACTIVITY

Read the Beatitudes for yourself. They're found in the first twelve verses of Matthew 5. How many times do you find the word *blesses?* (The word may be "blessed" or "happy," depending on the translation.)

March 3

Is it all right to say bad things if there is no one there to hear you?

Don't use foul or abusive language. Let everything you say be good and helpful, so that your words will be an encouragement to those who hear them.

Ephesians 4:29

JASON'S IMAGINATION

If something is wrong, then it is wrong even if no one else ever finds out about it. So swearing, lying, and saying bad things about others are wrong, even if our parents, friends, neighbors, or anyone else can't hear. God knows what we're saying, for he sees and hears everything.

That's why a true test of your character comes whenever you think no one else is watching or listening. If you really believe that swearing is wrong, you won't do it, period. You won't look for opportunities to do it when no one is around to catch you. Work hard at speaking what is good and right, even when no one else is around, because that's what really matters. And if anyone ever does find out what you said in private, that person will know you can be trusted. If you ask God to keep you close to him, his love will be in your heart. Then there will be no bad words to come out of your mouth.

ACTIVITY

Learn to communicate in a new way: sign language! Get an instruction book from the library and begin to learn letters and common words. Why not learn with a friend? Think about communicating positive things that are helpful and of thinking first before you "talk" with your hands.

March 4

Why don't I have time to play?

There is a time for everything, a season for every activity under heaven. Ecclesiastes 3:1

I'VE DECIDED THAT I JUST DON'T HAVE ENOUGH PLAYTIME BOOKED INTO MY SCHEDULE. I'M AFRAID MY CHORES WILL HAVE TO GO.

Schedules get packed with activities, lessons, sports, and schoolwork. Sometimes it seems as if there's no time to play. If this is a problem for you, talk with your parents about it. After you have done your homework and activities, you should find some time to play.

If your schedule is too full, you and your family can talk about the possibility of not doing some of the activities any more. Your parents want you to have fun. So does God!

ACTIVITY

Today's verse comes from a passage of Scripture found in the Old Testament. Look at the whole passage (Ecclesiastes 3:1-8). Then list all the activities that Solomon wrote, "There is a time . . . ," and, after each one, write an example or an explanation.

Why did the disciples tell the people that Jesus was too busy to see the kids?

Jesus said, "Let the children come to me. Don't stop them! For the Kingdom of Heaven belongs to such as these."   Matthew 19:14

Many parents brought their children to see Jesus, and Jesus always welcomed them. The disciples tried to stop them because they didn't understand how much Jesus loved children and wanted all people to come to him. Sometimes adults don't think children are important. Some grown-ups think that because children still have many things to learn, they just get in the way.

But Jesus thinks kids are very important. Even today. He thinks *you* are important. Don't be afraid to talk to him about anything.

ACTIVITY

Make a bookmark for your Bible. Take a long strip of construction paper or other fairly strong paper. Write on it, "Jesus loves kids!" Now decorate it with stickers or your own drawings. To make it last longer, cover it with laminating material or a clear, self-adhesive paper.

March 6

Do I have to let little kids in my room to play when I have special stuff?

Love is patient and kind. Love is not jealous or boastful or proud.
1 Corinthians 13:4

God is loving and kind, so he wants us to be loving and kind too, not stingy and selfish. If younger friends, brothers, or sisters want to play with your toys, you should let them if it's safe and OK with their parents.

Sometimes we act as though our toys, clothes, and other belongings are more important than our friends and family. But it's good to take turns and to let other people enjoy our "special stuff." When we do that, people will be able to see that we really love Jesus.

On the other hand, God wants you to be responsible, too. You don't have to let little kids do whatever they want to your things, especially if your special stuff is too hard for little kids to treat right. You should take good care of your things, just as you should respect everyone else's things. Try to let other kids have a turn with your stuff whenever you can. When you can't, be kind about it, and make sure you have a good reason. And thank God for your special stuff.

ACTIVITY
Invite a young friend over to play. Put today's devotion into practice by letting him or her play with your special stuff. But be sure to keep unsafe, breakable objects out of reach.

Is outer space hot or cold?

*[David is speaking:] When I look
at the night sky and see the work
of your fingers—the moon and
the stars you have set in place—
what are mortals that you should
think of us, mere humans that
you should care for us?*

Psalm 8:3-4

JASON'S
IMAGINATION

NASA

God created the universe with over a billion, billion stars. While the stars put out a lot of heat, anything not close to a star has almost no heat at all. The heat produced by our sun, the star that's closest to Earth, produces just the right amount of light and heat for us to live on our planet. The air on Earth keeps the heat in.

God created the earth with a climate that makes it possible for you, his special creation, to live here. Earth is your home, made just right by your heavenly Father.

ACTIVITY

Make an Earth light-catcher. Pour about one-third cup of white glue into a paper cup and add five drops of blue food coloring. (The glue will dry much darker.) Stir with a wooden stick until the color is completely mixed in. Pour the colored glue into a small margarine tub lid. Lay a paper clip in the glue to use as a hanger. (Have it extend over the edge of the lid.) Let the glue dry completely—this could take up to a week. Then peel the blue circle out of the lid and outline the continents with a permanent marker. Tie a piece of yarn through the paper clip, and hang your light-catcher in a window.

March 8

Were there any crimes in the Bible?

*The earth had become corrupt in
God's sight, and it was filled with
violence.* Genesis 6:11

Ever since Adam and Eve sinned against God, sin (and there-fore, crime) has been in the world. In fact, every person ever born has been born a sinner. This means that it is natural for boys, girls, men, and women to do wrong—to lie, cheat, steal, and hurt others. So crimes have been committed by people since the beginning. That's why we need Jesus.

Only Jesus can take away your sin, teach you to do right, and help you love and respect others. It all starts when you admit your sin, ask Jesus to forgive you, and invite him to rule your life. If every-one did that, and tried to obey God, the number of crimes would be reduced to almost zero! That's the way it will be in heaven, where there will be no sin.

ACTIVITY
Read the Ten Commandments, given in Exodus 20. Now look with a grown-up at the front page of today's newspaper. Which commandments were broken yesterday, according to the news-paper? How can teaching people about Jesus help to lower the crime rate?

March 9

When I ask a question, why do grown-ups always tell me what the Bible says?

All Scripture is inspired by God and is useful to teach us what is true and to make us realize what is wrong in our lives. It straightens us out and teaches us to do what is right. It is God's way of preparing us in every way, fully equipped for every good thing God wants us to do.   2 Timothy 3:16-17

The Bible is God's Word. When we read it, we learn what God is like and how he wants us to live. Think of the Bible as an instruction book. It's like the one for the family car. If we do what that book says, the car will run right. If something goes wrong, a mechanic can read the book and find out how to fix it.

The Bible is God's instruction book for your life. You need to read it and study it and do what it says. Then your life will run right and you'll know how to fix anything that goes wrong. And remember, you weren't just put together at a factory. Your heavenly Father made you! You are a one-of-a-kind model, and God has a plan just right for you.

ACTIVITY
Ask your dad or mom to let you look at an instruction manual for a car, a computer, a lawn mower, a VCR, or some other appliance in your home. Check out the way this manual helps you know how to run the machine or appliance and fix it. Name some ways the Bible is like this manual.

March 10

What is a conscience?

[Paul is speaking:] "I always try to maintain a clear conscience before God and everyone else."

Acts 24:16

G od has built into all people a way of helping them tell right from wrong. This inner voice is called a conscience, and we need to learn to listen to it. The conscience is a feeling inside about something we are thinking about doing. If what we are thinking about doing is not right, then our conscience can make us feel bad about it and give us the sense that we should not do it. Our conscience can also tell us when we *should* do something. When it does that, we get a strong sense that we should do what we're thinking about. God gave us our conscience to help us decide what to do. So it's important for us to listen to our conscience.

If you don't listen to your conscience, pretty soon you get into the habit of ignoring it. After a while you won't hear it at all. That can lead to trouble. Listen carefully to your conscience. What has God told you recently through your conscience?

ACTIVITY

Play "Whisper" with a brother, sister, or friend. Take turns whispering messages to each other across the room. See how quietly you can whisper and still communicate the message. Think of your conscience as God's whisper in your ear.

March 11

The kids around me in class keep getting me into trouble. What can I do?

Stay away from fools, for you won't find knowledge there.

Proverbs 14:7

You can ignore the other kids who are causing trouble. If you don't give them your attention, they probably will stop trying to get you to do what is wrong. If this doesn't work, ask the teacher to change your seat. To do your best in class, you need to be quiet and listen carefully to the teacher. Remember, no one can *make* you do something wrong or break the rules. Other kids can pressure you, but in the end, *you* always make the decision.

Decide that no matter what the kids around you do or how much they pressure you to do things that are wrong, you will do what is right. And you will do your best to focus on studying your lessons and listening to the teacher God has given you this year.

ACTIVITY

Write the letter *I* on a half sheet of paper or an index card and tape it to the cover of your assignment notebook or another note-book that you use often during the school day. It stands for "*I* am responsible." Make a colorful border around the letter. Let it remind you that *you* are the one who needs to be in control of your own behavior and do whatever you can to make good decisions at school.

March 12

When is Jesus coming back?

[Jesus is speaking:] "No one knows the day or the hour when these things will happen, not even the angels in heaven or the Son himself. Only the Father knows. So be prepared, because you don't know what day your Lord is coming."   Matthew 24:36, 42

Before Jesus left the earth many years ago, he promised to return someday. And after Jesus went up into the clouds, angels said he would come back. For Christians, this is a wonderful event to look forward to. Christ's return will be the beginning of the end for Satan and all evil in the world. Won't it be great to see Jesus in person! It could happen any day now. Although no one knows when Christ will return, he told us to be ready. This means pleasing God each day, using our time wisely, and telling others about Jesus.

What would you like to be doing when Christ returns?

ACTIVITY
Cut a large picture from a magazine, poster, or greeting card. Using a glue stick, glue the picture to a poster board or light cardboard and let it dry. Turn the picture over and draw wavy lines all the way down and all the way across to make jigsaw-puzzle pieces. Get an adult to help you cut along the lines. Then mix up the pieces and try to put the picture together again. At first you may wonder how it will turn out, but you know that it will. Jesus' return is also a mystery, but we know that everything will come together by God's design.

March 13

Why don't you let us watch certain TV shows?

Above all else, guard your heart,
for it affects everything you do.

Proverbs 4:23

Many TV shows encourage us to do things that are wrong. Most of the time the people who produce the television shows and the actors in the shows are not Christians. Because they don't know God, they will often do things on TV that are sinful, and those things are not good for us to watch. Some shows even encourage people to do wrong things. It is bad for us to watch people sin on TV because then we are tempted to sin in the same way.

Instead, turn the bad programs off so that you don't put bad ideas into your mind. Proverbs 4:23 talks about how you should "guard your heart," because what you think about and put into your heart will show up in what you do. So be careful, and turn off bad TV shows. God wants you to put good things into your mind so that you will do what is right.

ACTIVITY
Have you ever seen a Top Ten List? It is a list of someone's ten favorite items, whatever the topic happens to be. Make a Top Ten List of your favorite shows and movies ever. What you put on your list is entirely up to you. What kinds of things will you think about to help you make your choices?

March 14

Why are some people scared of angels?

Then the angel of the Lord touched the meat and bread with the staff in his hand, and fire flamed up from the rock and consumed all he had brought. And the angel of the Lord disappeared. Judges 6:21

In the Bible we read that some people became frightened when angels appeared to them. They were scared because they were amazed at the power and glory of the angels. God is great and holy and awesome, and sometimes angels appear as God's messengers, with a lot of light and noise. That can be quite scary.

Also, remember that most people have never seen an angel. So when one appears, it is quite normal to be surprised and fearful. God still sends angels to watch over us and protect us, but we don't need to be afraid of that! Angels do only what God wants them to do. So we can trust them to be helpful, loving, and powerful, just like God.

ACTIVITY

Before you go to bed, get a flashlight and set it up so that it stands by itself, shining against the wall. Then turn off the lights and see if you can make an angel by holding your hands just right, in front of the light and casting a shadow on the wall. You could try hooking your thumbs together and holding your fingers out, like wings. Thank God for angels that protect us and bring messages from him.

March 15

Is it all right to tell a lie once in a while?

Put away all falsehood and "tell your neighbor the truth" because we belong to each other.

Ephesians 4:25

We should always tell the truth because God always tells the truth. Would it be all right to touch a hot stovetop every once in a while? If you did, you would burn yourself every time. It is never right to lie, not even once in a while. God tells us to tell the truth because he is truth.

Lying also gets you into trouble. Usually one lie leads to another. It's much simpler to tell the truth than to have to remember the lies you have told so that you can keep them covered up. And lying makes others not trust you and want to avoid you. But people who are honest are free and joyful. This freedom and joy can be yours!

ACTIVITY

Cut out one-inch by six-inch strips of construction paper and make a "truth chain." On each strip, write a truthful phrase or sentence (for example, "God loves me," "I have a wonderful family," "I feel safe in my room," "I love basketball"). Take one strip of paper and form a circle—the first link of your chain. Tape or glue the ends together. Now take another strip, put it through the first link, and tape or glue the ends together. Continue until you have a long chain.

March 16

If lying is a sin, why did some people in the Bible tell lies?

You love to do the evil things [the Devil] does. He . . . has always hated the truth. There is no truth in him. When he lies, it is consistent with his character; for he is a liar and the father of lies.

John 8:44

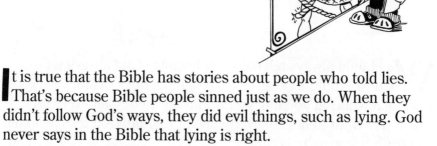

It is true that the Bible has stories about people who told lies. That's because Bible people sinned just as we do. When they didn't follow God's ways, they did evil things, such as lying. God never says in the Bible that lying is right.

God is truth, and he wants you to tell the truth. Honesty helps families, neighborhoods, cities, schools, companies, and friends get along together. Honesty protects you from danger and helps people to enjoy one another. If you choose to tell the truth, God will be very happy—and that's the truth!

ACTIVITY

Over the centuries people have sewn embroidery floss onto cloth to make pictures called samplers. Often they sew letters that spell out wise and true sayings. Take a piece of graph paper and *draw* a sampler instead of sewing one. Choose a saying about honesty, such as "Honesty is the best policy" or "It pays to tell the truth" or "God is truth." In the small squares on the paper, make *X's* to form the letters. Use a fine-point marker or colored pencil and fill in the squares on the graph paper. Draw other designs around the saying.

March 17

Why does God have rules?

Until faith in Christ was shown to us as the way of becoming right with God, we were guarded by the law. We were kept in protective custody, so to speak, until we could put our faith in the coming Savior. Galatians 3:23

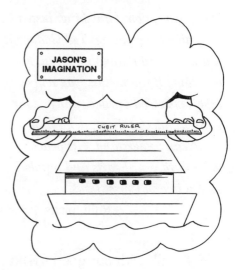

JASON'S IMAGINATION

CUBIT RULER

Some of God's rules are like a wall that protects us from danger. The wall stops us from going farther than we should and getting into trouble. Although we don't see the danger on the other side of the wall, God does, and he loves us so much that he wants to keep us away from it. God also has rules to help us grow to be like him. Think about a baby who doesn't like her food. We know that she needs to eat the food in order to grow and be healthy.

Like the baby, you don't know everything you need, but God does. God loves you more than you can imagine, and he knows what is best for you. His rules are for your benefit. That's why you need to trust him, obey him, and thank him for loving you so much that he gave you rules.

ACTIVITY

Go on the Internet with a parent or another grown-up that your parents trust, such as a librarian. Do a search for kinds of rules, such as "rules for games" or "rules of the road." What kinds of information did you find? People give us many rules. God's rules are even more important, and Jesus helps us obey them!

March 18

Why do we pray?

Don't worry about anything; instead, pray about everything. Tell God what you need, and thank him for all he has done. If you do this, you will experience God's peace, which is far more wonderful than the human mind can understand. His peace will guard your hearts and minds as you live in Christ Jesus.

Philippians 4:6-7

We talk with our good friends about all sorts of things. In the same way, we should talk to God about what is happening in our lives. God wants us to tell him what makes us happy, sad, and afraid. He wants to know what we would like him to do for ourselves and for others. Also, when we pray, we give God an opportunity to make good changes in us.

God has told us to pray. Our prayers show that we want to obey him and let him work in our lives.

ACTIVITY

You can talk with God any time, any place. But a special part of friendship is having a regular time and place to talk. Think about the best time for you to pray every day. Here are some suggestions: when you first wake up, while you walk to school or wait at the bus stop, when you first come home from school, right before you go to sleep at night. Next, make a prayer reminder that will help you remember to pray at the time and place you've chosen. For example, you could make a note card to carry with you, or you could place a picture of praying hands beside your bed.

One Year Book of Fun & Active Devotions for Kids

March 19

What should I say to God when I pray?

[Jesus is speaking:] "Pray like this: Our Father in heaven, may your name be honored. May your Kingdom come soon. May your will be done here on earth, just as it is in heaven. Give us our food for today, and forgive us our sins, just as we have forgiven those who have sinned against us. And don't let us yield to temptation, but deliver us from the evil one." Matthew 6:9-13

Prayer can become a habit in which we just say the same words over and over. Instead, we should think about what we are saying when we pray, and we should be honest with God. Also, we shouldn't pray to show off but to tell God our thoughts and feelings.

The Lord's Prayer (printed above) is a guide Jesus gave us for talking to God. Prayers should include thanking God for who he is and for what he has done. Through prayer you need to confess your sins, telling God you are sorry for the bad things you have done. You can ask God to help others and yourself, too. You can talk to God about anything on your mind.

ACTIVITY
Have you memorized the Lord's Prayer? It would be good to memorize the Bible version your church uses. You may want to write it down in your prayer journal. If you already know it by heart, find a quiet place now, close your eyes, and slowly pray the words to your Father in heaven.

March 20

Is it all right to laugh at dirty jokes?

Obscene stories, foolish talk, and coarse jokes—these are not for you. Instead, let there be thankfulness to God.
Ephesians 5:4

Some jokes are funny but not good. We should avoid laughing at dirty jokes. A "dirty" joke uses foul words or talks about sex to get a laugh. Jokes that make fun of other people, their race, skin color, religion, and so forth, are also bad. Why? Because God is holy and pure, and he wants us to be pure. Being like him is the key to living the way he meant us to live. Telling or listening to dirty jokes fills the mind with wrong thoughts and may cause others to feel bad.

If you are near someone who is telling jokes that are bad, go away from that person. You should do nothing to encourage the person who is telling them. There are plenty of good, clean jokes. Listen to those, tell those, and have fun!

ACTIVITY
Make today Funny Joke Day in your family! Tell as many good, clean jokes as you can, and learn some new ones. Read a joke book to learn some great jokes. You can probably find a good one at the library if you don't have one already. Here's a joke to get things started: *How can you tell if Godzilla is under your bed? Your nose is touching the ceiling!* Who has the best joke in your whole family?

March 21

How do I trust God for money?

[Jesus is speaking:] "Don't be troubled. You trust God, now trust in me."   John 14:1

Trusting God is no small thing. Many grown-ups have trouble remembering to trust him, especially when it comes to money. But that doesn't mean God isn't trustworthy! He definitely is.

First, pray. Tell God what you need, what you would like, and how you feel. But also tell him that you trust him to take care of you and to do what is best for you. Then put your mind at ease and do not worry. God promises to provide for his people. He also tells them to be content with what they have. You can be sure that God is doing what is best for you.

ACTIVITY

Take some money out of your wallet or bank—both paper bills and coins. Can you find the words about trust on each one? When you look at money, look at those words—"In God We Trust"—and let them remind you of God's many promises to take care of you. Remember that you can trust him because he never breaks his promises.

Why don't parents just let you pick your own friends?

Listen, my child, to what your father teaches you. Don't neglect your mother's teaching. Proverbs 1:8

> PERHAPS THAT'S NOT THE BEST WAY TO PICK A NEW FRIEND, JASON.

> ELEMENTARY SCHOOL YEARBOOK

Most parents try to let their children choose their own friends, but some of the choices don't seem very good. Also, parents usually know more about whole families, and they want their kids to hang around good and positive moms, dads, brothers, and sisters in other families.

God put your parents here for a reason. They know you well. Your parents can help you find good friends. Try to look at it like a team made up of God, your parents, and you. That will help you be the happiest and have the most fun in the long run.

ACTIVITY

Talk over with your parents what qualities in friends and friends' families they value. Write these qualities down together along the left side of a sheet of paper. Across the top of the paper list the names of your friends and other kids you think would make good friends. Make a chart by drawing vertical lines between the names and horizontal lines between the qualities. Under each name, put an *X* in the squares for the qualities that person has. Then look at the chart. Which kids will make the best friends? Why? Pray with your family for wisdom as you choose friends with whom you'll spend your time.

March 23

What's the difference between being best friends and just being friends?

After David had finished talking with Saul, he met Jonathan, the king's son. There was an immediate bond of love between them, and they became the best of friends. 1 Samuel 18:1

"**B**est friends" is a way of saying "very close friends." The difference between "very close friends" and others is that you spend a lot of time with very close friends and can talk to them about lots of subjects. Very close friends stick with you when you are having problems or are in a bad mood. You can have many friends, but you'll probably have just a few very close friends. Be careful about having just one "best friend" all the time because feelings get hurt very easily that way.

The kids you choose as your very close friends should want to please God and do what is right—like you do. If you made the chart described yesterday, you'll want to choose kids with the most *X*'s.

ACTIVITY
Close friends do lots of different things together. Has one of your close friends done something special lately—such as getting a good grade on a hard test in school, making a sports team, or recovering from being very sick? With your parent's help and the permission of your friend's parents, plan a surprise party. Arrange to gather your friends at a restaurant or your house, make a sign that celebrates the occasion, then surprise your friend by taking him or her to the party.

March 24

How did God create the earth?

In the beginning the Word already existed. He was with God, and he was God. He was in the beginning with God. He created everything there is. Nothing exists that he didn't make. John 1:1-3

Whenever we make something, like a craft, a drawing, a sand castle, or a dessert, we have to start with special materials, like string, glue, paper, crayons, sand, flour, and spices. We can't even imagine creating something out of nothing—by just saying the words and making it appear. But God is so powerful that he can do things that we think are impossible. That includes making anything he wants, even creating things from nothing. That's what it means to be God—he can do anything.

So we can't know the exact answer to the very good question, How did God create the earth? We know how he *didn't* do it—with a recipe or instructions from a book. And we can know that however he did it, the Creator did it with great love and power.

ACTIVITY

Take some Play-Doh or other soft modeling clay. Work at an art table to squeeze the clay and make it even softer. Close your eyes and feel its coolness. Now shape the clay into an animal, even if your Play-Doh is blue! Imagine the joy God had when he created new life on the earth. Now think about how God made the whole universe out of nothing. Our God is powerful.

How does God make the sun and moon go up and down?

[David is speaking:] The heavens tell of the glory of God. The skies display his marvelous crafts-manship.   Psalm 19:1

God made powerful laws for running the universe. These laws control the movements of the sun, moon, earth, and other planets and stars. For example, one law called *gravity* draws objects toward each other. Other natural laws control the weather. Many forces determine whether a day will be sunny or cloudy, warm or cold. These forces include the heat from the sun, the currents in the ocean, the wind, and many others. God set up the rules that make all of the forces work together. And because God controls the entire universe, he can interrupt the laws if he wants to—bring rain to dry land or bright sunshine to flooded areas. Just think how powerful God must be to control all that! Nothing is too hard for God.

ACTIVITY
Get the newspaper and find the weather forecast for today. Then see if the prediction is right. Weather experts use amazing instruments and computers to predict the weather. But are they right every day? God is the one who is powerful and in control.

Why didn't the bush burn up?

Suddenly, the angel of the Lord appeared to him as a blazing fire in a bush. Moses was amazed because the bush was engulfed in flames, but it didn't burn up. "Amazing!" Moses said to himself. . . . When the Lord saw that he had caught Moses' attention, God called to him from the bush, "Moses! Moses!"

Exodus 3:2-4

One day while watching sheep, a man named Moses saw a bush on fire that would not burn up. The burning bush didn't turn into ashes because God was present, doing a miracle to get Moses' attention. When Moses saw the bush and heard God's voice, he was ready to listen. Through the burning bush Moses learned about God's power. He discovered that God had the power to do what he said he would do—rescue the people of Israel from slavery in Egypt.

You probably haven't seen any burning bushes lately, but God still speaks to his people. He does this through his Word, prayer, other people, and circumstances. Can you hear him? Are you ready to be God's helper to carry out his plans?

ACTIVITY

Go with a grown-up to a forest preserve or other nature area away from the noise of cars, trucks, and yelling people. Take a listening walk to practice keeping your ears in shape to hear God's world. What noises do you hear from animals? from water? from the wind? from other parts of nature? Also listen to what God might be saying to you in your heart.

March 27

What's so bad about cheating in sports?

[Jesus is speaking:] "Unless you are faithful in small matters, you won't be faithful in large ones. If you cheat even a little, you won't be honest with greater responsibilities." Luke 16:10

Cheating in sports is bad because it deceives others and ruins the game. Sometimes, on TV or even in school, it can seem as though winning a game is the most important thing in the world. But nothing can be so important that it's OK to cheat to get it. God wants us to be honest, truthful, and fair in *all* that we do. That's why we should also play clean. Some people think that playing dirty (hurting others in a game) is OK as long as it doesn't break any rules. But Christians should respect others as well as obey the rules.

These are the best reasons to play in sports activities: (1) to improve your skills and physical condition; (2) to learn about teamwork and how to win *and* lose; (3) to have fun. When you play in any sport, you should do your best and enjoy the game. That's much more important than winning or losing. God is on your side no matter what the scoreboard says.

ACTIVITY

The next time you watch a sports events—in person or on TV, kids or professionals—keep a "good sport" score. Write down each time a player does a positive, sportsmanlike thing, such as applauding an opponent's good play, making sure somebody else didn't get hurt, and not arguing over a close play.

March 28

Why do I feel bad when I do something wrong?

I am no longer sorry that I sent that letter to you. . . . Now I am glad I sent it, not because it hurt you, but because the pain caused you to have remorse and change your ways. It was the kind of sorrow God wants his people to have, so you were not harmed by us in any way. For God can use sorrow in our lives to help us turn away from sin and seek salvation. 2 Corinthians 7:8-10

When we do something wrong, we may feel bad because it hurt others. Or we may feel frustrated because we didn't do what was best. Also, we may feel guilty because we have let God down.

God wants you to do right, so he built a warning system in you to alert you when you are about to do something wrong. That warning system is called a conscience. If you get too close to a fire, the heat warns you to move away before you get hurt. Your conscience warns you that doing bad things will hurt you if you do them. Your conscience is a gift from your loving God. Sometimes we don't listen to our conscience, so people need to help us pay attention. That's what Paul did when he wrote a letter to the people in Corinth (see the verses above).

ACTIVITY
Watch the movie *Pinocchio* and look for the character named Jiminy Cricket. Listen to the song he sings to Pinocchio about the value of a conscience.

Why do my parents get mad at me if they have Jesus in their hearts?

"Don't sin by letting anger gain control over you." Don't let the sun go down while you are still angry.   Ephesians 4:26

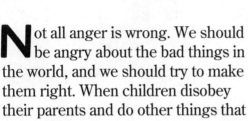

Not all anger is wrong. We should be angry about the bad things in the world, and we should try to make them right. When children disobey their parents and do other things that are wrong, sometimes their parents get angry. Good parents want their children to do what is right, so they try to teach children right from wrong.

Sometimes, of course, parents get angry at children for the wrong reasons. Maybe the parents are grouchy because they've had a bad day. Or maybe they misunderstood what their child did. Parents are human and make mistakes. Even Christian parents who have God living in them and guiding them sometimes do what is wrong. That happens when they don't do what God wants them to do. No matter how your parents act, you should love them and pray for them.

ACTIVITY
Do a role play with your mom or dad. But this time, you be the parent and make Mom or Dad the child! Act out a scene like this: The child comes into a room and the parent thinks the child has been disobedient. How would you act? After the role play, talk with your parent about how you feel when he or she gets angry with you.

How can God be everywhere?

[King Solomon is speaking:] Who can really build [God] a worthy home? Not even the highest heavens can contain him! So who am I to consider building a Temple for him, except as a place to burn sacrifices to him?

2 Chronicles 2:6

God is spirit, not just a big person. That is, God is not limited to space and time. He has no body that can be only here or there. Also, God is *all*-powerful, not just *very* powerful. That is, he can do anything. He can be all places at once just by wanting to.

We human beings have physical bodies. That means we can be in only one place at a time. But God is not like that. He is everywhere, always ready to love, help, and listen to everyone's prayers. And God wants you to know this: You don't ever have to be afraid that he won't be there for you when you need him.

Think of it—God is everywhere all the time. Isn't that amazing!

ACTIVITY

On a piece of paper, list the places you've visited: cities, states, perhaps even other countries. Maybe you've lived in more than one city already. Put down those places also. Now just think about some of the places you have not visited. God is there already—he is God of the whole universe!

March 31

Why do we go to church if God is everywhere?

Let us not neglect our meeting together, as some people do, but encourage and warn each other, especially now that the day of his coming back again is drawing near.   Hebrews 10:25

In the Bible, God tells Christians to worship with other Christians. It is possible to worship God by ourselves. And we *should* spend time alone, praying and reading his Word. But it is also very important to get together with others who follow Christ. We can encourage and strengthen each other, pray for each other, and learn from each other. We can sing and praise God together. We can serve and help each other. All of this can happen in church.

Church is also a place where Christians of all ages and types can come together—babies, grandparents, children, poor, wealthy, brown, black, white, weak, strong, and so on. The church is more than a building. It's all these people, who are like one huge family—God's family. And family members need one another.

ACTIVITY
Everyone in your church is needed, just like each of the ingredients of a cake are needed. Christians come together to make up the church, just as different ingredients come together to make a cake. Get out a recipe book and make a cake with your mom. As you add the flour, salt, sugar, and so on, think of all the different people who add something special to your church. When the cake is baked, write "Thank you, God, for my church!" in icing on top of it. Then enjoy!

April 1

Why do God and Jesus love people?

God showed his great love for us by sending Christ to die for us while we were still sinners.

Romans 5:8

God loves people because God *is* love (1 John 4:16). God doesn't love people because they're good or nice. In fact, no one could ever be good enough to be worthy of God's love.

Isn't it amazing that God loves us even though we sometimes ignore him and disobey him? He even sent his own Son, Jesus, to die on a cross and take the blame for the bad things we do. That's real love from God the Father and God the Son.

And we can love others because God loved us. Some people act loving only because they feel guilty if they don't, or somebody is making them, or they want others to think they are nice. We should love one another because God tells us to. We can love others because God commanded us to, and because *he* loves them.

ACTIVITY

Think of two or three people in your neighborhood or church who would appreciate an encouraging word. Maybe they're older people who are lonely. Or maybe they have been sick or have experienced other problems. Ask a parent for some stationery and write each one a note of encouragement. Tell them that you love them, God loves them, and you are praying for them. Then be sure you *do* pray!

April 2

What does God want us to do?

They replied, "What does God want us to do?" Jesus told them, "This is what God wants you to do: Believe in the one he has sent."   John 6:28-29

In God's Word, the Bible, God tells us how he wants us to live. Although there is a lot of information in the Bible, God's four main instructions for our lives are:

Believe in Jesus; trust him every day.
Obey Jesus; do what he says.
Love God and others.
Do what's fair and honest, and live for God without being proud about it.

These four instructions are hard and easy. They're hard because we're human, and human beings make mistakes. But they're also easy because they are very clear and because God has sent the Holy Spirit to help us obey.

How well are you doing what God wants you to do?

ACTIVITY
Take a piece of construction paper or a large index card. Write at the top: "God's Instructions for Me." Then use four different colored markers to write this list:

Believe in Jesus.
Obey Jesus.
Love God and others.
Do what's fair and honest.

Put the list where you will see it every morning—perhaps on your bulletin board, mirror, or refrigerator. It will be a good reminder of how to do what God wants.

April 3

Why wasn't Moses afraid to go to Pharaoh?

[God is speaking to Moses:]
"Now go, for I am sending you
to Pharaoh. You will lead my
people, the Israelites, out of
Egypt." Exodus 3:10

Moses *was* afraid to go to Pharaoh, but he went anyway out of obedience to God. At first Moses tried to get out of the job by using all sorts of excuses. He said he wasn't the right person, the people wouldn't believe that God had sent him, and he wasn't a good speaker. Moses pleaded: "Lord, please! Send someone else" (Exodus 4:13). But God wanted Moses to go, and Moses *did* go—God gave him strength and stayed with him, helping him lead God's people out of slavery and to the Promised Land. The Bible doesn't say Moses wasn't afraid—it says he obeyed God.

It's all right for you to be afraid at times, too. Just don't let your fear stop you from obeying God. Be honest with God about how you feel, and trust him to help you.

ACTIVITY

If you have a computer, ask your mom or dad if you can change the screen saver to a message that will inspire you to be like Moses—something like "God can use me! God will help me!" If your mom or dad doesn't want a new screen saver, you could make a small sign or poster with this message and put it on the corner of your mirror.

April 4

Why wouldn't Pharaoh let the people go?

"This is the finger of God!" the magicians exclaimed to Pharaoh. But Pharaoh's heart remained hard and stubborn. He wouldn't listen to them, just as the Lord had predicted. Exodus 8:19

The pharaoh or king in charge of Egypt when Moses lived was different from the pharaoh whom Joseph had served—that pharaoh had been kind to the Israelites. But this pharaoh was mean, forcing the Israelites to serve the Egyptians as slaves. When Moses asked Pharaoh to let the Israelites leave Egypt to worship in the wilderness, Pharaoh was very angry. He was too proud to give in to a slave, and he refused to give up his slave laborers.

A person doesn't have to be a pharaoh to be stubborn. When have you been stubborn? Maybe you wouldn't listen to a brother, sister, or friend. Perhaps you refused to do a chore for no good reason. Don't be afraid that you'll be a sissy or a wimp. Doing what's right pleases God, the Creator of the universe! So keep your heart open to God and to your family.

ACTIVITY
If the weather is OK, go outside and look for a rock in the shape of a heart. Clean it up and put it where you can see it to remind you of the pharaoh's rock-hard heart. Ask God to show you if you're being stubborn today. Ask him to soften your heart so that you will want to please him.

Is it OK to slam the door when you're mad?

It is better to be patient than powerful;
it is better to have self-control than to
conquer a city.   Proverbs 16:32

God wants us to control our emotions, not let them control us. So no door slamming. Emotions are good, and it is good to understand what we are feeling. In other words, if we are angry, we shouldn't pretend we aren't. But we should also think about why we are angry, talk to God and others about it, and work at changing what caused the anger. And we have to be careful about how we express our anger—yelling, screaming, calling names, hitting, and slamming doors don't help and can even hurt other people, making the situation worse.

The Bible says that you should have self-control. That means controlling your anger and not letting it control you. If you are cheerful and polite, people will be more likely to listen and care about your concerns. And you'll feel better without all that slamming noise!

ACTIVITY
Write down on a piece of paper the things that make you mad. Now take that list to your bedroom and stand by your door. Read one out loud and quietly close the door. Then open the door and read the next thing on the list, quietly closing the door again. Do the same for the rest of the list. It *is* possible to stop slamming the door, isn't it?

April 6

Why is it wrong to complain when my mom asks me to do something?

*In everything you do, stay away
from complaining and arguing.*
Philippians 2:14

Remember, the Bible tells us to honor our parents. This means being polite, having a good attitude, and showing them respect, even when we disagree with them. If you don't agree with your parents, you can tell them how you feel without complaining or hurting them with words.

Also, think about how much they do for you. That will help you have a thankful rather than a complaining attitude. People who complain a lot don't have many friends, are usually unhappy, and just feel generally miserable. The more they complain, the worse it gets. You can choose to be content and to make the best of every situation. Won't that make life more enjoyable for you, too?

ACTIVITY
Spread some newspapers on your work table. Create a sponge-painting Mother's Day card by dipping small sponges into a small amount of poster paint. Make an interesting design with different colors. When the paint is dry, write a thank-you message inside for your mom, grandma, or aunt.

April 7

Why isn't a dollar worth a dollar any more?

The Lord will not let the godly starve to death, but he refuses to satisfy the craving of the wicked.
Proverbs 10:3

When people say that a dollar isn't worth a dollar any more, they mean that it doesn't buy as much as it used to. Let's say that ten years ago a dollar bought ten chocolate chip cookies. But today you get only seven cookies for your dollar. So you get less for your money than you used to.

This happens for many reasons, but it's often like a circle of dominoes. The store owner, the baker, the chocolate-chip maker, and the cocoa-bean farmer are all dominoes in the circle. If a hurricane wipes out the farmer's cocoa-bean crop, he has to raise his prices. The chocolate-chip maker has to pay more for cocoa, so she then has to raise her prices. The baker has to pay more for chocolate chips, so he has to raise his prices. And the store owner has to pay more for cookies, so she has to raise her prices.

Do not worry about it, though. No matter what a dollar is worth, God is in control and you can trust him to take care of you. Price changes don't take him by surprise.

ACTIVITY
Ask your mom or dad how much money different items cost when they were your age. How much did cereal cost? a soft drink? a hamburger? What were movie prices?

April 8

Is it OK to beg for things from your parents?

Even when you do ask, you don't get it because your whole motive is wrong—you want only what will give you pleasure.

James 4:3

It is OK to *ask* your parents for things, but not to *beg*. For example, you could ask for a special treat, birthday presents, or permission to go to a friend's house. You should ask politely and explain your reasons. But if your parents say no, you should accept their answer with a good attitude. Don't beg. That is, don't ask over and over to try to get them to give you something they can't afford or something they know wouldn't be good for you.

The key is to respect your parents. They gave the answer they thought was best for you. If you wear them down, you may get what you want and then regret it later. God gave you parents to protect you and to provide for you. If you talk them into going against their first answer, you step outside that protection. Respect and obey your parents. You'll be safer and, in the long run, happier.

ACTIVITY

Decide today that you will not beg or ask twice for things for the next three days. Write out on an index card, "Don't beg." Put the card on your bedroom mirror or bulletin board. Now start your experiment. After the three days, you'll probably find it easier to stop begging than you thought!

Why did God put scary stories in the Bible?

All these events happened to them as examples for us. They were written down to warn us, who live at the time when this age is drawing to a close.

1 Corinthians 10:11

The Bible tells true stories about real people who actually lived and died. Sometimes those stories seem scary, especially when they reveal the bad things that can happen when people choose to do evil.

God included those stories because he wanted to teach us something from them. That is, they weren't put there to scare us. Instead, they can warn us of what to avoid and show us what we *should* do, helping us learn how to please God each day. Even scary stories can show how important it is to listen to God and obey him.

ACTIVITY

Today you can see what life was sometimes like in Bible times. Read in Acts 9:1-30 the story of Paul persecuting Christians, meeting Jesus, and then *being* persecuted. It is scary because Paul goes through a hard time. But as you read, you will see how God protected the Christians from Paul. Then, you'll see how God protected Paul after *he* became a Christian.

100

Why did God send plagues on Egypt?

*"Go back to Pharaoh," the Lord com-
manded Moses. "Tell him, 'This is what
the Lord, the God of the Hebrews, says:
Let my people go, so they can worship
me. If you continue to oppress them
and refuse to let them go, the Lord will
send a deadly plague.'"*   Exodus 9:1-3

God sent terrible events called *plagues* to Egypt to punish
Pharaoh and to show God's power. The plagues were miracles—fantastic demonstrations of God's power. Each time
Pharaoh refused to let God's people go, God sent a plague to the
Egyptians but not the Israelites. After each plague Pharaoh agreed
to release the Israelites, but then he said no. After the death of the
oldest boy in each Egyptian family, the Israelites were allowed to
leave. But even then, Pharaoh chased after them.

Pharaoh found out the hard way that God keeps his promises,
even his promise to punish those who disobey him. God means
what he says!

ACTIVITY

Look at Exodus 7–12. If you read the chapter headings, you will see
all ten of the plagues. Make a list so you can see them together.
Try to recreate how scary these plagues might have been. To illustrate the first plague, mix red food coloring in a bowl of water.
What if all the water in your house turned into real blood? Next, try
the ninth plague, darkness. Go into the darkest room in your house
and make sure that you can't see any light at all. Imagine if your
whole neighborhood were that dark all day. God's miracles are
amazing! What a powerful God we have.

April 11

What does Passover mean?

[Moses is giving God's instructions:]
"Continue to celebrate this festival.
Then your children will ask, 'What
does all this mean? What is this
ceremony about?' And you will reply,
'It is the celebration of the LORD'S
Passover, for he passed over the homes
of the Israelites in Egypt.'"

Exodus 12:25-27

Just before Jesus died, he had a Passover meal with his disciples. Passover is the special celebration that Jewish people hold every year to remember when the Israelites left Egypt and started their trip to the Promised Land. Moses had told Pharaoh that because he wouldn't let the Jews go, all the first-born Egyptian boys would die. But God told Moses to have each Jewish family put the blood of a lamb along the top and sides of their door. Then the angel of death would pass over them and keep the Jewish children safe.

Today many Jewish people still celebrate Passover to remember God's protection in Egypt. Christians celebrate the Lord's Supper (Holy Communion) rather than Passover. Communion pictures Jesus, the Lamb of God, dying on the cross so that we can have eternal life. Rejoice in what Jesus did for you!

ACTIVITY
Learn about Passover traditions from library books, the Web, or Jewish friends. What is the traditional dinner, called a seder, like? Also read 1 Corinthians 5:7 to learn about Jesus, the Passover Lamb of God who takes away the sins of the world.

Why did Judas betray Jesus?

Judas Iscariot, one of the twelve disciples, went to the leading priests and asked, "How much will you pay me to betray Jesus to you?" And they gave him thirty pieces of silver.

Matthew 26:14-15

Judas turned against Jesus and betrayed him because Judas did not care about what Jesus had come to earth to do. Judas had hoped that Jesus would be a military leader and free the Jewish people from the Romans. Also, Judas loved money, and the religious leaders who wanted to kill Jesus offered Judas money to help them capture Jesus. If Judas had been one of Jesus' true disciples, he would not have betrayed him. Afterward, when he saw that Jesus was going to be killed, Judas was so upset over what he had done that he killed himself.

There is nothing wrong with money, for we need it to buy things. But money must never become more important to us than people. Money is not what is truly important. Love and friendship matter a million times more! You can be a good friend to Jesus by loving him and his people. Never put money or the things that money can buy ahead of Jesus.

ACTIVITY

Ask your parents, brothers and sisters, and sitter about the good things that money *cannot* buy. What is on this list for you?

Why did they beat up Jesus?

The soldiers took him into their head-quarters and called out the entire battalion. They dressed him in a purple robe and made a crown of long, sharp thorns and put it on his head. Then they saluted, yelling, "Hail! King of the Jews!" And they beat him on the head with a stick, spit on him, and dropped to their knees in mock worship. Mark 15:16-19

Some Jewish leaders got very angry at Jesus because he was speaking against the bad things they were doing. They tried to get Jesus to do what they wanted. Instead, Jesus did what God wanted him to do, and he told everybody how bad those leaders were. Finally the leaders got so angry at Jesus that they wanted to kill him. And eventually, that's what they did. They had the government officials arrest Jesus and the Roman soldiers beat him up.

Jesus is the Son of God. He didn't have to come to earth as a person, but he did. He suffered in many ways because he loves us. He was willing to let people beat him up and kill him to take the blame for our sins. Always remember how much God, the Father and the Son, loves you.

ACTIVITY

Find out more of what happened to Jesus. Turn to chapter 15 of the Gospel of Mark, and read verses 1-20. Jesus was hurt very badly that day, but he let it happen to take our punishment. Say thank you to Jesus for what he suffered.

Why did the people say, "If you are the Son of God then come down off the cross"?

The people passing by shouted abuse, shaking their heads in mockery. "Ha! Look at you now!" they yelled at him. "You can destroy the Temple and rebuild it in three days, can you? Well then, save yourself and come down from the cross!"

Mark 15:29-30

The people who said this didn't believe in Jesus. They thought he was lying when he claimed to be God and their Messiah. Actually, Jesus had the power to come down from the cross, but he stayed there because he loved us and wanted to die for our sins. When Adam and Eve sinned, everybody became separated from God. Jesus died so people could be forgiven and be with God again. If Jesus had saved himself by coming off the cross, you couldn't be saved from your sins. Jesus showed his power in a much greater way—by rising from the dead. Aren't you glad Jesus stayed on the cross?

ACTIVITY

Here's how to turn a cross (suffering) into a diamond (reward):

Tie two Popsicle sticks together in a cross shape by holding them together in one hand and wrapping a 36-inch piece of yarn around the middle. Wrap it on the diagonal about fifteen times in one direction and then fifteen times in the other direction. Now you can begin weaving. Knot another piece of yarn (perhaps another color) to the end of the piece in the middle. Move clockwise, wrapping the yarn over and around the first stick and then over and around the next stick. Continue doing this, making a diamond pattern. Knot on new colors of yarn as you use up each one, tying the last piece around the stick.

April 15

Did Jesus know that he would come to life again?

[Jesus is speaking about himself:]
"They will mock him, spit on him,
beat him with their whips, and
kill him, but after three days he
will rise again."   Mark 10:34

He sure did! He told his disciples about it at least three times. But the disciples didn't seem to understand what he was talking about, so they were totally shocked by his death. They didn't expect Jesus to come back to life and didn't recognize him at first. But when he talked with them and ate with them, they knew he was Jesus. After the Resurrection, Jesus appeared to Mary Magdalene in the garden. Later he appeared to two men on a road and then to the disciples gathered together in a room. He appeared to hundreds of others, too.

You can be sure that Jesus' death didn't take him or his Father in heaven by surprise. Neither did his resurrection. You can be glad that we have such a Savior!

ACTIVITY
Check out a book about butterflies from your local library. Find pictures that show the development of a caterpillar into a butterfly. When the caterpillar is inside its cocoon, it seems to have died. But new life will come when it breaks out as a butterfly.

April 16

Why did Jesus go up to heaven instead of staying here on earth?

[Jesus is speaking:] "There are many rooms in my Father's home, and I am going to prepare a place for you. If this were not so, I would tell you plainly. When everything is ready, I will come and get you, so that you will always be with me where I am." John 14:2-3

Jesus is the Son of God, and his home is in heaven. Jesus left his Father (and his home) to become a human being and live on the earth. So it's quite natural that Jesus would leave the earth and go back home. Jesus also went to heaven to prepare a place for his people. And though Jesus left us, he sent the Holy Spirit to take his place and be with us.

Although Jesus couldn't be in two places at once when he had a human body, the Holy Spirit can be everywhere. He lives inside all people who have trusted in Christ as Savior. Because Jesus went back to heaven, the Holy Spirit can be with you and in you, everywhere you go. He is always with you!

ACTIVITY

Talk with your mom, dad, or a grandparent about Christians you know who have died. They are in heaven now, and someday you'll be there also. Then you'll be back together. Find the word *heaven* in a concordance, and look up some of the verses to learn more about what heaven is like.

April 17

When is Jesus coming back to earth?

[Jesus is speaking:] "No one knows the day or hour when these things will happen, not even the angels in heaven or the Son himself. Only the Father knows. And since you don't know when they will happen, stay alert and keep watch." Mark 13:32-33

When Jesus ascended into heaven, angels promised that he would return, just as he said. But Jesus said that he would return when people least expect it. So no one knows exactly when he is coming back. It could be today, or it could be far, far in the future. Although no one knows when Jesus will return, we do know that every day brings his return closer. And when he comes, it will be a wonderful day for those who love him. He will create a new heaven and a new earth, where his people will live with him forever. He will put an end to all evil, suffering, pain, and death. We will get to be with family and friends who love Jesus, and all of us will be happier than we can possibly imagine now.

That is why Jesus said to be alert and ready for his return all the time. Stay close to God and always do what is right. He will help you do these things.

ACTIVITY
What if Jesus returned today—would you be ready for him? Make a list of what you should change about the way you live in order to be ready for Jesus' return.

Why didn't God just forgive everybody?

All have sinned; all fall short of God's glorious standard. Yet now God in his gracious kindness declares us not guilty. He has done this through Christ Jesus, who has freed us by taking away our sins. For God sent Jesus to take the punishment for our sins and to satisfy God's anger against us. We are made right with God when we believe that Jesus shed his blood, sacrificing his life for us. Romans 3:23-25

It would not be right or fair for God to just forgive everyone. There is a penalty that must be paid for doing wrong. The penalty for sinning against God is death—eternal death. But God loved us so much that he sent Jesus, his only Son, to pay our penalty, to die in our place. Now everyone can be forgiven by trusting in Christ.

This is why God's message is called the "Good News." If we all got what we deserved, we would be in *big trouble.* Instead, we can be forgiven and have eternal life by trusting in Christ. We can be sure of it!

ACTIVITY

Take out a piece of scratch paper and write down all the bad stuff you can remember that you have done over the past year. After you have finished that, draw a large cross over your list to show that Jesus paid the penalty for all of your sins. Then tell God you are sorry for your sins, rip up the paper, and throw it away to illustrate how God forgives and forgets your sins.

When did "Bible times" stop?

Confess your sins to each other and pray for each other so that you may be healed. The earnest prayer of a righteous person has great power and wonderful results. James 5:16

The last book in the Bible was written about seventy years after the time Jesus lived on earth. That's a very long time ago—almost two thousand years. In one way that's when Bible times stopped. But in other ways we are still in Bible times. God still speaks to us through his Word, he still cares about us, and he still does miracles.

We may not see God divide a sea like he did for Moses, and we may not see anyone walk on water like Jesus did, but God still answers prayer and changes lives. That kind of "Bible times" will continue until Jesus returns. Aren't you glad!

ACTIVITY
Take a sheet of paper and title it "Bible Times." Divide the paper into two sections: "Answered Prayer" and "Changed Lives". Then ask a parent for suggestions of what to write in each section. Add your own ideas. Later, share your findings with the whole family.

Why does Jesus want us to follow him?

Jesus said to the disciples, "If any of you wants to be my follower, you must put aside your selfish ambition, shoulder your cross, and follow me. If you try to keep your life for yourself, you will lose it. But if you give up your life for me, you will find true life."
Matthew 16:24-25

Jesus told people to follow him because he is the way to God, heaven, and eternal life. In fact, he is the *only* way to God. When Jesus was on earth, the disciples and others followed him by walking close to him and listening to his words.

Today we follow Jesus by giving our lives to him in faith. We continue to follow him by copying his example and doing what he says. The Gospel books of the Bible—Matthew, Mark, Luke, and John—tell the story of Jesus' life on earth. We can read the Gospels and see how he was kind, fed the hungry, and got upset when people were mean to others.

ACTIVITY
Want to be a copycat? Sit on the floor across from a friend. Pretend that you are a mirror. Have your friend slowly move one hand around in a circle. Try to do the exact thing your friend is doing, reflecting back the exact movement—do funny faces, move both arms, and so on. After a while, have your friend be the mirror. It's easiest to copy someone when you watch the person very carefully—just like following Jesus by carefully learning all about him.

Why do some moms and dads divorce?

Jesus replied, "Moses permitted divorce as a concession to your hard-hearted wickedness, but it was not what God had originally intended. And I tell you this, a man who divorces his wife and marries another commits adultery—unless his wife has been unfaithful."

Matthew 19:8-9

God's plan is for a husband and wife to stay together and not get divorced. But all people have weaknesses. No one is perfect. That is why troubles arise in all relationships, even between two people who love each other very much.

When a man and a woman get married, they promise to stay with each other for life. But when the arguments and pressures come, some people don't know how to handle them. Usually the problems start small and then grow. Eventually, these problems can become so big that the husband or wife or both give up and decide to end their marriage. Some people don't try very hard; these couples divorce because they choose not to work out their problems.

But God wants Christians to stay married and work things out. He knows that when they do, their lives will be better for it. Do you know people who are divorced? Perhaps even your own parents? Always remember that they each love you, no matter what happened to their marriage. And God loves you most of all!

ACTIVITY

Divorce is probably the hardest thing that families have to face. Think of parents who are divorced—either your own or a friend's. Pray hard for them. Ask God to help them continue to be good and wise parents.

April 22

If we are running out of trees, why doesn't God just make more?

God said, "Let us make people in our image, to be like ourselves. They will be masters over all life—the fish in the sea, the birds in the sky, and all the livestock, wild animals, and small animals." Genesis 1:26

God *is* making more trees, but it is up to us not to use them faster than he replaces them. Some trees are cut down and used for wood, paper, and other products. Other trees are cut down to make room for houses, shopping centers, roads, and other construction projects. Some say that we are running out of trees. When God created trees and other plants, he made them with the ability to make new ones. They do this by producing seeds that fall to the ground or are planted and then grow. But it takes many years for a tree to grow big and tall. So people should be careful not to cut down more trees than can be replaced by the seeds.

God has given human beings the job of taking care of the earth. This includes using the trees well and planting new ones. We should take care of all that God has given to us.

ACTIVITY
Because paper is made from trees, one way to care for trees is to recycle newspapers. Most towns and cities have recycling trucks that pick up newspapers. If not, there will be a recycling center near you where you can take them. Make collecting newspapers and seeing that they are recycled one of your family chores.

How much does recycling help?

"Now gather the leftovers," Jesus told his disciples, "so that nothing is wasted." John 6:12

R ecycling helps a lot. It is important because we're using up our natural resources very rapidly. For example, oil heats homes and makes gasoline for cars and trucks. Many other products also come from oil, including plastics, tires, and jet fuel. Yet there is only so much oil in the earth. When it is used up, it will all be gone. Recycling used paper, oil, plastic, and rubber makes these resources stretch. We are able to use the materials again to make other things.

God does not want people to be wasteful. At the same time, you don't need to fear running out of the things you need. God created you and this earth. He put you here to enjoy all that he has created. He provides everything you need. If the oil runs out, God will still be in charge and will always provide what we need. So recycle and don't be wasteful, but don't be afraid of running out of things either. Just be a responsible user of God's resources.

ACTIVITY

Call up your local telephone company and find out where old telephone books can be deposited. With a grown-up's help, get your friends together and offer to pick up your neighbors' old telephone books. Then take the books to the drop-off place. The paper can be recycled, and trees will be saved.

April 24

Why does God let people die?

We know that when this earthly
tent we live in is taken down—
when we die and leave these
bodies—we will have a home
in heaven, an eternal body made
for us by God himself and not
by human hands.

2 Corinthians 5:1

People die because sin came into the world when Adam and Eve sinned. In fact, everyone dies eventually. Some people die when they're young, some die when they're old, and some die when they're in the prime of life. But no matter how long a person lives, his or her life *will* come to an end. God can heal people and stop them from dying, and sometimes he does. But even a person who has been healed through a miracle from God will someday die.

God's people know that death is not the end of the story. This life is not all there is. People who know God will go to live with him in heaven after they die. Are you ready to meet him when you die? God wants you to be sure. If you haven't asked Jesus into your heart yet, you can do it today.

ACTIVITY

Make a bookmark from a scrap piece of wallpaper, part of your earthly home. Cut a long rectangle, about two inches by six inches. With a ballpoint pen (or any pen that won't smear on the wallpaper), write "We will have a home in heaven—2 Corinthians 5:1." Now draw an outline of a house or a roof to remind you of your heavenly home.

April 25

Can't we pray anywhere?

Pray at all times and on every occasion in the power of the Holy Spirit. Stay alert and be persistent in your prayers for all Christians everywhere.   Ephesians 6:18

THANK YOU FOR THE SUNNY DAY AT THE BEACH.

Yes, we can pray anywhere.

Prayers do not have to be spoken aloud, so you could pray while sitting at a desk with your eyes wide open or anywhere else. You can pray in school, on the playground, at basketball practice, in a choir concert, in church, at home, on vacation . . . anywhere! You can pray silently because God knows your thoughts.

God is glad when you ask him for help right when and where you need it—any time, any place!

ACTIVITY

Get on the phone and take a survey. Call your pastor, Sunday school teacher, best friend, and other Christian adults and relatives and ask them, "Where is the most unusual place that you have prayed?" Write down the answers you get, and share them with your family at dinner some evening. Then ask them to give their answers to your survey question.

April 26

Why do some white and black people hate each other?

There is no longer Jew or Gentile, slave or free, male or female. For you are all Christians—you are one in Christ Jesus.

Galatians 3:28

Hate is caused by sin in the world. People get angry and hate others for many reasons. They may be upset over something a person said or did. They may be bitter about what a person's relatives did in the past.

But hate is wrong, for God tells us to love, not hate. If someone hurts us, we should forgive that person and try to fix the relationship.

Some people hate others for very silly reasons. They may not like another person's religion, nationality, neighborhood, school, or skin color. For many years, some white people have hated black people just because they are black. And many black people have hated white people just because they are white. Others have been mean and cruel to such people as Hispanics, Japanese, or Irish.

That is not God's way. His way is for all kinds of people to live, work, and worship together. Show love and respect to all people, no matter how different they are from you. God created everyone, and Jesus died for everyone. If you live God's way, he will help you not hate anyone.

ACTIVITY

Using a black pen or pencil and a white sheet of paper, draw a picture or diagram of white people and black people getting along.

Should I tell on other kids?

Take no part in the worthless
deeds of evil and darkness;
instead, rebuke and expose them.

Ephesians 5:11

If a law will be broken or someone may be hurt, then it is right to tell a grown-up. God puts adults in positions of authority to protect you and others against wrongdoing. If those adults don't know about a problem, they can't provide protection. Tell a parent, teacher, coach, counselor, police officer, or another caring adult if someone is stealing, vandalizing, doing drugs, selling drugs, drinking, planning to break the law, talking about committing suicide, or making threats. There's nothing wrong with telling on kids like that.

But there *is* something wrong with "telling on" kids you don't like just to get them in trouble. Also, if you need to tell on someone, don't brag about what you did. God's purpose for us is to serve him and help others, so bragging is out of place. Quietly pray for that kid and his or her family.

ACTIVITY

Have you ever written a letter to God? He doesn't have a real mailbox, but you can still write out your thoughts and feelings. Take pen and paper and do it. "Tell on" yourself. That is, tell God that you know you are a sinner. Be honest about the ways you sin and disobey him. Then thank him for Jesus, who is bigger than your sin.

Why are some people mean to animals?

The godly are concerned for the welfare of their animals, but even the kindness of the wicked is cruel. Proverbs 12:10

Some people who don't care about animals are mean to them for fun. Some hurt animals without meaning to when they are angry or frustrated. For example, someone might be having a very bad day. Then, when this person comes home and his or her pet has done something annoying, the person takes out his or her anger on the pet. Some people even let their pets run away when they don't want to care for them any more.

We don't always know why other people are mean, but you can ask God to help you be kind and not mean. Also ask him to show you what you can do to take good care of his creation. You can be one of his special helpers for your part of the animal world!

ACTIVITY
Take a family field trip to an animal shelter (sometimes called a humane society). This is where homeless animals, especially cats and dogs, are cared for until they can find a good home. See how the animals are cared for. If your family is getting a pet, think about getting one from a shelter.

April 29

Why do some animals look funny?

[God is speaking:] "Take a look at the mighty hippopotamus. I made it, just as I made you. It eats grass like an ox. See its powerful loins and the muscles of its belly. Its tail is as straight as a cedar. The sinews of its thighs are tightly knit together. Its bones are tubes of bronze. Its limbs are bars of iron. It is a prime example of God's amazing handiwork."
Job 40:15-19

Some animals look funny because they are built a certain way to help them live in their environment and to get food. An armadillo, for example, has a hard shell that protects it from other animals. A lizard has a long, sticky tongue to help it catch flies to eat. An anteater has a long nose to help it eat ants. The giraffe's long neck helps it eat leaves in tall trees. God made all animals with amazing features that help them live, and that's just one of the wonders of God himself.

God is very creative. He made a huge variety of plants and animals. This variety is part of God's creative genius. It is part of the beauty he built into the world. You are a beautiful part of the world, too.

ACTIVITY
Wouldn't the world be boring if all animals looked the same? Gather up some magazines and make a Funny Animals Collage. Cut out pictures of humorous animals or animals doing funny things and glue them onto a big piece of paper. God won't mind— he has a sense of humor, too!

April 30

Why does the world have different religions?

JESUS LOVES THE LITTLE CHILDREN, ALL THE CHILDREN OF THE WORLD...

[God is speaking:] "Do not worship any other gods besides me."   Exodus 20:3

All cultures know about God, but many don't really know God and have tried to explain him in their own ways. Some people do not want to believe that Jesus is the only way to God, so they start their own religion.

Within Christianity itself are many denominations or groups of churches. Some of these groups formed because the people were all from a certain country. Other denominations exist because some like formal worship services and others like informal worship.

The Bible tells us that Jesus Christ is the only way to God. Christians may go to many different churches as long as their beliefs and worship center on Christ and God's Word. God wants all Christians to love and appreciate each other and to bring the Good News about Jesus to people of different religions.

ACTIVITY

Make a chart about your church. Label one column "What We Believe" and write down your church's teachings on the Bible, Jesus, prayer, and other important subjects. Label the second column "How We Worship" and describe a worship service. Tell how often communion is served, identify the musical instruments and the types of songs you sing (hymns, choruses), and name other ways you praise God together. Ask your parents, your church leaders, or your minister for information to help you fill out the chart.

May 1

Why did God make heaven?

[Jesus is speaking:] "There are many rooms in my Father's home, and I am going to prepare a place for you. If this were not so, I would tell you plainly. When everything is ready, I will come and get you, so that you will always be with me where I am."

John 14:2-3

God has only one use for heaven, and that is to share it with his people. God is everywhere, not just in one place. But when we talk about heaven, we are really talking about where God lives. We think of heaven as a place because that's where we know we're going to be with God.

In the Bible, the word *heaven* can refer to several places. It can mean (1) the home or place of God, (2) the New Jerusalem, (3) "the heavens" or sky.

Just before Jesus left the earth, he said he would go and prepare a place for us, a place where we can live with him. Someday he will come back and set it all up for us—he will destroy this world and create a new one. That new world will be for all those who love him. That's the "heaven" that God will make for you and for all believers so that you can live with him in peace forever.

ACTIVITY

Gather some magazines and cut out pictures and words that remind you of heaven. Make a heavenly collage by gluing the pictures and words on a big piece of paper.

One Year Book of Fun & Active Devotions for Kids

Is Jesus the only way to heaven?

Jesus told him, "I am the way, the truth, and the life. No one can come to the Father except through me."   John 14:6

Yes, Jesus is the only way to heaven. Notice that Jesus said, "No one can come to the Father except through me." Just as the only correct answer to 2 + 2 is 4, Jesus is the only correct answer to every person's need for forgiveness. He is the only one who has the *right* to take away anyone's sins because he died to pay the penalty for sin. He is the only one who has the *power* to take sin away because he is God. And he is the only one who can be perfectly fair to every single person, from babies to the most wicked person who has ever lived, for he is just and merciful.

Jesus died in our place. His death paid the price for the sins of each and every human being who trusts in him. Isn't it great that Jesus has offered such a clear way to heaven for us? Just think— eventually you will be in heaven because you have trusted in Christ as your Savior. You learned about God's way and followed it. Wow!

ACTIVITY
Open your Bible and get ready to solve a mystery. Turn to John 3:1-17. Who was Jesus talking to? Did he decide to follow Jesus? Find out what he eventually did by turning to John 19:38-42.

How did Moses part the Red Sea?

Moses raised his hand over the sea, and the Lord opened up a path through the water with a strong east wind. The wind blew all that night, turning the seabed into dry land. So the people of Israel walked through the sea on dry ground, with walls of water on each side! Exodus 14:21-22

After Moses and the Israelites left Egypt, Pharaoh sent soldiers to bring them back. When the fleeing Israelites came to the Red Sea, there seemed to be no way across. But Moses held his rod over the edge of the sea, and God made the waters part. Then the people marched to the other side on dry ground. So Moses didn't part the Red Sea—it was a miracle that God did through him.

It may be hard to imagine how God did such a great miracle. But it reminds us how great God's care for his people really is.

ACTIVITY
Water is very powerful, especially when used by our all-powerful God. Take off the labels and rinse out two large (two-liter), clear plastic soda pop bottles. Fill one bottle three-quarters full of water. Add a few drops of red food coloring. Turn the other bottle upside down and put it on top of the first bottle, with the openings together. Wind strong, waterproof (electrical) tape tightly around the necks so that no water can leak out. The top bottle should be securely balanced on the bottom one. Now hold them with both hands and swirl the water around. Turn the bottles upside down and watch what happens.

May 4

Why are animals becoming extinct all over the world?

[God is speaking:] All the animals of the forest are mine, and I own the cattle on a thousand hills. Psalm 50:10

The main reason for animals becoming extinct is disruption of their habitat (where they live). People move in and take away the land used by the animals. Some people don't seem to care what happens to the plants and animals of the earth. They just do whatever they want, regardless of the consequences in nature. But God has given human beings the job of taking care of the world. That means taking good care of all of it, animals included.

You can do your part if you take good care of your pets, don't litter so that animals have a clean place to live, and act as a good caretaker of the rest of God's earth. After all, everything belongs to God, and caring for his world is a special job God has given each of us. He is pleased with you when you do your part well.

ACTIVITY

Grab a grown-up and go on a nature walk to see all the new life that God is creating. Look in ponds, under big rocks, and up at the buds in trees. Notice the flowers starting to grow. Spend some time bird-watching, too. Notice the kinds of things birds eat and how they need trees so they can build nests to care for their young.

Why can't I see Jesus now?

[Jesus is speaking:] "But it is actually best for you that I go away, because if I don't, the Counselor won't come. If I do go away, he will come because I will send him to you."   John 16:7

Jesus went back to heaven to be with his Father, but he has *not* forgotten about his people. In fact, he is preparing a place for all who believe in him so it will be ready for them when they die and go to be with him. Also, Jesus is acting as our high priest—like in the Old Testament. Whenever his people sin, he presents his own death as a payment so God can forgive them.

The Bible calls Satan the "Accuser" (Revelation 12:10). That's because he accuses believers before God, to get God to reject them. (Read an example in Job 1:6-11.) Whenever the devil accuses a believer, Jesus defends that person. That's one reason why you can't see Jesus now—he's very busy working to help you. Meanwhile, Jesus has sent the Holy Spirit to be with his people wherever they go. That's why Jesus said, "It is actually best for you that I go away." When Jesus comes back, he will take all believers to live with him forever. Then you'll be able to see Jesus in person.

ACTIVITY

Read more of what Jesus said about how the Holy Spirit would come. In John 15:26–16:15, you can find the teaching he gave his disciples in the Upper Room before he was arrested.

May 6

Why doesn't God answer prayers right away?

There is a time for everything, a season for every activity under heaven.   Ecclesiastes 3:1

YES, OPERATOR – COULD YOU TELL ME THE TIME DIFFERENCE BETWEEN HERE AND HEAVEN? I AM EXPECTING AN IMPORTANT ANSWER TO PRAYER AND...

God knows not only *what* is best but also *when* is best. Sometimes we do not have to wait at all—God answers our prayers even before we put them into words. At other times, however, we have to wait.

God has good reasons for his timing. Sometimes he wants to bring people and situations together like a big team. Or God may know that we are not ready for the thing we want, so he takes time to help us grow and get ready. Other times, God waits to answer in order to test our faith and trust in him.

Will you keep trusting him even when it looks as if he is not answering? If so, when the answer finally comes, your faith will become even stronger. And you'll be even happier as you trust God more and more.

ACTIVITY

Check out a garden or a park with a grown-up. What flowers do you see? When were they planted? (Hint: Spring flowers such as tulips and daffodils were probably planted as bulbs last fall. Other flowers may have just been planted.) Different flowers take different times to grow, just as God's answers to prayers take different amounts of time.

May 7

Why do we have to study computers?

Wise people treasure knowledge, but the babbling of a fool invites trouble. Proverbs 10:14

Computers are becoming a very important part of society, and they are getting easier and easier to use. Almost every kind of store and business uses computers—from grocery stores to car-repair shops. By using computers, people can keep learning more and more about almost everything there is to know. So studying computers will become more and more important.

As you grow up, computers will be part of your life. People who know how to use computers will get good jobs and will be able to help others. And a person who helps others is God's helper in the world.

ACTIVITY

Most computers have many different software programs on them, such as games, learning software, and writing software. Chances are you haven't used all of them on the computer you use at home, in your school, or at the public library. The next time you use that computer, try to learn how to use a new software program or at least a feature you haven't tried before. Ask a parent, teacher, or librarian for help if you need to.

May 8

Is the Internet bad?

Whatever you eat or drink or whatever you do, you must do all for the glory of God.

1 Corinthians 10:31

The Internet itself is not bad. It is simply a very big network of networks. Just like any other tool, such as a hammer, a book, or a phone, it can be used for both good and bad. Almost anything can be used in a bad way, even things that are usually used for good. A hammer, for example, can be used to drive a nail or to destroy things. The Internet, too, can be used for bad purposes, just as it can be used for good purposes. Sadly, some people do use it that way.

Whether the Internet is used for good or bad is up to you. It has great potential for good. You need to do your part and use it rightly—to the glory of God.

ACTIVITY

If you have a computer at home, you may get onto the Internet through one of the popular on-line services (also called Internet service providers). They usually have a kids' section, like a "door" to the many good and safe parts of the Internet. Explore this with your mom or dad. If you use a computer at the library, ask your librarian how you can best get to the good and helpful parts of the Internet.

May 9

Do all people lie?

All have sinned; all fall short of God's glorious standard.
Romans 3:23

A ll people sin, and one of the most common sins is lying. So, yes, all people lie at one time or another. In fact, some people lie so much that they become confused and think a lie is the truth. But at the beginning, lying is a choice people make to deceive others. Jesus, of course, never sinned, so he never lied.

Sometimes people don't know all the facts, so they say something that's not true. That's not the same as lying. But it's good to check the facts to make sure that what we say is correct.

To be a person who wants to do things God's way, you need to make a decision not to tell lies. If you do lie, be sure to ask God for forgiveness, admit your lie to the people involved, and try not to do it again. God will help you.

ACTIVITY
Maybe you'd like to make a reminder for yourself to tell the truth when you are tempted to lie. You could write in big letters on a folded sheet of paper, "Tell the truth!" Decorate your paper, and stand it on your dresser.

May 10

Why should we always have to save our friends when they get in trouble?

"Lord, help!" they cried in their trouble, and he rescued them from their distress. Psalm 107:6

G od says that we should help those who are in trouble, even our *enemies*. That's what it means to love, and it's how we can show others God's love. You can help your friends when they are in trouble. You can be a very good friend to them.

There's a limit to what you can do, however. Parents and other adults may need to help. You should never lie for friends or make excuses for them. Sometimes letting friends learn to solve their own problems is the best thing to do. Ask God to show you what it means to be a good friend to each of your friends.

ACTIVITY
Pretend that one of your friends has asked you to lie. Make a pretend phone call to your friend. Tell him or her that you care about your friendship but that you will not lie—for yourself or for anyone. (If this has really happened to you, then you won't have to pretend—use that experience and make a real phone call.)

If God says that salvation is free, why do we have to buy a Bible?

If you confess with your mouth that Jesus is Lord and believe in your heart that God raised him from the dead, you will be saved. For it is by believing in your heart that you are made right with God, and it is by confessing with your mouth that you are saved. Romans 10:9-10

We pay for Bibles because it costs money to produce them. The publishers who publish the Bibles, the printers who print them, and the stores that sell them all need to pay their workers. God tells us to pay what we owe (Leviticus 19:13), and the price we pay for a Bible pays the workers' wages. It's reasonable to pay for something as important as God's Word.

Salvation, on the other hand, is free. But that has nothing to do with money. The penalty for sin is death, so sinners should be separated from God forever. But God sent his only Son, Jesus, to die on the cross in your place. If you ask God to forgive your sins and you believe that Jesus died in your place, God will forgive you. You become his child. So salvation is free because you did not have to pay the penalty for your sins. Jesus did!

ACTIVITY

Make a computer poster. (If you can't get to a computer, make a poster with markers and stickers.) Choose a style of letter (called a font) that reminds you of someone saying important things. Type out in big letters, "Salvation is free, but it's priceless!" Put a border on it, if you like. Print it out and put it on your refrigerator.

May 12

Why did God give Moses so many laws for the Israelites to obey?

Moses called all the people of Israel together and said, "Listen carefully to all the laws and regulations I am giving you today. Learn them and be sure to obey them!" Deuteronomy 5:1

Moses led the Israelites to Mount Sinai, where God met with Moses and gave him laws that are recorded in the books of Exodus, Leviticus, Numbers, and Deuteronomy. It seems as if God gave the Israelites a lot of laws to obey. Actually, most cities and towns today have far more laws than are recorded in the books of Moses. Some of the laws that God gave the Israelites helped organize them into a nation; some helped keep the people healthy; others told them (and us) how to live.

God knows and wants what is best for us. That's why he gave so many instructions. Be thankful that God's rules come from his love and care for you. God's list of rules may seem big, but his love is even bigger!

ACTIVITY
The Ten Commandments are God's most famous laws. Turn to Exodus 19 and read the story of how God gave them to Moses. Read also the commandments themselves in chapter 20. Next, make a list of the Ten Commandments so that you can remember God's ten important rules. Put a star by the ones that you think may be easy for you to follow. Circle the hard ones that you have to work on. Pray for God to help you.

May 13

If God owns everything, then why do people sell stuff like it is their own and charge however much they want for it?

[David is speaking:] "Who am I, and who are my people, that we could give anything to you? Everything we have has come from you, and we give you only what you have already given us!"
1 Chronicles 29:14

Yes, God owns everything because he created everything and is in charge of everything. But God trusts people with things and money. He makes people managers of the things they have. A manager is someone who takes care of something that belongs to someone else.

God has given you your toys, for example. Those toys are yours to take care of. As part of that responsibility, you may decide one day that you are too old for them and want to sell them or give them away. If your parents say it's OK, you can sell those things and use the money for other things. Just remember that honest people set fair prices. Be known as a person who treats others honestly.

ACTIVITY
Will your family be having a garage sale this spring or summer? Think hard about the toys you don't use anymore and could sell. Work hard on the set-up, and price things fairly. Talk with your parents about what share of the profit you should get. Have a plan beforehand about what you will do with your money: Decide in advance how much to save, how much to give to a good cause, and how much to spend on new things.

One Year Book of Fun & Active Devotions for Kids

Why do some kids get their allowance free and others have to earn it?

Work brings profit, but mere talk leads to poverty! Proverbs 14:23

In some families, children have to do jobs around the house in order to earn their allowances. In other families, children receive money just for being part of the family. Some don't get any allowance at all. It's all up to the parents. Some kids don't like having jobs to do around the house. But those jobs teach you how to be a good worker and a valuable member of a team. Be thankful for opportunities to help at home.

One reason God has placed you in your family is to help you learn to manage your money wisely. Be careful about comparing your parents and family with others. God has given your parents the responsibility of rearing *you,* not your friends. And other kids' parents are not in charge of you.

ACTIVITY
Does your family have a chore chart? If not, talk with your family about making one. Some families use stars or check marks when chores get done each day. If you do have a chart, talk about who does what jobs and why. Work out ways to switch jobs once in a while, if your parents agree. Be creative and cooperative to make your family the best chore team on the block!

May 15

What should I do when kids are mean to me?

Do what the Scriptures say: "If your enemies are hungry, feed them. If they are thirsty, give them something to drink, and they will be ashamed of what they have done to you."   Romans 12:20

This will be difficult, but you should be kind to kids, no matter how mean they are to you. That's what God expects his people to do. God's way always works out best. You may think that you'll feel better by getting even, but you won't. If you respond God's way, you'll feel better about yourself. You may even help those kids change when they see your good example. If you have to, avoid the mean kids. Don't let their meanness get to you. If they threaten to hurt you physically, you should tell an adult right away.

Also, you should pray for them. God cares very much when people are mean to each other. He cares about you *and* those being mean.

ACTIVITY
Today's verse comes from the apostle Paul's letter to the Romans. Read the whole section of good advice about getting along. You'll find it in Romans 12:14-21. When you're done, make a collage of words that remind you of the good advice you just read about. Write the words on one sheet of paper, cut them out, and paste them to another sheet.

What part of the body of Christ am I?

Just as our bodies have many parts and each part has a special function, so it is with Christ's body. We are all parts of his one body, and each of us has different work to do. And since we are all one body in Christ, we belong to each other, and each of us needs all the others. Romans 12:4-5

The Bible uses word pictures to explain how Christians relate to each other. We are a "family," with brothers and sisters in Christ. And we are a "body," with each person serving as a special part. God talks about us being a body to show how Christians should treat each other and work together. God has given each Christian special gifts. That means each person has talents and abilities that can be used to help other believers.

In Romans 12:6-8, you can read about some of the gifts God gives his family. You can see what part of the body of Christ you can be right now and what part you might play as you grow up. The gifts include: helping others, teaching, sharing money, being a leader, and showing kindness.

ACTIVITY
Press your thumb on a stamp pad with washable ink and make a thumbprint on a piece of sketch paper or computer printer paper. Now make prints of your other fingers. These will be bodies of thumbprint people. With a fine-point pen, make the arms, legs, heads, and faces. Each body has many parts, and each part is special—one-of-a-kind—just like God's family, the church.

How much should a person give to the church?

You must each make up your own mind as to how much you should give. Don't give reluctantly or in response to pressure. For God loves the person who gives cheerfully. 2 Corinthians 9:7

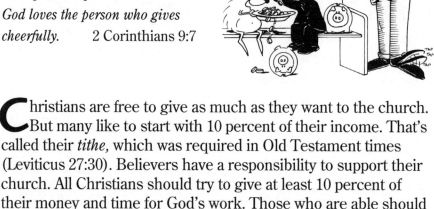

Christians are free to give as much as they want to the church. But many like to start with 10 percent of their income. That's called their *tithe,* which was required in Old Testament times (Leviticus 27:30). Believers have a responsibility to support their church. All Christians should try to give at least 10 percent of their money and time for God's work. Those who are able should give even more. The money we give beyond our tithe is called our *offering.* We should give offering money to other people and ministries that serve God.

Some people need to ask themselves: Why am I not giving anything to the church? If they can't bring themselves to give 10 percent, they can start smaller and pray that God will help them increase their giving. It's more important that we give *something* rather than waiting until we have a lot to give anything.

ACTIVITY
Ask your mom and dad how they got started giving to the church. Ask how they determine the amount to give. Christian Financial Concepts (CFC) has produced a plastic bank with three different compartments: Giving, Sharing, and Spending. For each ten pennies, you'll want to put at least one penny in the *Give* bank. That will be your Sunday school offering money.

May 18

How could the angel unlock Peter out of jail without keys?

The night before Peter was to be placed on trial, he was asleep, chained between two soldiers, with others standing guard at the prison gate. Suddenly, there was a bright light in the cell, and an angel of the Lord stood before Peter. The angel tapped him on the side to awaken him and said, "Quick! Get up!" And the chains fell off his wrists. Acts 12:6-7

The angel freed Peter through God's power. Herod wanted to kill Peter to make some of the other leaders happy. He had Peter arrested and sentenced to death. The night before Peter was scheduled to be killed, God sent an angel to rescue him. The angel woke Peter up, and the chains fell off Peter's wrists. Then Peter and the angel walked away from the soldiers without awakening any of them. God made the iron gate open up when they walked up to it. The angel left when they got outside. Peter could hardly believe what had happened—and neither could his friends who were praying for him (Acts 12:12-16)!

You can believe in God's power, too. And you can pray for God's people who are in prison today.

ACTIVITY

In many parts of the world, Christians are treated badly—even put into prison—for their faith. This happens a lot in China, Pakistan, Afghanistan, and parts of Africa. Find these countries on a world map or globe. Then write a reminder in your prayer journal to pray for these persecuted believers and their families.

What happens to the bad people when Jesus comes back?

They will be punished with everlasting destruction, forever separated from the Lord and from his glorious power.

2 Thessalonians 1:9

When Jesus returns to earth, people who know Jesus will be glad. But people who don't know Jesus will be very sad and afraid because they will be judged for their sin. Those who did not believe in Jesus as their Savior will be punished and sent to a place far away from God called hell. That is one of the reasons God urges us to tell our friends about Jesus—so they can join us in heaven someday.

God is loving and fair—both. He will make the right decision about every person. So to be certain about your own future, trust in Jesus as your Savior. And tell other people the good news that he can be their Savior, too.

ACTIVITY

Take a grown-up (or a teenager your parents trust) on a walk through your neighborhood. Make it a prayer walk. This means praying for each family, each person, as you pass apartment buildings, houses, and stores. Ask God to bless the people of your town and to help them hear and understand the good news about Jesus—maybe you'll be the one to tell them!

If you say *Jesus* when you're mad, isn't that like praying?

[God is speaking:] "Do not misuse the name of the Lord your God. The Lord will not let you go unpunished if you misuse his name." Exodus 20:7

No. It is one thing to talk to God. It is another to say his name as a swearword.

When and how we say a word can help tell what we mean by it. We pray and worship using God's name. In Sunday school classes and with friends, we talk a lot about Jesus. Those are good ways to use God's name. But some people say his name in anger, in frustration, or just in passing. That's called swearing or using God's name *in vain*—it's misusing God's name. God says that's wrong. So it's not OK. God's name is very important.

We should only say "God," "Jesus," or "Christ" when we are being serious about God, praising him, or praying to him. We shouldn't even say "My God!" when we're surprised. Treat God with respect. Honor his name.

ACTIVITY

God is such a creative God that he has many different names in the Bible. See how many you can find, and write them down in a "Names of God" list. The following Bible verses will get you rolling: Psalm 3:3; 18:2; 23:1; 144:2; Isaiah 9:6; 33:22; 40:28; 49:7; 64:8; Zechariah 14:5

May 21

Why is it that some teachers are nice to other kids but mean to me?

SUSY, DON'T WORRY.
EVERYTHING WILL
BE FINE. JASON,
START WORRYING!

My child, never forget the things I have taught you. Store my commands in your heart. . . . Then you will find favor with both God and people, and you will gain a good reputation. Proverbs 3:1, 4

Most teachers try to be fair and to treat all their students the same, but there are a few situations that make it seem otherwise.

- It's easy to be nice to students who listen carefully, try to learn, do their assignments on time, and stay out of trouble. And it's natural to *not* be attracted to kids who seem to have bad attitudes.
- God gave people different personalities. Thus, although we love everyone, we get along better with some than with others. This is also true with teachers. You'll find that you will get along OK with some teachers and great with others.
- Some kids get nervous wondering how a teacher feels about them. Therefore, they misinterpret some of the teacher's words or actions as being negative toward them.

If you have a problem with a certain teacher, pray and do your best to cooperate and learn. That combination often works wonders.

ACTIVITY

Tonight after dinner, get your family together to name the teachers all of you have had. Talk about the different personalities and ways of teaching represented by these teachers. Then thank God for the teachers who have helped you and your family members learn.

May 22

Will I have a bedroom up in heaven?

[Jesus is speaking:] "There are many rooms in my Father's home, and I am going to prepare a place for you. If this were not so, I would tell you plainly."

John 14:2

Jesus told his disciples that the place where his father lived had many rooms and that he was going to prepare a place for them there. But we don't know exactly what that place or those "rooms" will be like. The Bible tells us that in heaven we will have "new bodies" (Romans 8:23). And when Christ returns, "we will be like him" (1 John 3:2). We will be able to recognize others, but we won't need food or sleep. We won't have bedrooms in heaven like the ones we have here. Instead, we'll have very special places, each one prepared for us by Jesus.

Can you picture not having to worry about the weather? The temperature will always be perfect in heaven. We won't even have to be concerned about what to wear—God will give us special clothes. Heaven is a wonderful place filled with joy, love, and happiness!

ACTIVITY
Write a poem or draw a picture that describes what you know about heaven. Let God know how you feel about the wonderful place that he is preparing for you.

May 23

Why are doctors so smart?

Moses told Bezalel and Oholiab to begin the work, along with all those who were specially gifted by the Lord. Exodus 36:2

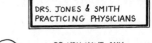

DRS. JONES & SMITH
PRACTICING PHYSICIANS

DO YOU HAVE ANY
DOCTORS THAT ARE
FINISHED PRACTICING?

God gives every person special talents and abilities. And he makes each person unique—one person has this skill, another person has that skill. People who become doctors have the talents and abilities to do what doctors do. But people aren't born being doctors. They have to get a lot of training. They have to go to school for a long time and study hard. They have to learn from other doctors who have a lot of experience. Only after they have done all that are they "so smart." They know a lot because they've learned a lot.

God helps your parents choose which doctors will have the responsibility of helping care for you. Doctors do their part by learning and being in training for many, many years. Are you learning new things at school each day so that you can do what God wants you to do when you grow up?

ACTIVITY
On your next doctor visit, do a mini-interview with your doctor. Ask him or her two questions:

- Why did you become a doctor?
- How did you learn to be a doctor?

You may get some interesting answers and find out how God leads people to different careers.

What does cloning mean?

[David is speaking:] You made all the delicate, inner parts of my body and knit me together in my mother's womb. Psalm 139:13

C*loning* means making an exact copy of a living thing's DNA, or genetic code. It involves taking the genetic code of a plant or animal and making another plant or animal from that code. Cloning bypasses the usual means of reproduction from a male and female. It's like making a photocopy of a living plant or animal, or building two houses with the same measurements. No one could ever make an exact copy of a person, though. Cloning can copy only a body—not a soul, spirit, or the experiences that make a person who he or she is.

Even if someone could make an exact physical copy of your eyes, knees, and brain, the clone would still be different from you. Your personality, experiences, desires, dreams, choices, and relationship with God can never be copied. All of these things together make you one of a kind. There will never be anyone exactly like you. Isn't that great?

ACTIVITY
Choose three friends and write a special card or letter to each one, telling your friends what you appreciate about each of them. Include characteristics such as "your great smile," "the way you encourage me," "your singing," "your friendship," "your skill at basketball," and so forth. At the bottom you can write, "You are special! —Psalm 139:13." Then mail these messages.

May 25

Why do people put garbage in their heads by watching bad movies?

I will refuse to look at anything vile and vulgar. I hate all crooked dealings; I will have nothing to do with them. Psalm 101:3

Junk entertainment is like junk food—it tastes good even though it's bad for us. Many people watch garbage on TV and in the movies because they like it, even though it is bad for them. Also, many people watch bad shows because they like the advertisements for those shows. The ads make the shows look good, so they think, "That looks pretty good. I think I'd like to see that." But often, the ads are lies—the show is bad.

God wants us to be smart about what we watch. He wants us to recognize junk entertainment for what it is and avoid it, even if it seems fun or harmless. He wants us to be careful to do what is right even when something tugs at us to do what is wrong or unwise.

God gave you his Word so you could know what is good and what is bad. His Word gives you wisdom.

ACTIVITY
Have a family Academy Awards night. Talk about the movies you've all seen at the theater and on video. Come up with a list of the five best movies and be able to say why they were good.

Why can't we put new books in the Bible?

I solemnly declare to everyone who hears the prophetic words of this book: If anyone adds anything to what is written here, God will add to that person the plagues described in this book.

Revelation 22:18

We can't put new books in the Bible because the Bible is *God's* message, not ours. It contains his words, which he inspired his people to write in a special way. Some people have tried to put new books in the Bible, but others who recognized that the Bible is a special book kept them from changing it.

God's written story is complete. He has told us all we need to know to help us understand how much he loves us and how we can obey him. Just think, you can hold God's story in your hand and read it! Today, thank God for giving you his Word.

ACTIVITY

Begin memorizing the names of the books of the Bible. Start with the first five books of the Old Testament—Genesis, Exodus, Leviticus, Numbers, and Deuteronomy. Then memorize the names of the first four books of the New Testament—Matthew, Mark, Luke, and John—which are also called the Gospels. Can you find some of your favorite stories in these books?

Why do people worship idols instead of God?

[God is speaking:] "Do not make idols of any kind, whether in the shape of birds or animals or fish."
Exodus 20:4

Idols are simply pictures or statues of imaginary gods. Actually, most people who have idols don't worship the idols but the gods they represent. This is true of some other religions such as Hinduism and animism. Some people, however, think that an idol itself can help them. People want to believe in things that they can see and touch, so they make things they can see. But we cannot see God because God is spirit.

Anything that is more important to us than God can be considered an idol. As a Christian, do not let anything take your attention away from worshiping the one true God. Idols can include celebrities and possessions that you like a lot. If you're not careful, they can take the place of God in your life. But there is only one true God. He loves you and is the only one worth worshiping.

ACTIVITY
Look at a news magazine with a grown-up. What famous people are sometimes treated like gods in your country? in the world? Why is this wrong?

Why do people pray to idols?

Yes, they knew God, but they wouldn't worship him as God or even give him thanks. And they began to think up foolish ideas of what God was like. The result was that their minds became dark and confused. Claiming to be wise, they became utter fools instead. And instead of worshiping the glorious, ever-living God, they worshiped idols made to look like mere people, or birds and animals and snakes. Romans 1:21-23

Some people pray to idols because they believe or hope that their prayers will make a difference. That is, they believe in a false god. They believe that their god hears and answers their prayers. Other people pray to idols out of habit or superstition. In other words, they say their prayers as sort of a good luck charm. They do not really know or believe in their idol. They just hope something will happen if they pray.

Praying to idols is wrong because idols are just things. They are not alive and do not hear. They cannot answer your prayers or bring you good fortune. God wants you to place your trust only in him.

ACTIVITY

People have prayed to idols for thousands of years. Today's verse comes from Paul's letter to the church in Rome, where many people worshiped made-up gods and goddesses. In an encyclopedia or history book, read about a country where praying to idols is common—for example, India, China, or Peru. Pray that people who pray to idols will hear about the true God and learn to pray to him.

Why do countries fight wars with each other?

*What is causing the quarrels and fights
among you? Isn't it the whole army of
evil desires at war within you? You want
what you don't have, so you scheme and
kill to get it. You are jealous for what
others have, and you can't possess it,
so you fight and quarrel to take it away
from them.*   James 4:1-2

A war is fought when countries disagree and can't work out their problems by talking together. Sometimes a war will begin when both countries want the same thing, like a certain piece of land. Instead of talking it out, they fight. Other times, a war will begin when one country wants to take over another country.

Many wars could be avoided if everyone followed God's instructions for loving and getting along with others. If you choose to love God and others, you can prevent fights in your life and make the world a little more peaceful.

ACTIVITY

Get a parent's permission before doing this activity. Go outside with a friend, each taking a can of soda pop. Decide which of you is "It." Shake up your cans as you name things that make you mad. Now "It" takes his or her can, points it away from both of you, and opens it. What a mess! You can clean it up with damp paper towels. Ask each other what happens when you yell and hit before you think. Are you like an exploding can? Now slowly count to thirty. Have the other person open his or her can. It didn't explode, did it? How is this like thinking before you get angry?

May 30

Is God happy for one country and sad for the other at the end of a war?

The Lord will settle international disputes. All the nations will beat their swords into plowshares and their spears into pruning hooks. All wars will stop, and military training will come to an end.   Micah 4:3

God is saddened by all sin and death. In most wars, nobody wins. People are hurt and killed. Property is destroyed. Countries, cities, neighborhoods, and families are torn apart. God is not happy with any of it. He is sad about all the destruction caused by sin, including war.

But sometimes, God does send war as a punishment for evil. The Old Testament explains that some nations suffered in wars as a punishment for their sins against others. And sometimes war seems to be the only way to stop an evil dictator or an evil government. But that doesn't mean God is happy to see nations go to war. He much prefers that people avoid war.

Ask God to help you grow up to be loving and wise. Thank him for the people who have died for our country's freedom. Ask him to comfort their families.

ACTIVITY

Today is the traditional celebration of Memorial Day in the United States. We honor those who have died while serving their country. Did any of your relatives die in a war? Ask your parents if you can visit a cemetery and find the graves of people who gave their lives for their country. Put flowers by their graves as you thank God for them.

What's a parable?

*[Jesus] used many such stories
and illustrations to teach the
people as much as they were able
to understand.* Mark 4:33

Good Samaritan
PAIR APPLE

A parable is a short story with a surprise ending that makes a point. Jesus told many parables, for two reasons: (1) to hide the truth from people who weren't really interested, and (2) to teach the truth to listeners who were interested and wanted to learn. Whenever Jesus told parables, those who weren't interested or who wouldn't listen didn't understand. But those who wanted to learn asked Jesus to explain the story, and then they got the point.

We can learn from the Bible if we want to do what God says. But if we don't want to listen to God, the Bible won't make much sense. Listening to stories and telling stories are great ways to learn.

ACTIVITY
Read one of the most famous parables, the Good Samaritan. It's found in Luke 10:30-35. (The verses before and after tell how Jesus decided to use this story to teach an important lesson.) Now rewrite the parable and set it in your town, today. Who would the characters be? Write out the story or say it onto a cassette recorder. If you have friends or brothers and sisters around, act out the story.

Why do we have marriage?

*[Jesus] said, "This explains why a
man leaves his father and mother
and is joined to his wife, and the
two are united into one."*

Matthew 19:5

God invented marriage because people need someone to be close to and to love and be loved by. He also created marriage because he knew it was the best way to bring children into the world. God knows what is best for us. He knows that babies and children need a mother and father to protect them and care for them. Marriage is good. In fact, God brought the first man and woman together in the Garden of Eden before any sin came into the world. God's best plan is that husbands and wives stay together, work out their problems, and be good parents.

If it's God's plan for you to get married someday, he has someone special in mind for you. When the time is right, you can count on God to bring the two of you together. Just ask God to help you know his plan for you. Then he will give you a happy marriage (or a happy life as a single person)!

ACTIVITY

Have you ever been to a wedding? If your family has a wedding album, look at the photographs. Ask if anyone remembers some of the words that were said during the ceremony.

June 2

If Jesus doesn't want us to get hurt, why did he tell us to chop our hands off and poke our eyes out?

[Jesus is speaking:] If your hand or foot causes you to sin, cut it off and throw it away. It is better to enter heaven crippled or lame than to be thrown into the unquenchable fire with both of your hands and feet.   Matthew 18:8

When Jesus spoke about cutting off a hand or poking out an eye, he was purposely exaggerating to make his point. It's like saying, "I'd give *anything* to have an ice cream cone"—even though there are many things you'd never give away. You just want everyone to know how badly you want ice cream. Jesus wanted people to know how bad sin is—it's so bad that we should get rid of *anything* that makes us sin.

Jesus doesn't want you to actually cut off anything—that won't get rid of sin in your life. But saying it that way shows how important it is to get rid of habits, friendships, or attitudes that cause you to sin. We should stay away from people and places that tempt us to disobey God.

ACTIVITY
Keep a list for a day of the bad things you are tempted to do, plus those you actually do. What made it easier to sin? Did a certain friend talk sassy to grown-ups and encourage you to do it, too? Don't spend so much time with that friend. Do the toy commercials on TV make you want things you shouldn't have? Don't watch these commercials. Ask God to help you stay away from the things that make it hard to obey him.

June 3

My parents want me to play a certain sport, but I hate it. What should I do?

Children, obey your parents
because you belong to the Lord,
for this is the right thing to do.
Ephesians 6:1

Your parents probably have a good reason for wanting you to play that sport. They may want you to learn teamwork and good sportsmanship and to stay in good physical condition. So give the sport a chance. If you still don't like it, talk it over with your parents. Be respectful and explain how you feel. Suggest other ways to have the same kind of experience—like playing another sport or being in a club that you would enjoy more. It's good to learn a wide variety of skills.

If you try hard regardless of how you feel and try to see it through to the end of the season, you will learn lessons and gain another skill that you may use in the future. Your parents are more likely to grant your request for a change if they know you gave 100 percent. God wants you to try your hardest, too.

ACTIVITY

What sport interests you the most? Who is your favorite professional player? Talk to a parent about the possibility of going to see him or her play. Hint: You may have to save your money to help pay for the tickets.

June 4

Why does my coach care so much about winning? It's not fun anymore.

I saw that there is nothing better for people than to be happy in their work. That is why they are here! No one will bring them back from death to enjoy life in the future. Ecclesiastes 3:22

Sometimes, winning becomes too important to people. In our society, being number one seems to be most important. Coaches and parents can get caught up in this pressure. It's good to win, but it's also important to have fun playing a sport. If winning seems to be more important to your team than having fun, talk to your parents. Then they can talk with your coach. If nothing changes, you may want to ask your parents what they think about helping you get on a different team.

Being on a team should be fun. Winning is nice, but that's not what matters most to God. He wants you to have a winning season in the fun column.

ACTIVITY
Write down your coach's name and your team members' names in your prayer journal. Pray that God will help your coach relax more so your team can have more fun. Watch to see how God takes care of you and your teammates.

June 5

Do we have to pray to be forgiven?

If we confess our sins to him, he is faithful and just to forgive us and to cleanse us from every wrong.

1 John 1:9

DEAR GOD, PLEASE FORGIVE ME FOR THE THINGS I DID WRONG TODAY. AND WOULD IT BE TOO MUCH TO ASK YOU TO FORGIVE ME IN ADVANCE FOR ALL THE MISTAKES I'LL PROBABLY MAKE TOMORROW?

When you do something bad, you should talk with God about it right away. Tell him that you know what you did was wrong. Then ask him to forgive you and show you what to do next.

The word *confess* means that you tell God what you have done, agree with him that it is wrong, and ask him to forgive you. Because only God can forgive sins, you need to confess to *him* in order to be truly forgiven. And you have his promise that he will always forgive you if you are truly sorry for what you have done. He is your loving, forgiving heavenly Father.

ACTIVITY

Borrow a hand mirror from a family member if you don't have one, and (with that person's permission) paint on the glass with black, green, and purple water colors, leaving only a few tiny places unpainted. It's hard to see yourself in the mirror, isn't it? Sin can make it hard to see yourself clearly, too. But God looks at your heart, even if it's smudged with sin. Now wash the paint off with water and clean it with a paper towel or rag. When you ask him to, God forgives you and cleans your sin away. He wipes away sadness, too. Thank God for his forgiveness and love.

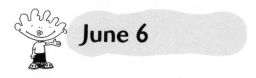

June 6

What are some good things to do when you're not in school?

I recommend having fun, because there is nothing better for people to do in this world than to eat, drink, and enjoy life. That way they will experience some happiness along with all the hard work God gives them. Ecclesiastes 8:15

There are many great things to do during a school break. Use your imagination. You could plant a garden, collect rocks or insects, take pictures, or check out the neighborhood to find some new friends. You could go to the library to read magazines and books or use the computers. You could organize a garage sale. You could ask your parents how you might help around your home.

Wherever you live, God has given you many interesting things to see and do. Don't just be lazy and say "I'm bored" all the time. Thank God for extra time to explore new ideas and new places!

ACTIVITY
Summer break may be coming up. Choose at least one activity from the list above that you can do, and take the first step toward doing it. For example, if you choose to plant a garden, you can buy a packet of seeds. If you decide to begin a rock collection, you could get a book that describes all kinds of rocks. Get started now!

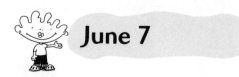

Will God be with me all the time in heaven?

I heard a loud shout from the throne, saying, "Look, the home of God is now among his people! He will live with them, and they will be his people. God himself will be with them."   Revelation 21:3

On earth, people cannot always be together with the people they love. They may be in a crowded place but not really know anybody. They might be by themselves a lot of the time. Or their best friends may move away. Or a favorite relative might die. Or perhaps they don't get a chance to meet their heroes.

This isn't the way it will be in heaven! There, you will get to go right up to God and talk to him. God will be with you all the time, and you will be with him. God will be your friend, and you will be his. Getting to be with God will be one of the very best things about heaven!

ACTIVITY
Make a list of everyone you will want to see in heaven. Think of Bible characters (David? Mary?), great Christians in history (Augustine? Luther?), and some of your own relatives. At dinner sometime, share the list with your family and see who the others would have on their lists.

Why does eternity last for a long, long, long, long time?

God has made everything beautiful for its own time. He has planted eternity in the human heart, but even so, people cannot see the whole scope of God's work from beginning to end.

Ecclesiastes 3:11

E ternity doesn't last a long time. It lasts forever, and that's longer than a long time. The word *eternity* means "infinite or endless time." It is impossible for people to understand eternity. It's beyond what our brains can imagine, because everything we imagine has limits.

But God knows because he has no limits. He is eternal. You can trust him to take care of all your tomorrows and your forever. You'll not only get to be with God in heaven, you'll get to be there with him forever!

ACTIVITY

Take an eyedropper and see how many drops of water it takes to fill a paper cup with half an inch of water. Next, do the math and figure out how many drops it would take for a foot of water (at the same width). Imagine how many drops it would take to fill a pond, a river, a big lake, or an ocean. The time that it would take to add all those drops together would be only the beginning of eternity.

Why do people kill animals to eat when they could just buy food at the store?

*God blessed Noah and his sons and told
them, "Multiply and fill the earth. All the
wild animals, large and small, and all
the birds and fish will be afraid of you.
I have placed them in your power. I have
given them to you for food, just as I have
given you grain and vegetables."*

Genesis 9:1-3

Many years ago everyone had to hunt for food. They would gather plants and kill animals. Some people began to raise fruits and vegetables and sell them. Others raised animals and sold them. Eventually there were grocery stores where people could buy the fruit, vegetables, milk, and meat they needed to eat. But for meat to be available at a store, someone has to kill the animals. No one can get meat at the stores unless someone kills the animals for food. It certainly is more convenient to buy meat at a store than to raise chickens or hunt wild pigs. But some people enjoy hunting, so they hunt deer, moose, pheasant, or some other animal or bird instead of buying all their meat at the store.

No matter where we get our food, we should always thank God for it. The food we have is part of what God provides for us so we can live. Be a thankful and healthy eater.

ACTIVITY
Draw a funny picture with a small fish being swallowed by a big fish that is being swallowed by a bigger fish that is being swallowed by an even bigger fish that is being swallowed by a huge fish. . . .

June 10

Why doesn't God just give us money when we need it?

"My thoughts are completely different from yours," says the Lord. "And my ways are far beyond anything you could imagine. For just as the heavens are higher than the earth, so are my ways higher than your ways and my thoughts higher than your thoughts." Isaiah 55:8-9

God does give us money when we need it. He always meets our needs. But he usually does it through jobs, people, and other ordinary means.

There is a difference between need and want. People often want a lot of things that they don't really need. All of us would have a better understanding of what real needs are if we lived in a land where no one received anything but the basic needs of food, clothes, and a home.

God wants you to work, to use well what he's already given to you, and to be responsible. The needs in your life help you learn these skills. For example, God may want you to use something that you already have, to make something, or to do without something. God isn't being mean—he's being your loving heavenly Father.

ACTIVITY

Can you remember what was on your wish lists for the past few Christmases and birthdays? Name as many of the things as you can. Did you receive all of the things? Probably not. Did you miss the things you didn't get? Again, probably not. So you didn't actually have a need for all those things. You just wanted them for a while. If you are thankful and content that God gives you what you *need,* you'll find that he also gives you some things you only *want.*

162

How do poor people get poor?

A poor person's farm may produce much food, but injustice sweeps it all away. Proverbs 13:23

Most people become poor by being born in poor families. In fact, many people in the world are born in a poor country where almost everyone is poor. It's not their fault that they are poor. There are many other reasons for poverty, too. Some people are born with a physical or mental handicap, or they are injured in an accident or in war. These people find it very hard to get a good job. Some people have a lot of bad things happen to them, and no one will help them. Some do not have a family to help them. Some are poor because they have been cheated by other people. And some people become poor because they made bad choices.

No matter what makes someone poor, God would like you to try to help. Isn't he kind to you, even when you make bad choices and mistakes? And you never know when you will need help. So you should be kind to others.

ACTIVITY

Read the fable "The Lion and the Mouse" by the ancient story-teller Aesop. It is a story about unexpected help. It ends with this moral (lesson): "Little friends may prove great friends."

June 12

Why did the Israelites who left Egypt have to wander in the wilderness until they died?

"Because the men who explored the land were there for forty days, you must wander in the wilderness for forty years—a year for each day. . . .' I will do these things to every member of the community who has conspired against me. They will all die here in this wilderness!" Numbers 14:34-35

Through Moses, God led the Israelites right to the Promised Land, the land he had promised to Abraham. Ten spies reported that the people there were giants, too big to fight. But Joshua and Caleb knew God would help them. They said, "Let's go at once to take the land" (Numbers 13:30). Unfortunately, the people listened to the ten, refusing to obey God and march into the land. Those Israelites never saw the Promised Land because they didn't have faith to do what God wanted.

God wants his people to have faith. You can trust him and follow him, even when other people doubt. God can do amazing things through you.

ACTIVITY

Ask your mom if she has a little glass saltshaker like the kind that restaurants have—one with a flat bottom and sloping sides. Pour a small pile of salt on a table, and set the saltshaker on its bottom edge in the salt until it balances at an angle just right. Gently blow away some of the salt around the shaker until only a few grains are left holding it up. If you tell your friends this really works, they'll probably say, "No way!" God can do lots more than saltshaker tricks—great things that make people who don't know him say, "No way!"

Is it OK to keep a toy that belongs to someone else if they don't ask for it back?

[Jesus is speaking:] "Do for others as you would like them to do for you."   Luke 6:31

Borrowing something from someone else but not giving it back is the same as stealing. We know that stealing is wrong. And it ends up hurting us even if no one finds out about it. Remember, God knows.

If a friend gives you something to keep, then that gift is yours. But if someone loans you something to use for a while, then you need to give it back . . . even if the person doesn't ask for it or forgets about it.

God has given the command not to steal because he wants to help and protect us from the penalties of stealing and from a reputation of being a thief. Besides, isn't that the way you would want to be treated? Wouldn't you want your toy or book or ball returned, even if you had forgotten about it?

ACTIVITY

Go on a "borrowed-toy hunt" in your room, looking through your belongings for other people's things. (Don't forget about things from your brothers or sisters.) Return things that don't belong to you. It may be hard to do, but apologize if you took something without asking or have kept a toy for a long time.

June 14

Who invented vegetables?

"Test us for ten days on a diet of vegetables and water," Daniel said. Daniel 1:12

God created vegetables—they were his idea. Our bodies need certain kinds of food, just as a car needs a certain kind of fuel. You wouldn't put hamburgers into a gas tank, would you? God gave us vegetables because that's one kind of fuel our bodies need.

In fact, vegetables have several very important jobs. First, they provide vitamins and minerals that help us grow and become strong and healthy. Vegetables also give us fiber, which is the part of plant cells that your body cannot digest. Fiber carries all the other foods through your digestive system.

God gave us fruits and vegetables to eat so that our bodies would work properly. You can thank God for wanting to keep you strong and healthy!

ACTIVITY

It's time to make alphabet soup . . . on paper! Write the letters of the alphabet down the left side of a piece of paper. Now try to think of at least one vegetable that starts with each letter. *A* is for asparagus, *B* is for beet, and so on. When you get stuck, move on to the next letter or ask other members of your family to help you. Then ask if you can add some of these items to next week's shopping list. You may even develop a taste for a new vegetable!

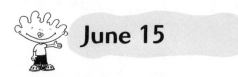

June 15

Do I really have to eat my vegetables or are my parents just making sure I clean my plate?

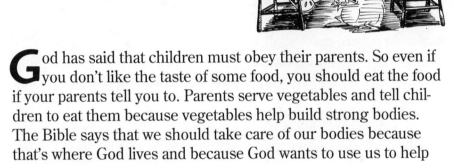

Don't you know that your body is the temple of the Holy Spirit, who lives in you and was given to you by God? You do not belong to yourself.   1 Corinthians 6:19

God has said that children must obey their parents. So even if you don't like the taste of some food, you should eat the food if your parents tell you to. Parents serve vegetables and tell children to eat them because vegetables help build strong bodies. The Bible says that we should take care of our bodies because that's where God lives and because God wants to use us to help other people.

So do what you can to stay healthy. Learn about nutrition. Eat good food, including vegetables. God (and your parents) want your body to be as healthy and good as it can be.

ACTIVITY
A dip can be a fun and tasty way to eat raw, peeled, and cleaned carrots, celery, radishes, or other veggies. Make and try one of these dips:

- Cheese dip: 4 tablespoons cream cheese softened in a microwave for 15 seconds, mixed with 2 tablespoons sour cream or plain yogurt, 1 teaspoon chopped chives, and a little bit of salt and pepper.
- Pink dip: 4 tablespoons mayonnaise, mixed with 2 tablespoons ketchup.

June 16

If we prayed to find something we lost, would we really find it?

As one of them was chopping, his ax head fell into the river. "Ah, my lord!" he cried. "It was a borrowed ax!" "Where did it fall?" the man of God asked. When he showed him the place, Elisha cut a stick and threw it into the water. Then the ax head rose to the surface and floated.

2 Kings 6:5-6

JASON'S IMAGINATION

LITTLE BO PEEP HAS LOST HER SHEEP AND DOESN'T KNOW WHERE TO FIND THEM, SHE PRAYED ON HER OWN THAT THEY WOULD COME HOME DRAGGING THEIR TAILS BEHIND THEM.

If we lost something and it was part of God's plan for us to find it, then, yes, we would find it. No job is too small for God. It is good to pray for what matters to us, even something small that is lost. God may help us find it right away or help us remember where we put it. He also might have us retrace our steps to find it so we will be more careful next time.

But prayer does not substitute for being careful. Don't say to yourself, "Oh well, if I lose it, I can ask God to find it for me." That would be using prayer the wrong way.

ACTIVITY

Ask a parent if you can make a family lost-and-found box. You can do this by decorating a medium-size box and labeling it "Lost & Found." Then, whenever a family member finds something lying around the house, he or she can put it in the box.

June 17

I want to be with my friends. Why do we have to go to church so much?

[David is speaking:] I was glad when they said to me, "Let us go to the house of the Lord."

Psalm 122:1

CHURCH SERVICE
Sunday School
Club Meeting
SPECIAL KIDS' SERVICE
Hosted by Jason
Meet at the WAVE POOL!!

Christians go to church to worship God, study the Bible, and be with other people who believe in Jesus. Church is a special place where you can learn more about God's love and how to please him. Churches also sponsor clubs and other children's activities.

Remember, you can bring your friends to church. You can also make friends at church. God doesn't want you to be lonely or bored at his house.

ACTIVITY

With your parents' permission, invite a friend to sleep over on Saturday night. Make part of the invitation going to church with you on Sunday morning. Be sure to ask your friend's parents if this is all right. You may have other activities at church that you would like to invite friends to attend also. Whenever friends come to visit and there is something going on at church, you can make the church activity part of the fun time that you have with your friends.

June 18

Do angels get tired?

Suddenly there was a great earthquake, because an angel of the Lord came down from heaven and rolled aside the stone and sat on it. Matthew 28:2

A ngels never get tired, not even a little bit, and they never sleep. They don't need sleep like you do because they don't have human bodies. Good angels are incredibly powerful and always ready to do what God tells them to do. Angels can open locked doors, roll away huge stones, and even wipe out whole armies. That's because they are God's servants, and God gives them the power they need to carry out his work. Angels are not all-powerful, however. The book of Daniel tells of a time when Satan stopped an angel for a little while, until the archangel Michael came to help him.

But you don't have to worry about angels getting tired, weak, or sick. You can also relax and be certain that someday they will fight in the final battle against Satan and his demons . . . and *win!*

ACTIVITY
Gather some friends to put on a mini-play about God and his powerful angels. One of you will play God, and the rest can be good angels. Have "God" whisper a job to do in the ear of one of the angels. Then the "angel" has to act that out. Take turns until all the angels have done the work that God has for each of them.

One Year Book of Fun & Active Devotions for Kids

What should I say if someone makes fun of the Bible?

Even if you suffer for doing what is right, God will reward you for it. So don't be afraid and don't worry. Instead, you must worship Christ as Lord of your life. And if you are asked about your Christian hope, always be ready to explain it. 1 Peter 3:14-15

If a friend makes fun of the Bible, you can politely explain how you feel and ask that person to stop. Your friend may not know how special the Bible is to you. This might give you a good opportunity to explain that the Bible comes from God, who created the whole universe, and it's very important to you. You might be the first one to help this person understand that the message in the Bible is for everyone in the world. If your friend doesn't want to listen, it's best to let it pass and just pray for him or her.

Politely but firmly defending God's Word is part of growing as a Christian. God will give you the courage and the words. That's what he's done for his people for thousands of years!

ACTIVITY
It takes practice to talk confidently about the Bible. Suggest to your Sunday school teacher that you do some role plays to practice defending the Bible. Take turns being the kid who brings up questions, and then practice being the kid who explains how special God's Word is.

What mean things does Satan do to people?

Be careful! Watch out for attacks from the Devil, your great enemy. He prowls around like a roaring lion, looking for some victim to devour.   1 Peter 5:8

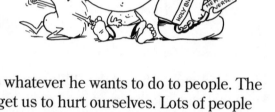

Satan does *not* get to do whatever he wants to do to people. The main thing he does is get us to hurt ourselves. Lots of people think that Satan only tempts people to do bad stuff. He does tempt us, but the worst thing he does is lie to us.

Satan hates God and does not want you to believe what God says. He wants you to sin. He wants you to believe what is false. He wants you to believe that you are no good. Satan lies to you about your worth and about what really matters, so you'll hurt yourself. But God loves you and wants you to be your best. God is the one to listen to.

ACTIVITY

With a parent or a grandparent, take a look at the front section of a daily newspaper or a newsmagazine. Find a story about someone who listened to Satan's lies and tried to hurt himself, herself, or someone else. Pray for that person. And ask God to help you keep listening to him.

Are demons red with horns and long tails?

I remind you of the angels who did not stay within the limits of authority God gave them but left the place where they belonged. God has kept them chained in prisons of darkness, waiting for the day of judgment. Jude 1:6

Sometimes the devil and demons are pictured as wearing red and having horns and long tails. But that idea of what Satan looks like came out of someone's imagination, not from the Bible. The devil is a bad angel. Since angels don't usually have physical bodies, no one knows how Satan looks. Like other angels, the devil can take different forms.

When Satan was created, he was good, but he later rebelled against God and was kicked out of heaven. While he is God's enemy, Satan is not as powerful as God. Jesus called him "a liar and the father of lies" (John 8:44). The Bible says he can make himself look like an "angel of light" (2 Corinthians 11:14). So you see, Satan can be very tricky—he tries to make bad look good. He usually does this by lying to you, not by scaring you with his looks. God will help you not be fooled, if you ask him.

ACTIVITY

Read the following: There is three errers in this sentence. What are they?

Do you know the answer? "Is" should be "are," and "errer" should be spelled "error." The third error is that there are only *two* errors! Did you get fooled? Many people do. Don't get fooled by Satan's clever ways. Keep thinking and keep trusting God.

June 22

Why did Jesus appear to Saul?

As he was nearing Damascus on this mission, a brilliant light from heaven suddenly beamed down upon him! He fell to the ground and heard a voice saying to him, "Saul! Saul! Why are you persecuting me?" Acts 9:3-4

S aul (later known as Paul) hated Christians so much that he got permission to capture them and put them in jail. But God had other plans for Saul's life. One day, while Saul was traveling to another city to look for Christians, he was blinded by a bright light. God used the light to get Saul's attention. Then Jesus appeared to him. Because of this experience, Saul believed in Jesus. He became a strong follower of Christ and a great missionary. Instead of trying to get rid of Christians, Saul went all over the world helping people *become* Christians. He wrote many letters to those Christians. Some of those letters are in the Bible.

God gives people a second chance and sometimes even more chances! And he can help people who trust him to totally change the way they live.

ACTIVITY

"Amazing Grace" is a famous hymn that tells about how God can change people. It was written by a man who should know! John Newton was a slave trader for many years until God helped him realize his actions were very wrong. He wrote the hymn out of thankfulness for how Jesus' power saved him. Find the song and read the words, thinking of John Newton and his changed life.

June 23

If I put money in a savings account, can I get it back?

[David is speaking:] If your wealth increases, don't make it the center of your life.

Psalm 62:10

Oh yes, you can get it back! The bank is just a holding place for your money. It's like a big piggy bank. To get money from a savings account, you just go to the bank and fill out a withdrawal slip. The teller gives you the money, and the computer keeps track of how much you took out. If you have a checking account, you can write a check anytime you like. If you have an automatic teller machine (ATM) card, you just go to the machine and follow the instructions. The money is yours, and you can always get it.

Remember, the purpose of a savings account is to save for the future. So try not to take money out until you've reached your goal. Don't just trust in your money, though. Trust in God, who owns everything. God will help you save, and he will take care of you no matter what. Remember that God—not money—is your provider. Place your trust in him.

ACTIVITY

Do you have a savings account? If not, ask your mom or dad to help you open one. If you have an account, decide how much of your allowance you will deposit each month. Also decide what percent of gift money you'll put away. Then set a goal for your money.

June 24

How is God always there?

[Jesus is speaking:] "Teach these new disciples to obey all the commands I have given you. And be sure of this: I am with you always, even to the end of the age."   Matthew 28:20

God can always be with us because he does not have a physical body. God is Spirit, so he does not have to stay in one place the way we do. We don't know exactly how this works, but that's OK. God is much, much greater and more amazing than we can imagine.

Wherever you go—to your home, to school, to church, to the store, to your friend's house, or anyplace else—God is right there with you. Isn't it great to know that God is there . . . and here?

ACTIVITY

The next time you wake up in the middle of the night, make a special point of remembering that God is with you, there, at that time. Listen to how quiet the house is. Everyone else is asleep. Everyone except for God! He's always awake; he's always there watching over you. Then thank him for being with you at all times and in all places.

How will the world end?

*I saw a new heaven and a new
earth, for the old heaven and
the old earth had disappeared.
And the sea was also gone.*

Revelation 21:1

We don't know exactly *when*
the world will end, but we know that it *will* end. This is not
bad news, for it's part of God's plan. And the world will not be
destroyed by people, or by things getting out of control. It will be
God's doing and God's timing. This world will end in a blaze of
fire! God will replace it with a new one.

This will not happen until Jesus comes back. He will return, just
as he promised, to judge all people who have ever lived and to set
up his kingdom. And he will replace our damaged world with a
new, perfect one, where his people will live with him forever. For
those who love him, the end of the world will really be a beginning—a wonderful, awesome beginning! You can be part of that
beginning if you trust him.

ACTIVITY

Today's Bible verse comes near the very end of the whole Bible.
But it talks about the new beginning. Read more about this in
Revelation 21:1–22:6. Then get a lump of clay and form it into a
"new world." Use a pencil or a piece of wire to outline countries
on the world. You can keep it as a reminder of the new world that
God will create someday.

June 26

Why doesn't God give us some things we pray for?

Trust in the Lord with all your heart; do not depend on your own understanding. Seek his will in all you do, and he will direct your paths.   Proverbs 3:5-6

God is much wiser than we are. He knows what will happen if we get some of the things that we pray for. He can see all that is happening all over the world in every person's life all the time. He wants the very best for each of us. And he has a special plan for every person. So sometimes, God does not give us what we pray for because it could hurt us or turn us the wrong way.

At other times, God doesn't give us what we ask for right away. He wants us to wait patiently for his timing. And sometimes, God has plans that we don't yet understand, so he waits or works something out that we cannot see.

Remember that God will never ignore your prayers. He loves you, hears your prayers, and works things out the best way possible. You can trust in God's great care for you. He always has a good, loving reason when he doesn't give you exactly what you prayed for.

ACTIVITY
Today's passage from the Bible is a favorite one for many people. Write it down on an index card and memorize it. Then, whenever you pray, do as verse 5 says: "Trust in the Lord with all your heart."

What happens to people who don't go to church?

Can we boast, then, that we have done anything to be accepted by God? No, because our acquittal is not based on our good deeds. It is based on our faith. So we are made right with God through faith and not by obeying the law.

Romans 3:27-28

Going to church doesn't get a person into heaven. And not going to church doesn't send a person to hell. A person becomes a Christian by faith, believing in Christ, not by doing good things. Most Christians go to church because of what happens there. At church, you can meet other Christians. You can find encouragement and help for your problems. You can learn from God's Word and help others. And you can experience wonderful worship, singing, and praying that glorifies God. People who don't go to church miss all that. They miss a very special meeting with God and the chance to grow with other Christians.

What do you enjoy most about church?

ACTIVITY
Push four toothpicks into a sweet potato around the middle of it. Put the sweet potato on the rim of a glass filled with water. Adjust the amount of water so that the bottom inch of the potato is in water. Set it in a sunny window. As the days go by, add water so that it always covers the bottom of the sweet potato. In about a week, the plant will sprout and grow. Christians can grow quickly, too. They grow to be like Jesus when they're in the water of God's Word and the sunshine of a church.

Is it all right to throw rocks at someone who threw rocks at you?

[Jesus is speaking:] "You have heard that the law of Moses says, 'If an eye is injured, injure the eye of the person who did it. If a tooth gets knocked out, knock out the tooth of the person who did it.' But I say, don't resist an evil person! If you are slapped on the right cheek, turn the other, too."

Matthew 5:38-39

It is not right to do something bad to someone just because that person did something bad to you. The Bible calls that returning "evil for evil," and Jesus says it is wrong. Instead of trying to get back at people who hurt us, we should talk about the situation with God and leave it with him. It's all right to protect ourselves, and certainly we should tell an adult, but it's not OK to get even. This may seem unfair, but only God knows how to judge fairly. So we need to let God take care of making things right. Getting back at others only makes matters worse.

Just because someone else is sinning doesn't give you the excuse to sin. You should always try to obey God. God's way is not always easiest, but it's always best.

ACTIVITY

Is there somebody who does mean things to you—maybe even hits you or throws rocks at you? God knows that it is hard not to try and get even with that person. But don't *get even*. Instead, *get out* . . . your prayer journal. Write down the person's name in the left column, pray hard for him or her, and be ready to watch God answer your prayers.

How much do investments cost?

[Jesus is speaking:] "Don't begin until you count the cost. For who would begin construction of a building without first getting estimates and then checking to see if there is enough money to pay the bills?" Luke 14:28

An investment is something you buy so you can sell it later at a higher price. Investments, like stocks, have all different prices. Some cost more than others. Most investments cost more than children can pay. That's why most kids have their money in bank savings accounts, not in stocks or other investments like that.

Some people say you can get rich quickly or easily by buying their investment. The Bible warns you to stay away from those kinds of tricks. God's plan is that you trust him and that you grow your money bit by bit. Greed causes us to listen to get-rich-quick ideas because we want more quickly. But trying to do it this way usually results in a loss, not a gain. Trust God and his way to grow your money.

ACTIVITY

Because your savings account is probably your main investment right now, take a closer look at it. Exactly how is your money growing? It earns interest—extra money that the bank puts in your account for letting them take care of your money. Find out from your mom or dad what interest rate you are earning, and figure out together how much money you can earn in a year.

June 30

What if the waiter gives me a kid's meal free because he thinks I'm younger than I really am?

Put away all falsehood and "tell your neighbor the truth" because we belong to each other.

Ephesians 4:25

It is important to do what is right, even if it costs you money. So if you get a children's price for a meal or a ticket and you are older than a "child," you should tell the truth. Tell the waiter, waitress, ticket seller, or whoever is in charge how old you really are. You can't put a price on honesty.

Remember that God is looking after you. He will meet all your needs and take good care of you if you do things his way. God's way is to be honest. It shows that you trust him.

ACTIVITY

Do a role play with a friend or brother or sister. Let one play the part of a child who's older than the usual kid's meal age. The other one can be a waiter or waitress. Then switch roles. What will you do? It's nice to save money, but don't forget that God values honesty above money.

July 1

Does God have a sense of humor?

A cheerful heart is good medicine, but a broken spirit saps a person's strength. Proverbs 17:22

Yes. One clue that God has a sense of humor is that people love to laugh. Genesis 1:26-27 says that God created people in his image. This means that in many ways we are like God—and he is like us. So if we have a sense of humor, God probably does, too. What's more, God's Word refers quite a bit to joy, happiness, fun, and laughter: "Sarah declared, 'God has brought me laughter!'" (Genesis 21:6); "We were filled with laughter, and we sang for joy" (Psalm 126:2); "Always be full of joy in the Lord. I say it again—rejoice!" (Philippians 4:4). It's clear that God wants his people to enjoy life.

But the fact that God has a sense of humor doesn't mean that he enjoys everything we think is funny or that he likes all our jokes. Some people are cruel with their humor. They laugh when people are hurt or make fun of others. That's wrong. You should laugh *with* people, not *at* them. Tell good jokes, laugh, enjoy life—God wants you to be filled with joy.

ACTIVITY

On one of the next weekend evenings, hold a Family Comedy Night. Let everybody have a turn. Tell jokes. Make funny faces. Do a skit. Sing a wacky song.

Why do my friends break their promises to me?

It is better to say nothing than to promise something that you don't follow through on.

Ecclesiastes 5:5

SO YOU'RE SAYING THAT IF I SIGN THAT CONTRACT, I CAN BORROW YOUR BASEBALL BAT?

FRIENDSHIP CONTRACT

SIGNATURE:

Only God is perfect and will never break his promises. Most people who make promises intend to keep them, but they may forget. Or circumstances may change. For example, a friend may say that you can visit anytime, but a baby brother arrives, and the family limits the number of visitors for a while. Sometimes, people make promises that are almost impossible to keep—like saying, "I will never get angry with you."

If a friend breaks a promise to you, let that person know how you feel, but try to be forgiving and understanding. Ask God to help you make only promises that you can keep. Then do your best to keep those promises.

ACTIVITY

Work on being a person who keeps promises. What promises have you made lately to God, to your parents, to your friends, and to yourself? Make a list and determine to keep them.

If the law says something is right but God says it's wrong, who's right?

Peter and the apostles replied,
"We must obey God rather than
human authority."   Acts 5:29

The Bible tells us to obey the government. But when a government law goes against what God wants us to do, we should obey God instead of the government. God is in charge of the government and not the other way around. God created and rules the universe. No one can have higher authority.

For example, if the government passed a law making it illegal to pray, you should break the law and pray anyway. The same would be true about worshiping, reading the Bible, and telling others about Christ. And if the government were to make it OK to lie and steal, you still shouldn't do those things because they go against God's law. So you must always obey God first. God knows that it might be hard for you sometimes, so he will help you obey his ways.

ACTIVITY

Imagine that the government made laws that said you couldn't worship God, read the Bible, pray, go to church, or tell others about Christ. How would your life change? What would you do? Write a story about some kids who had this happen to them.

It's a free country—why do we pay tolls?

For the Lord's sake, accept all
authority.   1 Peter 2:13

Living in a "free country" means that our highest laws guarantee our right to say and do certain activities, not that our country doesn't cost us anything. For example, the United States has freedom of speech, freedom of the press, and freedom of religion. That means U. S. citizens can say, publish, and worship pretty much whatever they want. But they don't have total freedom because their country needs laws and rules so that everything will run right. You can see that freedom works because it has limits.

That is why governments need money for paying leaders, police officers, firefighters, teachers, and other workers and for building and repairing things like bridges and roads. This money comes from taxes and tolls. The laws of a country are not the same as God's laws, but God tells us to respect the government and to obey the laws. So your family pays the tolls, wears seat belts, lets you drive only when the law says you're old enough, stops at red traffic lights, and follows the speed limits.

ACTIVITY

Save some loose change in a jar. The next time your family drives on a tollway, take this change with you. Then surprise your mom or dad and offer to pay the tolls.

Why are some kids so big and other kids so small?

The Lord said to Samuel, "Don't judge by his appearance or height, for I have rejected him. The Lord doesn't make decisions the way you do! People judge by outward appearance, but the Lord looks at a person's thoughts and intentions." 1 Samuel 16:7

People come in all different shapes and sizes. Just look at adults. Some professional football players weigh over three hundred pounds, and some professional basketball players are well over seven feet tall! Most people, however, are much lighter and shorter that that. Kids come in different shapes and sizes, too. They also grow at different rates. A girl might grow quickly and seem very tall compared to other kids. But in a few years, other kids will begin growing and pass her in height.

It can be frustrating to be very small or very tall right now, but eventually these things average out. Be patient. Size won't matter so much in the future when everyone has finished growing. Remember, too, that God is the one who's helping you grow— at the speed that's just right for you.

ACTIVITY

Do you have a growth chart in your home? If not, here's how you can make one. You'll need a long piece of paper to mark your height as you grow over the next few months. But make it wide enough to also write in your talents, hobbies, favorite books, and other things that show you are a special person made by God.

What if I don't like the music that everyone else listens to?

[Job's friend Elihu is speaking:] "Just as the mouth tastes good food, the ear tests the words it hears.'" So let us discern for ourselves what is right; let us learn together what is good."   Job 34:3-4

You don't have to enjoy certain music just because others do. It's like with food. What if everyone else liked French fries, but fries made you sick to your stomach? Would you eat French fries? You wouldn't have to. In the same way, you will develop your own taste in music. It may be the same as others, but it doesn't have to be.

You should respect others' tastes, of course. Don't yell at them to "turn off that stupid music" just because you don't like it. Pay attention to the words, however. If you know they aren't pleasing to God, let your friends know you have no interest in listening. True friends will respect you for your honesty. And God will be happy you wanted to please him.

ACTIVITY

Do you like to listen to classical music? rock? rap? traditional gospel? Music, even Christian music, comes in all styles. If you want to find music to fit your taste and honor God, go with your mom or dad to a Christian book and music store. You can probably listen on headphones to find an artist you like who's OK with your parents. Then buy the cassette or CD yourself, or put it on your birthday or Christmas present list.

July 7

In heaven, we don't just sing and worship all day, do we?

[David is speaking:] That I might sing praises to you and not be silent. O Lord my God, I will give you thanks forever! Psalm 30:12

JASON'S IMAGINATION

We read in the Bible about angels singing and praising God day and night, and we can't imagine doing that all the time. But they are singing because they are *glad,* not bored, tired, or old. They are expressing happiness and joy. No one in the universe is happier than God, so living in heaven with God is happy, joyful, cool.

Imagine that you're a tadpole. All your life you've lived only in the water. You know that someday you'll become a frog and get to live on land. But while you're a tadpole, if anyone tries to explain life on land to you, it won't sound very appealing. That's the way it is with heaven. Until you get there, it may be hard to understand what's so great about it. But once you get there, you will have a new, perfect body, and you'll be happier than you've ever been before.

ACTIVITY

Read Psalm 29. It was first written as a song of praise to God, but the music has gotten lost. Why don't you write a tune for the first four verses? Teach it to your family and your Sunday school class. If you have trouble writing a tune, you can sing the words to a familiar tune. Sing it to God, and then share it with your friends.

Why do I feel afraid if Jesus is with me?

May the Lord of peace himself always give you his peace no matter what happens. The Lord be with you all.

2 Thessalonians 3:16

Jesus is always with us. But we need to learn to trust him, to believe and know that he is there. It's natural to feel afraid. In fact, being afraid can be good. We should be afraid of danger. For example, fear can keep us a safe distance from a mean dog or something else that might hurt us. Being afraid should be a signal to trust Jesus and remember that he *is* always with us.

When are you most afraid? During those times, remember that Jesus is with you. Tell him what makes you afraid, and ask for his help.

ACTIVITY

Go on a trust walk! You won't need a map, just a scarf or bandanna and a guide. Your guide could be anybody your family trusts: an older brother or sister, a baby-sitter, a friend, your mom, or your dad. Fold the scarf or bandanna to make a blindfold, and tie it over your eyes. No peeking! Hold your guide's hand as he or she leads you around—inside or outside. Your guide must give you clues so you don't bump into things, walk into the street, or fall downstairs. The more you walk, the more you'll trust your guide. In the same way, the more you walk with Jesus, the more you'll trust him to guide you.

July 9

Was Samson a good guy or a bad guy?

[An angel is speaking to Samson's mother:] "You will become pregnant and give birth to a son, and his hair must never be cut. For he will be dedicated to God as a Nazirite from birth. He will rescue Israel from the Philistines."   Judges 13:5

S amson was one of Israel's judges. He served God and wanted to please him, but Samson wasn't perfect. God had chosen Samson to do a special service for the nation of Israel—to rescue his people from cruel enemies. Samson fulfilled that job well, but at times he also acted cruelly and foolishly (like most people). God didn't force him to do everything right.

Like Samson, you have the freedom to use your God-given abilities for good or bad. You can choose to go your own way instead of God's, or you can learn from Samson's mistakes and choose good.

ACTIVITY

Divide a piece of paper into two columns. An older kid or a grown-up can give you some help if you need it. Label the left column "My Gifts" and list the abilities that God has given you. Include abilities such as a good memory, friendliness, good at reading, good at sports, can make people laugh, and anything else that that God helps you do. Next, label the right column "Ways to Use Them" and list ways you can use each ability for good. For example, if you have "can make people laugh" as one of your abilities, you can use it for good by telling jokes and making people happy. Choose to use your abilities for good.

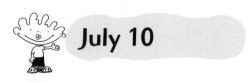

July 10

Why did Samson tell Delilah his secret?

Day after day she nagged him until he couldn't stand it any longer. Finally, Samson told her his secret. "My hair has never been cut," he confessed, "for I was dedicated to God as a Nazirite from birth. If my head were shaved, my strength would leave me, and I would become as weak as anyone else."   Judges 16:16-17

Samson was in love with a woman named Delilah even though she was a friend of his enemies. When some of those enemies offered Delilah money to help them capture Samson, she agreed and asked him for the secret of his strength. At first, Samson gave the wrong answers, but Delilah nagged and prodded until finally Samson told her the truth—his strength came from God as part of a vow that included not cutting his hair. Samson told Delilah that if his hair were cut, the Lord and his strength would leave him. Samson let himself be tricked because he was blinded by his feelings for Delilah.

Be careful about your friends. Choose them carefully. Even people you care about and like a lot may want you to do something wrong. Whenever that happens, you should obey God.

ACTIVITY

Are you still keeping your prayer journal that you started on February 10? God wants you to be with kids who will help you please him. Write a note in your prayer journal to pray about having good friends. Thank God for the good friends you have, and pray about others who might become your friends.

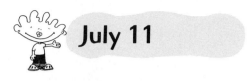

July 11

If I break something that belongs to someone else but fix it, do I have to tell what I did?

[Jesus is speaking:] "Do for others what you would like them to do for you. This is a summary of all that is taught in the law and the prophets."   Matthew 7:12

How would *you* feel if a friend broke something of yours and didn't tell you, even though your friend fixed it? You probably would be upset, especially if you found out later. Treating another person the way you want to be treated is called the Golden Rule. Jesus taught that this is the way we should always act.

Letting the person know what you did is not only telling the truth, it's also respecting that person. If you break something that belongs to someone else, it *is* important to fix it or to pay to have it fixed. But you should let the person know what you did and not try to hide it. If you're honest, people will know you are responsible, and they will trust you more. But if you try to hide it and they find out, they won't trust you anymore. God wants you to be a person who can be trusted. You'll feel good about this, too!

ACTIVITY

Get a wooden ruler and some small stickers that you can write on. On twelve stickers, write short reminders of how to treat others—"Respect others," "Tell the truth," "Be kind," "Be a good listener," etc. Place the stickers on the inch marks, and use your "golden ruler" to remind you how Jesus would like you to act.

July 12

Why can't I have everyone as a friend?

Jesus took Peter, James, and John to the top of a mountain. No one else was there. Mark 9:2

There are too many kids and not enough time for you to be a good friend to everyone. Actually, there are many different kinds of friendships. Some friends who are very close will be your very good friends. Some kids, however, you will just know by name—they are called acquaintances. Even if you don't know someone's name, you can be friendly to that person. It's good to like everybody and be friendly, but don't expect everyone to like you the same way and to be really close friends. Friendship takes time.

Be friendly with everyone, but work at having a few very close friends. Keep in mind that even Jesus, who loved everyone, had just three very special friends—Peter, James, and John. Jesus will guide you to the friends who will be the most fun and helpful to be with.

ACTIVITY
Think of your three closest friends. Pray for them right now. Then write them each a note, thanking them for their friendship.

July 13

Why do I have to give money to church?

I can testify that they gave not only what they could afford but far more. And they did it of their own free will. 2 Corinthians 8:3

It is part of God's plan for Christians to give money to the church so they can worship God, do his work, and help others learn how to follow him. Like families and businesses, churches have bills to pay—electric, phone, water, and so on. Churches also have to pay salaries to pastors, secretaries, organists, and others. The church's money pays for Sunday school materials, the support of missionaries, and special events. Churches don't sell tickets for the worship services or sell products, so they get their money from people in the congregation who give freely and generously.

God's people have always given money to those who lead in worship and service to God. Abraham did it. The Israelites did it. Jesus did it. The apostles did it. Everyone who loves God does it. Leading God's people is a lot of work, so pitch in and help pay for it!

ACTIVITY

Identify some of the expenses at your church—bills, salaries, ministry programs, missions. Then talk with your family or Sunday school teacher about the possibility of raising money for a special need that your church has right now, such as paying for VBS materials. With your family or friends, plan a way to earn money for this project.

July 14

Where does the money I give to church go?

In the same way, the Lord gave orders that those who preach the Good News should be supported by those who benefit from it.

1 Corinthians 9:14

It goes to the church's bank account, where it stays until the church treasurer writes checks to pay for all the church's expenses. The church has to pay for the building, heat, light, phone bills, postage, Sunday school supplies, pastors' salaries, staff salaries, missions, and other ministries and expenses. Some people send their gifts to church in the mail or drop them by the church office. Most people put their money in the offering plate when it is passed during the church service every Sunday. After every offering, the money is collected, counted, and deposited in a bank.

A gift to God's people is a gift to God. Give because you are thankful for all God has given you, and he will take care of you.

ACTIVITY
It is good to be a responsible and cheerful giver. Buy a small spiral notebook and make it your "God's Money Record." Write down the date and amount of your offering each week (or month, if you decide to give once a month). Make sure you increase your giving as your allowance and other income goes up. Use the notebook as a reminder to give your offering.

One Year Book of Fun & Active Devotions for Kids

Why do some people die before they are old?

To me, living is for Christ, and dying is even better. Yet if I live, that means fruitful service for Christ. I really don't know which is better. I'm torn between two desires: Sometimes I want to live, and sometimes I long to go and be with Christ. That would be far better for me.

Philippians 1:21-23

D eath entered the world when sin came in. Ever since Adam and Eve, pain and death have been part of life. Eventually, everything that is alive in our world has to die. Plants die. Animals die. People die. Death can come from a lot of different causes: automobile accidents, sickness, old age, and many others. And life is short, no matter how long a person lives. Just ask someone who is sixty or seventy or eighty.

Because life is short, we should make the most of every day we are alive. Each breath is a gift from God. But also remember that this life is not all there is. After we die, we can live forever with God. Won't that be great?

ACTIVITY

Ask your parents what an "obituary" is. With their help, look through a newspaper to find a write-up about someone who passed away recently. Notice the loving things the family says about the person who died. Pray for the family, that God will help them in their time of sorrow.

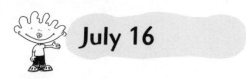

Why hasn't God told us when Jesus is coming back?

[Jesus is speaking:] "No one knows the day or the hour when these things will happen, not even the angels in heaven or the Son himself. Only the Father knows."

Matthew 24:36

Jesus promised his disciples (and us) that he would return to earth some day. But when they asked the dates for different events, Jesus told them, "They are not for you to know" (Acts 1:7). Rather than be concerned with the time when Jesus will return, we should always live as though he will return at any moment. In other words, we should always do what is right and tell others about the salvation God offers everyone through Jesus. Although God has never said exactly when Christ will return, he did say that certain things would take place first. One of these is that Christ will not come back until the gospel has been preached to the whole world.

God has promised that Jesus *will* return, and every day that passes is a day closer to his return. If Jesus came back today, would you be ready?

ACTIVITY

Read all about it! Actually, why not write all about it? Work with a couple of your friends or family members to create a newspaper telling about Jesus. Call it *The Good News Paper* (the word *gospel* means "good news"). Write some news stories about Jesus and the disciples. Illustrate the stories with your own drawings.

How will I know what I want to do when I grow up?

If you need wisdom—if you want to know what God wants you to do—ask him, and he will gladly tell you. He will not resent your asking. James 1:5

It is good to think about what you want to do when you grow up. God has made you good at doing certain things. He has given you talents, interests, and abilities. As you get older, you will learn more and more about your abilities. Your parents and other people who know you well will help you uncover and develop your talents.

But don't wait for them to tell you what to do. Whenever you get interested in something or do well in something, keep working at it. Find out more about it. Ask questions about it. Read books about it. Take an extra class. Ask God to guide you and give you a desire to keep learning. God has a plan for your life. He created you and loves you. He knows exactly what you will be best at and enjoy most and where you fit in his plan. Keep asking God to direct you, and he will do it.

ACTIVITY

Today's Bible verse is a great one to memorize. Write out the verse on an index card, including the Bible reference. Keep the card with you and learn it by heart. God will help you keep this truth in your heart the rest of your life! And he will give you this wisdom whenever you ask for it!

Should people stay at a good paying job that they don't like?

"I know the plans I have for you,"
says the Lord. "They are plans for
good and not for disaster, to give
you a future and a hope."

Jeremiah 29:11

Whether a person should stay in a yucky job depends on the person and the job. What matters most is doing what God wants. When you become an adult and have a family, God wants you to take care of them. You may have to stay in a job you don't like so you can do this. That doesn't mean that you must have a job you don't like. If you follow God's guidance and do what he says, he will lead you to your job. Every job is hard sometimes and can get boring other times. So it's important to learn to be content.

Pray about your future job, and ask God to guide you in your education. Trust God to help you find work that suits how he made you. Life on earth will never be perfect, and you may not always have a fun job. But if you ask God to help you please him and learn to be content, God will take care of you.

ACTIVITY

Talk to your parents about your career choices. If you want more information, go to the library and find some books that talk about the profession you're interested in. If one of your relatives or someone in your church is in that line of work, explain that you want to learn about this job. Then ask what he or she likes best about the job, how he or she got the job, and so forth.

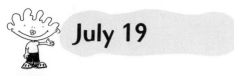

Why is there a universe?

By faith we understand that the entire universe was formed at God's command, that what we now see did not come from anything that can be seen.

Hebrews 11:3

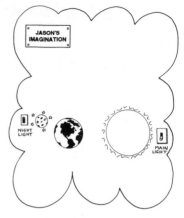

U niverse is another word for the creation—everything that God created. God created every star, every galaxy, every black hole, every atom. And God created everything very good. We don't know why God created the universe, but we do know he had a good reason. We also know God designed the universe for us to live in it. The Bible says that God placed the stars and the moon in the sky to give light during the night. He made the sun to give light during the day. God had us in mind when he created these things—he designed them so that we could live on this earth. They are a sign of God's care and love for us.

The Bible also says that the creation is evidence of God's existence (see Romans 1:20). When you look around and see the earth and all the stars, you can know what a wonderful, powerful Creator God is.

ACTIVITY

A planetarium is an amazing place to visit. See if you can plan a school or family field trip (bring a friend!) sometime soon. If you don't live near a city with a planetarium, check out the Internet. For example, the Sommers-Bausch Observatory and the Adler Planetarium have Web sites that are the next best thing to a visit there.

Why do people want to fly to other planets?

It is God's privilege to conceal things and the king's privilege to discover them.　　Proverbs 25:2

COLLECTING FOR NASA'S SPACE STATION

Some people want to travel to other planets because they want to know how the universe began. Even those who believe that God created everything are curious about how he did it. The stars, the planets, and all the universe are marvelous displays of his handiwork. Other people are simply curious. They want to travel to other planets to see them up close, to see what it would be like to go there, and to learn all they can. It certainly would be an adventure!

Not everyone is meant to be an astronaut. But perhaps you are interested in space and astronomy. Find out all you can about God's universe. Stay alert in math and science class. And say yes to whatever adventure God has for you!

ACTIVITY
Go to the library and read about some of the world's pioneer astronauts, such as Yuri Gagarin, Alan Shepard, Sally Ride, John Glenn, and Neil Armstrong. You can find articles about them in magazines and encyclopedias and in books about the space program.

Why is it wrong to be bad?

*We are God's masterpiece. He has
created us anew in Christ Jesus,
so that we can do the good things
he planned for us long ago.*

Ephesians 2:10

It is wrong to be bad because God created us to do good. Think about bicycles. They are made for riding, for helping us go from one place to another faster and easier than walking. If a person decided to use a bike for shoveling snow or for cooking, that would be very foolish because that's not the bike's purpose.

In the same way, God designed you to do what is good and right, to bring honor to him. When you do bad things, you do what you were not created to do. God created everything. So he knows what works and what doesn't, and he knows what will make you happy and what will hurt you. And he loves you! If you trust him, you will do things his way. Today, thank God for making you his "masterpiece."

ACTIVITY

Ask Mom or Dad what a masterpiece is. Look up the word in a dictionary, too. Now draw your own masterpiece—a picture of your family. Think about some of the good things you can do by yourself and with your family. Then make plans to do at least one of those things.

Is God sad when I do something wrong?

Do not bring sorrow to God's Holy Spirit by the way you live. Remember, he is the one who has identified you as his own, guaranteeing that you will be saved on the day of redemption.
Ephesians 4:30

God is sad whenever we do bad things. In fact, he is more upset and grieved over the sins of the world than anyone else. God is sad because he knows and sees how much sin hurts us and others.

But don't give up hope when you do something wrong. God realizes that you are growing and that you make mistakes. He will keep on encouraging you if you will let him. He loves you so much that he will not give up on you or stay sad forever if you want to change. You can be sure of it!

ACTIVITY
Draw a circle face that looks like a person frowning until you turn it upside down. Then it looks like a person smiling. Let the face remind you of God's sadness when you sin and his happiness when you do better next time.

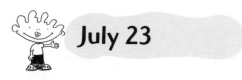

July 23

What does God want me to do when I do what's wrong?

If we confess our sins to him, he is faithful and just to forgive us and to cleanse us from every wrong.

1 John 1:9

The first thing we should do is to pray and admit to God what we have done. That is what the word *confess* means. We should tell him that we are sorry and that we want him to help us not do it again. Also, we should ask God to help us learn from the experience. Admitting our sins to God brings us back close to him. Remember, God wants to protect us and to provide all we need for living.

So stay close to God and talk with him about everything. Try praying when you first think of doing something wrong or even while you're doing it. God can help you avoid or get out of trouble. If your sin has hurt others, talk to them, too. Say you're sorry, and ask for their forgiveness.

ACTIVITY

When we sin, it often causes us to suffer. Some people have to suffer a lot before they're sorry. The Prodigal Son had to end up in a foreign land dressed in dirty rags and eating pig food before he was sorry. Want to have a funny photo that you can use to witness to unsaved friends? Find an old piece of clothing, rip it up and wear it, then mess up your hair, cover yourself in mud, and look really sad. Hold up a beat-up cardboard sign that reads, "I'm sorry now! I wanna go home!" Then show the photo to your friends.

July 24

Why are some people different from others?

"Teacher," his disciples asked him, "why was this man born blind? Was it a result of his own sins or those of his parents?" "It was not because of his sins or his parents' sins," Jesus answered. "He was born blind so the power of God could be seen in him."

John 9:2-3

B ad things happen in this world, and people suffer. Some people are hurt in accidents. Some are injured in sports. Some are born with physical or mental problems. You can probably think of many ways that people can be harmed, making them different from others. Today there are many doctors, nurses, and other people who can help us when we are hurt or need special help. They can give us medicine and bandages and operate if necessary. And scientists are always working on special tools to help. Glasses, wheelchairs, hearing aids, and artificial legs are just a few of their wonderful inventions. These doctors and scientists are gifts from God.

ACTIVITY

Think about your parents, brothers and sisters, and other relatives. Each person is different, with something special about him or her. Who wears glasses? Who uses a hearing aid? Do you know someone who has trouble learning new things? Do any of them use a cane or a wheelchair? Can you think of other physical or mental problems? What about the kids and teachers at school? People at your church? Thank God that he knows how each person is made and that he has given doctors and scientists ways to help people.

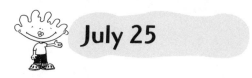

July 25

Is it OK to tell people to shut up if they are being jerks?

A gentle answer turns away wrath, but harsh words stir up anger. Proverbs 15:1

When someone does something annoying or wrong, you shouldn't do something bad to that person in return. God wants people to be loving and kind to others. So the rule is to be respectful, not bossy or rude. It's *good* to tell friends that they're not being nice or that they are being mean. But it's *not* good to talk just like them.

Responding to cruelty with kindness can build friendships. But when you respond to cruelty with cruelty, you just make more conflict. So the best way to make someone stop annoying you is to do things God's way and be nice to the person, not mean.

ACTIVITY

Make a sweet-smelling pomander as a gift for someone who has been unkind. With a nail, poke holes in an orange or a lemon. Gently put a whole clove, stem first, into each hole. In a paper bag, mix one teaspoon each of cinnamon and nutmeg. Carefully place the piece of fruit in the bag and shake it gently. Put the fruit in a shallow bowl and let it dry for several weeks. After it dries, place it in a square of netting material (like from an onion bag) and tie a ribbon around it. It will smell great hanging in your unkind friend's closet and may help to make your friend's words sweeter, too!

Why are some countries rich and others poor?

Hard workers have plenty of food;
playing around brings poverty.

Proverbs 28:19

Wealthy countries often have many natural resources, such as oil, gold, rich fisheries, or tourist attractions. They also have economic systems that reward people for making and selling goods and services, so they attract buyers with the things they make and sell. And they have laws that protect people from being cheated.

Other countries don't have the natural resources that people want to buy. Or perhaps they have the resources, but the economic system makes it difficult for people to sell them or for buyers to buy them. Some countries have been ravaged by war, hurricanes, earthquakes, famines, or other tragedies.

Be thankful for all that God has given your country. Pray for the Christians in poor countries and those hit by natural disasters.

ACTIVITY

We often hear in the news about disasters such as famines, mudslides, earthquakes, or hurricanes. Soon we forget those news bulletins, but the people in those countries can't forget—recovery can take months or even years, especially if the country was already poor. Check newspapers or the Internet for articles about a recent disaster in another country, and find out if there are organizations that are collecting money to help there. Pray about sending money to them.

July 27

My friend's parents are getting a divorce. What can I do?

[Job is speaking to Eliphaz:] "I would speak in a way that helps you. I would try to take away your grief." Job 16:5

HERE'S MY WALKIE-TALKIE. I JUST PUT FRESH BATTERIES IN IT. CALL ME WHENEVER YOU NEED A FRIEND.

Be a good friend—listen to your friend and give your support. Pray for your friend and his or her parents. Remember, you can't do anything about the parents' relationship with each other. They will have to work that out. You probably don't know much about what has been going on in your friend's family, and that's OK.

Being a friend means just being there to talk, listen, and care. Right now your friend really needs you. God will show you how he wants you to help your friend—he cares about your friend more than you could imagine!

ACTIVITY
Make a card that communicates how much you care for your friend. Perhaps you have a card-making program on your computer. A possible message inside could be one of the following: "I care about you. I'm praying for you." "Want to talk? I will listen." Then mail or hand the card to your friend.

July 28

Doesn't God ever get tired of answering prayers?

O Israel, how can you say the Lord does not see your troubles? How can you say God refuses to hear your case? Have you never heard or understood? Don't you know that the Lord is the everlasting God, the Creator of all the earth? He never grows faint or weary. No one can measure the depths of his understanding.

Isaiah 40:27-28

G od never gets even a little bit tired of answering prayers. He loves to hear from us because he loves us. Jesus died for our sins so that we could have friendship with him. That does not change no matter how often we ask things of him.

God wants to work in your life to change your behavior, thoughts, and habits. Don't worry that you are wearing him out with your prayers, even when you pray the same thing over and over. That is because he wants to keep being a part of your life. A very close and loving part of your life.

ACTIVITY

Today's verses come from the prophet Isaiah, the biggest book of prophecy in the Bible. To find out more of what Isaiah was saying about how God doesn't get tired of anything, especially our prayers, read Isaiah 40:25-31.

July 29

Does it matter how much faith we have?

*"You didn't have enough faith,"
Jesus told them. "I assure you,
even if you had faith as small as
a mustard seed you could say to
this mountain, 'Move from here
to there,' and it would move.
Nothing would be impossible."*

Matthew 17:20

J esus said that even if we have a very tiny amount of faith, we can accomplish great things in prayer. Having faith just means that we believe God is faithful. In other words, we decide to trust that he loves us and will do what he said he would do. Great faith in God comes from having a little faith and deciding that God is faithful and that we are going to trust him no matter what.

Put all your trust in God and depend on him. Human words, strength, or clever plans are not dependable. If you trust even a little in God, it will make a huge difference. He alone is truly mighty and worth your trust.

ACTIVITY

Get a small seed and tape it to a card. Above the seed write *FAITH* to remind you of the "seed faith" that Jesus spoke about.

Have you ever seen a mustard seed? The next time your family goes to a grocery store, look in the spices aisle for it. (Look for the whole seeds, not the ground-up powder that most people use in recipes.) How big is a mustard seed? Think about Jesus' words: even this tiny amount of faith in our big God is enough!

July 30

Is it selfish to save money?

Don't be selfish; don't live to make a good impression on others. Be humble, thinking of others as better than yourself.
Philippians 2:3

PIGGY BANKS FOR SALE

Saving money can be selfish, but it doesn't have to be. We need to plan ahead and save for future needs, so we need to save. If we don't, we are being foolish. But we also need to give. We need to trust God to meet our needs. If we try to save all our money and never share any of it, we aren'st trusting God—we're trusting in our money. That's called hoarding, and God doesn't like it. Saving should always meet a future need. It should not just make us richer.

Most selfish people show their selfishness by spending all their money on themselves, not by saving it. If you spend all your money on candy and toys for yourself and then ask other people to supply all your needs, that's really selfish. God will help you find the balance between saving and spending.

ACTIVITY
Go on a "loose-change hunt" in your house. Check under all the cushions and in the desk drawers where stuff tends to accumulate. Look on closet floors, too. Put all the change in a family savings jar or envelope.

July 31

Why do some people spend every cent they get right away?

The wise have wealth and luxury, but fools spend whatever they get.

Proverbs 21:20

Some people spend all their money right away because they have no self-control. They have no discipline or patience. They don't save money because they convince themselves that they have to buy things they don't really need. This is not good. God wants his people to use well what he has given them. God also wants people to take care of each other. It would be wrong for parents to spend all their money on themselves and forget about the children. It would be wrong for Christians to spend all their money on themselves and neglect the church.

God wants you to control your spending, not let your spending control you. He will care for you and help you be happy if you learn this.

ACTIVITY

Make a milk-bottle bank that will help you save and not spend all your money right away. Take a plastic milk bottle, either a half-gallon or gallon size. Keep the cap. Rinse out the bottle and the cap well and let them dry. Put the cap back on. Ask a grown-up to help you cut a slot in the side of the bottle. Decorate the bottle with stickers and construction paper. (Many markers and crayons will either wipe off or not show up well on the bottle. But experiment to see if some will work for you.)

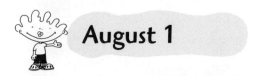

August 1

What's so bad about wanting to wear clothes that are in style?

[Jesus is speaking:] "Don't worry about having enough food or drink or clothing. Why be like the pagans who are so deeply concerned about these things? Your heavenly Father already knows all your needs, and he will give you all you need from day to day if you live for him and make the Kingdom of God your primary concern."   Matthew 6:31-33

It's all right to wear nice clothes that are in style. But we shouldn't think that having the latest clothes will make us happy and gain us friends. And we should remember that nice clothes don't *make* a person nice. It's what's on the inside of the person that really counts.

Some people who design and make new clothes broadcast clever ads on TV and radio to make people want to buy their clothes. They change the styles every season and say that everyone should wear the latest style. Often the most stylish clothes are also the most expensive.

Work with your parents to buy what you can afford. And remember that God wants you to put him in first place in your life, so don't make clothes and other things more important than him. God loves the real you—that's what's most important.

ACTIVITY

Sit down with a paper and pencil and talk with your parents about clothes shopping. Decide together about what you really need. Be creative about what items may be bought at a resale shop or garage sale. Keep two thoughts at the front of your mind: "God loves the inside me," and "I want to be a thankful person."

August 2

If you don't like something a person wears and they ask you if you like it, are you supposed to tell them the truth?

We will hold to the truth in love, becoming more and more in every way like Christ, who is the head of his body, the church.

Ephesians 4:15

We are not supposed to lie, but that doesn't mean we have to be mean or hurtful. There are many ways to tell the truth. We need to learn *tact,* which is saying the truth in a nice way without hurting the other person's feelings.

For example, suppose you don't like a person's coat. You don't have to say, "I *hate* that ugly coat!" You can say something good about it: "It looks warm." Practice saying what you think in ways that respect people's feelings. God will help you find tactful ways to say things.

ACTIVITY
Being tactful can take a lot of creativity! Do a role play with another family member. Practice responding tactfully in these situations:

1. Your best friend comes back from vacation as bright red as a lobster. She says to you, "Don't I look great with a tan?" You say . . .
2. Your neighbor paints his front door hot pink. He asks you, "How do you like my door?" You say . . .

August 3

How was God created?

In the beginning the Word already existed. He was with God, and he was God. He was in the beginning with God. He created everything there is. Nothing exists that he didn't make. John 1:1-3

God was not created—he always was. God had no beginning, and he has no end. He always was, and he always will be.

Imagine going on a deep-sea dive and being able to talk to a fish on the floor of the ocean. If you explained what life is like above the surface of the water and on land, the fish would not be able to understand. Everything the fish knows is in the water. You can breathe air and walk on the land, but the fish knows nothing about that. So the fish thinks it's silly or impossible.

That is the way it is with God. God created everything we know, including time. Beginnings and endings are limitations of our world, but not of God. That is one of the great things about him— he is so much greater than we are! He is a God you can count on!

ACTIVITY

Do you know the praise song "Our God Is an Awesome God"? Perhaps you sing it at church. Ask your mom or dad, or perhaps a song leader at your church, to teach it to you if you don't know it. How great that we have "an awesome God" who rules us with his power and his love.

How can God be three persons and one person at the same time?

[Jesus is speaking:] "Go and make disciples of all the nations, baptizing them in the name of the Father and the Son and the Holy Spirit."　　　Matthew 28:19

We don't know how God can be three persons at the same time, but we know he is because the Bible tells us so. We can understand what God has told us about the Trinity (three in one), but it's difficult to figure out how it works.

In some ways God is like a family with father, mother, and child—three persons and one family. Remember, however, that the Trinity does not mean that we have three gods. There is one God with three persons. The Trinity also does not mean that God wears three hats, or takes on three roles, at different times. All three persons—Father, Son, and Holy Spirit—have always existed. Keep thinking and trusting, and God will help you with hard questions like this.

ACTIVITY

Some people use the example of water to describe the Trinity. With a grown-up's help, put an ice cube (water as a solid) in a small pan. Heat it over low heat on a stove. Soon the cube will melt (water as a liquid). Then it will boil, and steam will form (water as a gas). Whether liquid, gas, or solid, it's still water. Whether Father, Son, or Holy Spirit, God is still God.

August 5

How did God make Adam and Eve?

The Lord God formed a man's body from the dust of the ground and breathed into it the breath of life. And the man became a living person. So the Lord God caused Adam to fall into a deep sleep. He took one of Adam's ribs and closed up the place from which he had taken it. Then the Lord God made a woman from the rib and brought her to Adam.

Genesis 2:7, 21-22

God made Adam and Eve, the first human beings, by using material that he had already made. God formed Adam and then brought him to life. God made Eve from part of Adam so that she would match him perfectly.

Human beings started from a miracle. And human life continues to be a miracle because we have such a creative God. What's even more amazing is that God made people in his own image. That doesn't mean that you look just like God. It does mean that you are like God in ways that animals are not. His image shows through us!

ACTIVITY

Make some leaf rubbings that show the image of leaves in an interesting way. Collect different leaves and arrange them on a hard surface. Place a thin piece of paper—like tracing paper or typing paper, but not construction paper—over the leaves. Gently rub different colored crayons over the leaves and watch the images show through. Do you let God's image show through you?

One Year Book of Fun & Active Devotions for Kids

Why did Eve disobey God when she knew she would die?

[Jesus is speaking:] "You are the children of your father the Devil, and you love to do the evil things he does. He was a murderer from the beginning and has always hated the truth. There is no truth in him. When he lies, it is consistent with his character; for he is a liar and the father of lies."   John 8:44

E ve disobeyed God because Satan *fooled* her. That is, the devil used lies and tricks to get her to disobey God. God had said that Adam and Eve would die if they ate of the "tree of the knowledge of good and evil" (Genesis 2:15-17), but Satan said they wouldn't (Genesis 3:4). Eve believed Satan. Another trick Satan used was to promise that eating the fruit would do great things for her—he said that if she did it, she would be "just like God" (Genesis 3:5). That sounded good to Eve, and so she did what Satan suggested.

Satan still deceives people by twisting God's words and making people believe lies. Satan wants us to think that once we sin, God won't forgive us. But even though Eve sinned, and even though we sin, God made plans for taking away our sin. That plan was to send Jesus—which he did!

ACTIVITY

Act out a short play about what happened in the Garden of Eden. Have four characters—God, Satan, Adam, and Eve—played by you and some stuffed toys in your room. The real story is found in chapters 2 and 3 of the book of Genesis.

August 7

Are Satan and Jesus still at war?

Put on all of God's armor so that you will be able to stand firm against all strategies and tricks of the Devil. For we are not fighting against people made of flesh and blood, but against the evil rulers and authorities of the unseen world, against those mighty powers of darkness who rule this world, and against wicked spirits in the heavenly realms. Ephesians 6:11-12

Jesus and Satan are definitely enemies, but Jesus will win. (By the way, when Jesus says to love your enemies, he's not talking about loving the devil. He's talking about loving people.) The devil will do everything in his power to try to stop people from believing in Jesus and living for Jesus.

But you don't have to be afraid of Satan because God protects his people against Satan's power. Jesus never loses. You are on the winning side when you belong to Jesus.

ACTIVITY
Soldiers today don't wear armor like they did in Bible times or in the time of knights. But we can see what Paul had in mind in his letter to the Ephesians when he talked about "God's armor." Draw a picture of a knight in full armor—use a reference book if you need to see what the iron pieces looked like, and make sure to include all the pieces listed in Ephesians 6:13-17. Notice how each piece protects a different part of the knight's body. God's armor protects all of you, too.

How did computers get so smart?

The Lord grants wisdom! From his mouth come knowledge and understanding. Proverbs 2:6

Computers are machines and do not think, so they aren't smart in the way that human beings are smart. They simply process information very, very fast. They get and send electrical signals according to a set of rules, called instructions, built into the main chip. The computers of today seem "smarter" than older ones because they run much faster and because they have more instructions built in. But they still just process information according to a set of rules.

Some people think that human beings are very special computers, with the "main chip" in their head, but this is not true. You are much more than just a brain, and a brain is much more than a big computer chip. You are a combination of body, soul, and spirit. You are created in the image of God.

ACTIVITY

Go to your computer and create a "Happy (day of the week)" card for each member of your family. Include a favorite Bible verse. Did your computer make the card, or did you?

August 9

Is it wrong to copy computer games?

If you are a thief, stop stealing.
Begin using your hands for honest
work, and then give generously to
others in need. Ephesians 4:28

If a computer game is copyrighted, then yes, it is wrong. (You'll see the copyright symbol—©—plus the date.) What does *copyright* mean? It means that the person (or company) who created it is the only one with the right to copy it. People copyright their work so that other people can't sell or misuse it. The law says that anyone who *does* take or sell someone else's copyrighted work is guilty of stealing.

Just as you can steal an object, you can also steal information. When a person creates a computer game, the information about how to play that game belongs to him or her. Other people can have a copy of the game only if they *buy* it.

Some people make illegal copies of computer software, but that doesn't make it right. It is wrong because it goes against God's nature and his laws to steal. Say no to copying copyrighted software. God will honor your honesty.

ACTIVITY

Uncopyrighted software is called *shareware.* It's OK to copy software only if it is not copyrighted. To remind yourself of this, make a sign to place next to your computer: DON'T COPY IT IF IT'S COPYRIGHTED. Then offer to be the official "registration card filler-outer" for your family when you buy software.

How did Noah build a boat that was so big?

Noah did everything exactly as God had commanded him.

Genesis 6:22

We don't know exactly *how* Noah built the huge boat (which we call the "ark"). But God told him what size to make the boat and what materials to use. Noah obeyed God's instructions exactly. The boat had to be very large because it would have to hold Noah, his children, their families, and hundreds of animals. It had to be a boat because God was going to flood the whole earth. It took a long time for Noah to build the boat. He probably had his whole family help with the building project.

How good are you at following instructions? Do you listen to your parents? teachers at school? teachers at church? God gives us people to guide us, and he uses the Bible to give us his instructions. Be a good listener and doer of God's plans.

ACTIVITY

Practice following instructions. *Recipes* are sets of instructions for cooking. Ask your mom, dad, grandparent, or baby-sitter to help you pick out a recipe. It could be slice-and-bake cookies from the store, a cake mix from a box, or whatever you and a grown-up decide you can make. Read through all the instructions first. Make sure you have all the ingredients and tools you'll need. Then carefully make your food creation. Following instructions can be fun . . . and delicious!

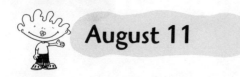

August 11

Why did God flood the whole earth?

The earth had become corrupt in
God's sight, and it was filled with
violence. Genesis 6:11

G od made the rain fall and the water rise so that all the evil
people in the world would drown. God was sorry that he had
created human beings. People were evil, mean, cruel, and violent.
God gave them 120 years to improve. Instead, they got worse.
Only Noah and his family were trying to live God's way—just one
family in the whole world! Noah tried to tell people about God,
but no one would listen.

Are you listening to God? And are you telling other people about
him?

ACTIVITY

To build a model of the ark, get a piece of card stock about 3 feet
long. Ask a parent to help you draw a pattern 30 inches long by
5 inches wide. Then make flaps on all four sides that are 3 inches
high. Cut out the ark and fold the flaps up. On your card stock,
draw another pattern 30 inches long by 5 inches wide for the roof.
Cut it out and tape the edges to the ark. Now draw a man 3/8 of
an inch high on the side of the ark to show how small Noah was
in comparison to the ark.

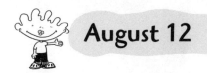

August 12

Why did God put a rainbow in the sky?

God said, "I am giving you a sign as evidence of my eternal covenant with you and all living creatures. I have placed my rainbow in the clouds. It is the sign of my permanent promise to you and to all the earth."

Genesis 9:12-13

After the rains stopped, the flood waters went down. Noah, his family, and the animals were able to leave the ark. God promised that he would never again send a flood to destroy the earth. Then God put a rainbow in the clouds as a sign of this promise.

Whenever you see a rainbow, let it remind you of the Flood. Think about the reason for it. But then think about God's promise never to flood the earth again. You can be certain about this because God keeps his promises!

ACTIVITY

Make your own rainbow-colored sun catcher. Draw shapes on the underside of a paper or foam plate and cut out the shapes. Cut a white tissue paper circle large enough to cover all the cutout designs. Spread glue on the inside of the plate around the cutout designs, and press the tissue onto the plate. Let it dry. On the inside of the plate, use different color markers to color the tissue paper over each cutout design. Make a hole near the edge of the plate and tie a string through the hole. Hang your sun catcher from the string in the window, with the underside of the plate facing you. Let your sun catcher remind you of God's promise never to flood the earth again.

One Year Book of Fun & Active Devotions for Kids

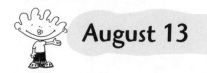

August 13

Why doesn't God take rich people's money and give it to the poor people?

Yes, you will be enriched so that you can give even more generously. And when we take your gifts to those who need them, they will break out in thanksgiving to God.

2 Corinthians 9:11

God wants more than just to end poverty. He wants us to love each other as much as he loves us. Just imagine how awful it would be if everyone had plenty of money and no kindness. Money alone would not make anybody kind. But if everyone would obey God and love one another, we would be better people and better off.

That is why God has chosen to work through his people to help others instead of just making everyone rich. God has a lot in mind for you. He wants you to learn to be kind, generous, and wise. He wants you and other people to help each other. And there's something more: He knows this will make you happy, too!

ACTIVITY

It's time to start getting your school supplies ready. But many families don't have enough money to buy all that their kids need—especially if they have more than one kid. Many churches, YMCAs, YWCAs, and other organizations collect school supplies to help these families. Check in your local newspapers to see if there's a collection near you. Find out what's needed, and then help by buying and donating supplies so that other kids can start the school year off well.

One Year Book of Fun & Active Devotions for Kids

August 14

Do angels watch television?

[Jesus is speaking:] "I tell you that in heaven . . . their angels are always in the presence of my heavenly Father."

Matthew 18:10

JASON'S IMAGINATION

LITTLE HOUSE ON THE PRAIRIE

Angels spend all their time serving God and praising him. They don't take time to relax or do things just for fun. Keep in mind that angels don't need to relax because they don't get tired. And they enjoy their service to God so much that stopping to do something else wouldn't be fun for them anyway.

Why would angels want to watch the stuff on TV when they can see the stars up close, fly through the universe doing errands for God, and watch God doing miracles in people's lives? Angels have much better things to do than watch TV—they help us!

Think about a time when you helped your mom or dad with an emergency or took care of a sick pet. Remember the good feeling inside? That feeling is much, much better than what you get while watching television. Now you know a little of how an angel probably feels about doing God's work. Even the best show ever can't compare!

ACTIVITY

Write a short poem or story about angels helping God. Use scratch paper and pencil first until you get the words the way you want them. Then rewrite the words in color and draw angels around the outside as a border. At dinner, display and explain to your family what you wrote.

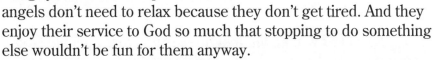

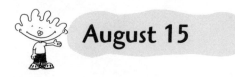

August 15

Why is there so much fighting on TV?

Good people enjoy the positive results of their words, but those who are treacherous crave violence. Proverbs 13:2

One reason for all the fighting on TV is that there is so much fighting in real life! Some people have not learned to control their tempers, so they fight. God wants us to overlook insults and stay calm when people try to make us mad. Too many people think they have no choice but to blow their tops.

Another reason TV has a lot of fighting is that many people like to see other people fight. So the studios produce programs with fighting, and the networks show them. The TV and studio bosses often say they show fighting because they have to be realistic. That may be true, but the bigger reason is money.

God wants you to see good examples of people working out their problems. Fighting and violence are not for you. So don't let them be part of your TV watching either. God will help you find good examples on TV.

ACTIVITY
One good thing that TV can do (even though it doesn't always do it) is provide good examples. Real people have real problems. Write down your ideas for a good TV show that would show people working on their problems without fighting. Who would be the main characters? Where would they live? What problem would they face on the first episode?

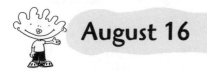

August 16

Does God only give us things that we need?

[David is speaking:] Praise the Lord, I tell myself, and never forget the good things he does for me. He fills my life with good things. My youth is renewed like the eagle's!   Psalm 103:2, 5

God gives us much more than just what we need to get by. The Bible says that every good thing comes from God (James 1:17). If it is good, it came from God. That includes all of the things that we need plus all of the extras that he has given so kindly to us. And he is able to give us much more than we could possibly hope for or imagine (Ephesians 3:20).

Jesus said that even sinful people know how to give good gifts to their children. So God is much more able to give us good gifts, such as the help of the Holy Spirit (Luke 11:11-13).

God loves you and really enjoys giving you good things. He is your heavenly father, and he wants you to be his friend. He delights in blessing you. So sometimes he lets you have more than just what you need—good things that make you glad.

ACTIVITY

Be an investigative reporter. Try to track down the extra blessings that God has given to your family. Check with your parents, brothers and sisters, grandparents, and aunts and uncles. Ask them: "When did you ask God for something and he surprised you with something even better?" Write down the answers. Try this at a big family dinner sometime. God is good!

August 17

Do children have to pray with an adult?

[David is speaking:] You have taught children and nursing infants to give you praise. They silence your enemies who were seeking revenge.   Psalm 8:2

I'M GOING TO PRAY FOR SOME REALLY BIG THINGS! I THINK IT WOULD HELP IF YOU FILLED OUT THIS CONSENT FORM.

Jesus said, "Let the children come to me. Don't stop them!" (Luke 18:16). Any believer, no matter how old or young, can talk alone with God. You don't need to have anyone else with you when you pray—you can talk to God on your own. God loves to hear from his children. He welcomes all sincere prayers.

Go ahead and practice praying to God all by yourself. You can start by telling him what is on your mind and asking him to help you solve your problems. You can also ask him to teach you to pray better. You do not have to do it a certain way. It is like talking to your friends—you just say what you want to say in your own words. Then thank God for understanding what you want to say, even if you don't know how to say it.

ACTIVITY
Let's try out the ideas above about prayer . . . right now. It's OK to start out simply if you've never prayed by yourself. Try these three steps: (1) Greet God. (2) Tell him you want to learn to pray better. (3) Thank him for understanding what's in your heart already.

August 18

How does God answer our prayers?

[David is speaking:] You faithfully answer our prayers with awesome deeds, O God our savior. You are the hope of everyone on earth, even those who sail on distant seas. Psalm 65:5

God is all-powerful, so he can use anything he wants to work out his plans. One of the ways he answers prayer is through other people. For example, God often works through doctors and medicines to bring healing. He answers the prayers of people in need through the money that generous Christians give. Sometimes God directs angels to intervene in some invisible, miraculous way. He also uses events and natural forces of nature.

And sometimes, God will simply change *you*. For example, you may ask for more money, and God may answer by showing you how to use what you have more carefully. In other words, God gives you wisdom and teaches you. He works inside you to make you more like Christ in the way you think, talk, and behave. And he does it the most loving way he can.

ACTIVITY

Make a sandwich for yourself. What different kinds of bread could you use? What might you put inside? Place the ingredients and utensils out on a table and put the sandwich together. How many ways could you cut the bread? Triangles, rectangles, squares, cookie-cutter shape? However you make your sandwich, it's still a sandwich. As you eat it, think about the different ways God can put together an answer to your prayers.

When we're bad, can we still pray?

*[Jesus is speaking:] "The tax
collector stood at a distance and
dared not even lift his eyes to heaven
as he prayed. Instead, he beat his
chest in sorrow, saying, 'O God, be
merciful to me, for I am a sinner.' I
tell you, this sinner, not the Pharisee,
returned home justified before God.
For the proud will be humbled, but
the humble will be honored."*

Luke 18:13-14

A person can pray at any time and in any need. When people do bad things or make mistakes, they need God more than at any other time. When we do something wrong, we need to talk with God about it. We need to admit that what we did was wrong, say that we're sorry, and ask him to forgive us. That is the first thing we should pray when we do something bad. Then God can help us do better next time. God knows we are not perfect, and he wants to help us by giving us wisdom and a desire to change.

If you wait until you are good enough to pray, you will never pray. And God wants you to talk with him. He doesn't want you to miss out on something so great and exciting—a close friendship with him.

ACTIVITY
Today's Bible verse comes from a story that Jesus told, which many call "The Parable of the Pharisee and the Tax Collector." (The Pharisees were important religious leaders.) Read the whole parable and see what Jesus was teaching about prayer. You can find it in Luke 18:9-14.

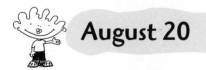

Why do some kids say bad things about others?

They must not speak evil of anyone, and they must avoid quarreling. Instead, they should be gentle and show true humility to everyone. Titus 3:2

Some kids say bad things about others because they think it's fun. They might be jealous of other kids or angry with them. They might be in competition with them. Or they may not have learned yet that it's unkind. Whatever the reason, saying bad things about people, calling names, spreading rumors, or making fun is not right. Unfortunately, a lot of humor these days is based on making fun of someone.

Laughing at someone is a cruel way to joke around. Don't do it. A good rule to follow is to make sure that everything you say about people will make them feel good. Pretend that they are present to hear what you're saying about them, even if they're not.

ACTIVITY
Picture in your mind some of the kids on your school bus, kids who sit closest to you in school, or kids in your Sunday school class. Think of at least one good thing about each one. It could be anything from their smiles to the way they can memorize Bible verses. Get in the habit of looking at the good things about people and talking about these things instead of bad things.

Is it wrong to spread rumors?

A troublemaker plants seeds of strife; gossip separates the best of friends.   Proverbs 16:28

A rumor (or gossip) is a story about someone that may or may not be true. Sometimes rumors are lies, spread to hurt someone else. Sometimes rumors are totally false, but they are spread because somebody got the wrong information. Sometimes rumors are partially true, but they don't tell the whole story. Even if a story started out to be true, after a few people tell it, usually it gets changed and is only partly true. Rumors almost always do much more harm than good.

If you hear a story about someone, don't just pass it on. First, try to find out if it is true or not. If you find out that the story is true, you have two good choices: (1) you can drop it and forget the whole thing; (2) you can talk to the person that the story is about and try to help him or her. Passing along gossip—spreading rumors—is not loving or kind. God wants us to be loving and kind to others.

ACTIVITY

Has one of your friends done a good thing lately? Something good in school or in sports? Maybe created a nice painting? Tell another friend—in person, by phone, or by E-mail. Be the one to spread good stories.

August 22

Is it all right to pray to God for money?

This same God who takes care of me will supply all your needs from his glorious riches, which have been given to us in Christ Jesus.

Philippians 4:19

Please drop money here

Alternate drop site

Yes, it is fine to pray to God about money. The Bible tells Christians to "pray about everything" (Philippians 4:6) and gives the reminder that "the reason you don't have what you want is that you don't ask God for it" (James 4:2). There is no better person to ask than God whenever you need anything, including money. You should ask God for the money you need.

Just be sure that you want the money for a good reason. God promises to provide what we need, but Jesus warned against greed and love for money. God probably won't give you money just because you want something badly. But if you need the money for something good, ask God for it, and God will provide it. It's not a good sign if you *never* pray for God to supply money. If you're not praying, you're not depending on God.

You can also be an answer to another person's prayer about money. If you know someone who really needs money and you have money to give, then give some.

ACTIVITY

It's easy to say, "Give me more, Lord!" Instead, ask God to give you a generous heart. Ask him also to show you what your true needs are. And ask him to show you how you can help someone else with your money.

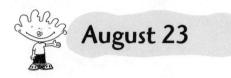

Is money one of the most important things in life?

Being wise is as good as being rich; in fact, it is better. Wisdom or money can get you almost anything, but it's important to know that only wisdom can save your life. Ecclesiastes 7:11-12

Money is both very important and not at all important. Money makes it possible for us to pay bills, to buy food, and to get other things we need. Money also helps us support God's work in the world. We can use money to help feed hungry people, clothe poor people, and share the good news about Jesus with people all over the world. We need money to do these things.

Money is not most important, however. The most important thing in life is our relationship with God. Only God can forgive our sins, and only God can teach us how to live. Next come the people whom God has put in our lives. They are way more important than money. Money can't buy you a new mom or dad, good friends, good health, or good neighbors. Money can't buy you any of the things that matter most in life.

ACTIVITY

Make a list of people and things that are really important in your life. Is God at the top of your list? Then should come your family and friends. Then put everyone else God created. And then put money underneath all those. Use money to serve people, not the other way around.

One Year Book of Fun & Active Devotions for Kids

August 24

How should I treat kids who are different?

The woman was surprised, for Jews refuse to have anything to do with Samaritans. She said to Jesus, "You are a Jew, and I am a Samaritan woman. Why are you asking me for a drink?" John 4:9

Kids differ in many ways. They may be from different races or cultures, or they may be different sizes. Some children may be mentally or physically handicapped. People in a school or neighborhood may even speak different languages. It's never right to make fun of people or ignore them because of those differences. Just because people are different doesn't mean that they are wrong or to be feared.

Remember, God loves all people. In fact, he is the one who made the differences! Even if people have different ideas about God, he still wants you to be kind and to respect them. God wants you to treat everyone in the way that you would like to be treated.

ACTIVITY
Make a list of the ways that kids are different in your school, neighborhood, and church. The differences could include race, culture, nationality, language, religion, physical disability, clothing styles, and so forth. Choose one or more of these differences and look up information about it. For example, if a student in one of your classes is from another country, you could look for information on that country. Or if someone has a physical disability such as muscular dystrophy, you could find out more about that condition.

Why was it against the law to make friends with a Gentile?

Peter told them, "You know it is against the Jewish laws for me to come into a Gentile home like this. But God has shown me that I should never think of anyone as impure." Acts 10:28

Gentile was anyone who was not a Jew. It *wasn't* against the law to make friends with a Gentile. God simply wanted the Jewish people not to copy Gentiles and be like them because they didn't follow the Jewish laws and didn't worship the true God. Some Jewish people wouldn't even walk through Gentile towns. Jews did accept some Gentiles into their religion. These converts were called "God-fearers."

God wanted to give everyone, including Gentiles, the opportunity to follow Jesus. So God let Peter know it was OK to visit and talk with Gentiles. By breaking down the barrier to Gentiles, the message about Jesus could be taken to everybody.

God wants us to accept all people and not think we're superior just because we know that Jesus is God's Son. You can share the message about Jesus with your friends. This is a special job from God that you can do!

ACTIVITY

Get a magazine and see how many different types of people you can find. Look for differences in age, sex, nationality, race, and economics. If it's all right, cut out the pictures and make a collage on a piece of poster board. Across the top or bottom, write *Jesus loves everyone.*

What happens if a person doesn't pay a credit card bill?

[David is speaking:] The wicked borrow and never repay, but the godly are generous givers.

Psalm 37:21

A person who doesn't pay a credit card bill on time is charged interest. Sometimes the bank will charge extra penalty fees, too. If someone keeps on refusing to pay a credit card bill, the small bill will turn into a huge one. Not paying credit card bills goes on a person's credit record. It shows that the person cannot be trusted with money. That will hurt the person if he or she ever wants to get a loan from a bank.

People who continue refusing to pay their bills get in big trouble with the stores, the banks, the law, and God. God wants us always to be honest and to do what we say we are going to do. When we don't pay the bills we agreed to pay, we are being dishonest. It is important that we borrow money only if we know we can pay it back.

ACTIVITY

Ask your mom or dad to show you a credit card statement. Have them explain how much interest is charged when the bill isn't paid in full. (It's all explained in the small print on the statement.)

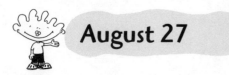

August 27

What do prayer warriors do?

Timothy, I thank God for you.
He is the God I serve with a clear
conscience, just as my ancestors
did. Night and day I constantly
remember you in my prayers.

2 Timothy 1:3

Some people use the term "prayer warrior" to describe people who seem to pray all the time. They pray for others and for God's work on a regular basis. They know that prayer is important. Because these people care about God's work in the world, they make sure that they pray about it often.

God wants all believers to pray for those who don't know Jesus, for Christian leaders, and for the growth of God's kingdom. But some people feel that God has given them an extra special task of spending a lot of time doing this. You can learn a lot about prayer from these special people of God. And as you grow up, you can become a prayer warrior, too!

ACTIVITY

Ask your minister for the name of a person in your church who is an extra-strong person of prayer. Talk with that person about prayer. Ask him or her: When do you pray? Why do you pray? What do you pray for? How has God answered your prayers in the last year?

August 28

Will there be a Bible "hall of fame" in heaven?

[Jesus is speaking:] "See, I am coming soon, and my reward is with me, to repay all according to their deeds." Revelation 22:12

Some people think that heaven is just like earth, with shopping malls, schools, athletic stadiums, and airports. But heaven is very different from earth. The focus in heaven is on God, not people. We will praise and worship God because no one's fame can compare with his.

People *will* be honored in heaven, however. The Bible says that believers will receive rewards for their good deeds. The greatest reward, of course, is just getting there. God gives salvation—a free gift made possible by Jesus' death on the cross—if you put your faith in Christ. He will give other rewards if you do good deeds for God on earth. Everyone's service will be rewarded. Including yours!

ACTIVITY
Make a book and title it "God's Hall of Fame." Draw pictures of some of the men, women, and children of the Bible who served God. Write a couple of sentences about each person under the picture you draw. For some ideas, look at Hebrews chapter 11. You can add more recent heroes of the faith also, plus people you have actually known.

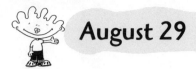

August 29

Why do people litter?

God said, "Let us make people in our image, to be like ourselves. They will be masters over all life— the fish in the sea, the birds in the sky, and all the livestock, wild animals, and small animals."

Genesis 1:26

Some people litter because it's a habit. Others are just careless or don't really care. No matter why people litter, it is against the law and hurts the environment. Littering shows a lack of respect for others and their property and makes everything look ugly. Christians should respect other people, other people's property, God's creation, and the law. So we should not litter.

When you go for a walk or ride your bike, think about the world that God has given you. Remember what a responsibility you have to help take care of it. And be thankful for what a caring God you have.

ACTIVITY
Ask a grown-up to take you and some friends to a park or playground. Before you play, look around for litter. Pick up scraps of paper and put them in the trash. (The grown-up with you can help you identify things that may not be safe to touch.) When you're done, have a good time on the swings and slide!

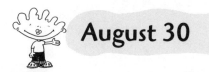

August 30

Why is it wrong to do something if all the other kids do it?

Live no longer as the ungodly do, for they are hopelessly confused. Their closed minds are full of darkness; they are far away from the life of God because they have shut their minds and hardened their hearts against him. They don't care anymore about right and wrong.
Ephesians 4:17-19

If something is wrong, it is wrong, no matter how many people do it. Suppose a group of your friends started throwing stones through windows in the neighborhood.

Would it be OK just because everyone did it? Of course not! It would be wrong whether one person or everyone in school did it.

If a lot of kids swear, cheat, lie, do drugs, drink, smoke, vandalize, disobey their parents, shoplift, or do something else that is wrong, don't think that you have to do it, too. You should do what is right, even if you are the only one. That's what God wants. If the group you hang around with does things that are wrong and pressures you to join them, find another group. Get away from kids who are always tempting you to do what is wrong. God will help you find good friends who are fun, too. No question about it!

ACTIVITY
Get out your prayer journal. Start a new page and write "Friends" at the top. Next, record a prayer asking God to help you make and keep the right kind of friends this school year. Then pray your prayer, and keep praying it over the next few weeks. Watch for God's answers, and record the answers, too.

If I swear, will I go to hell when I die?

God saved you by his special favor
when you believed. And you can't
take credit for this; it is a gift from
God. Salvation is not a reward
for the good things we have done,
so none of us can boast about it.

Ephesians 2:8-9

Although we should watch what we say, the place where we spend eternity is not based on our speech. Instead, each person's forgiveness and eternal life are based on the death and resurrection of Jesus Christ. If we trust Jesus to save us, we are forgiven. Of course, that doesn't make it all right to swear.

Some kids say bad words to try and impress others. Some people swear when they're angry or upset. But that's cheap talk. Instead of swearing, we should use good, positive words, letting the light of Christ shine through us.

ACTIVITY

Make a light-catcher picture. Tear off a 24-inch piece of aluminum foil. Fold it into thirds, with the shiny side out. Fold each edge of the foil in about half an inch, and pinch it together. With a marker, draw a simple design (such as a star) on the foil. Fold a towel and put the foil on the towel. Carefully poke a pencil through the foil on the drawn lines, making the holes about one-half inch apart. In a dark room, shine a flashlight against the light-catcher. Tilt the foil to make the picture move around the room, just like the light of Christ can shine through your words and actions.

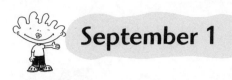

September 1

Why do we have to pray when God already knows what we are going to pray?

[Jesus is speaking:] "When you pray, don't babble on and on as people of other religions do. They think their prayers are answered only by repeating their words again and again. Don't be like them, because your Father knows exactly what you need even before you ask him!" Matthew 6:7-8

The main reason that we should pray is because God tells us to. We don't know exactly how prayer works, but we know it does. God says that he hears the prayers of his people and that those prayers make a difference.

God designed the universe, and prayer is part of his plan for how it works. One of the most important reasons to pray is for the person praying to be changed. So when we pray, we find ourselves becoming more the way God wants us to be. Also, God wants to have a friendship with us. No one would say, "Why do we have to talk to our friends?" Talking with God just grows out of loving him.

Pray with confidence that something good will result. Believe and trust that God knows what is best and that he will work in your life.

ACTIVITY

In today's verse, Jesus tells his followers that God the Father knows what they need even before they think to ask for something. In your prayer journal, create a praise list, writing down everything you can think of that you're glad God knows about you. Examples: "He knows what I'm like," "He knows what I want most in life," and "He knows what I'm afraid of."

September 2

Why did people kill animals for church?

Our High Priest offered himself to God as one sacrifice for sins, good for all time. Hebrews 10:12

Before Jesus came, God's people had to sacrifice animals in worship to make payment for their sins. All people sin against God, and that sin must be paid for. The sacrificed animal took the person's place. (Not all sacrifices involved killing animals—some people would offer grain as a praise offering to God.) But Jesus was the perfect and final sacrifice—he died for all the sins of all who believe in him. That's why John the Baptist called him "the Lamb of God who takes away the sin of the world!" (John 1:29). The sacrifice of animals in Old Testament times represented Jesus' future death for his people—the animals could not actually take away sins, as Jesus could (see Hebrews 10:4-7).

Because Jesus died and then rose from the dead, people never have to sacrifice animals again. Instead, we can worship and praise Jesus for all he's done for us. And he is worth our praise!

ACTIVITY
God is holy and perfect. When Bible people sacrificed animals, they did it just the way God told them to. Check out Leviticus 1–5 and Numbers 28–29. Read just the headings in the chapters. Make a list of all the different kinds of offerings that God told the Israelites to give. Then thank God for sending Jesus as the final offering.

Why did Cain kill his brother?

We must not be like Cain, who belonged to the evil one and killed his brother. And why did he kill him? Because Cain had been doing what was evil, and his brother had been doing what was right.   1 John 3:12

The story of Cain and Abel shows the effects of sin in the world. You can read the story in Genesis 4:1-16.

The first sin was when Adam and Eve disobeyed God and ate from the tree of the knowledge of good and evil. After that, every person has been born a sinner—someone who does not please God in thoughts, words, or actions. Both Cain and Abel had presented gifts to God, but Abel's gifts had pleased God, while Cain's had not. Cain had become jealous and very angry (Genesis 4:5). Cain's jealousy and anger led him to kill his brother.

You can see from this story that jealousy and anger can cause people to do terrible things, sometimes even hurting people they love. Watch out for those feelings, and take care of them before they hurt you, too.

ACTIVITY

Is there something in your family that makes you angry? Perhaps you are upset with a younger brother or sister for breaking one of your toys. Maybe you think your mom or dad wasn't listening at dinner. Draw a picture about what makes you angry. Then ask God to help you not be so angry. Show the picture to your mom or dad, describe what you have drawn, and tell about your prayer.

September 4

Can I ask God to help me pass a test?

Work hard and cheerfully at whatever you do, as though you were working for the Lord rather than for people. Remember that the Lord will give you an inheritance as your reward, and the Master you are serving is Christ.
Colossians 3:23-24

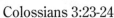

We can talk with God about anything. But God wants us to always do our best and not expect him to do the work for us. We go to school and work as part of God's plan, relying on him for strength and wisdom, but not asking him to do everything for us.

We should study for tests and do what the teacher says. Then, at test time, we should ask God to give us a clear mind, helping us to relax and remember what we have studied.

Remember that the point of taking tests is to find out how well you have learned what you were supposed to learn. Don't just pray for God to rescue you from a lack of studying. Ask God to help you study. He is willing to help you learn.

ACTIVITY

On a piece of paper, list all your school subjects. Leave a few lines between each subject. Now pray through each subject, one at a time, asking God to help you do the work and learn a lot in that subject. Write down on the paper any tests or projects that are coming up in each subject. God will help you be a good student.

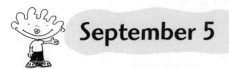

September 5

Why are grades so important?

Work hard so God can approve you. Be a good worker, one who does not need to be ashamed and who correctly explains the word of truth. 2 Timothy 2:15

Tests and grades help teachers check to see what students have learned. Grades also help students and their parents see how well the kids are doing at school. Use your grades as a tool to help you see where you need to work harder.

Remember that grades don't make a person better or worse than anyone else. Doing your best and learning the material are more important than grades. That's the kind of effort that most pleases God.

ACTIVITY

Make a poster to describe what you are—a hard-working student. Use bright-colored markers and write in bold letters: "Look out! Student at work!" Put an interesting border around your poster. Then hang it on your bedroom door or near the place where you do your homework.

September 6

I want to get A's, but my friends say getting good grades is dumb. What should I do?

It is senseless to pay tuition to educate a fool who has no heart for wisdom. Proverbs 17:16

HOW DID YOUR TEST GO, JASON?

TERRIBLE, MOM. I GOT AN "A".

It's always important to do what is right and to do your best no matter what others think or say. Some kids make fun of getting good grades because they don't want to work hard to get those grades. Others may think that it's not cool to seem smart. They're wrong. It's really cool to do well in school. Doing well now will lead to doing well in high school and college, which will lead to doing well in adult life.

Your friends who think that it's not cool to get good marks may think that they are somehow cheating the system, but they are only cheating themselves. Don't listen to them. Listen to God, and ask him to help you do your best.

ACTIVITY
Make a special sign that you can stand just above your television screen. The sign should read, "Study first!" Make it colorful and easy to read. It will remind you to get your studies done before any TV shows.

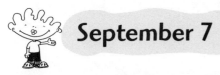
Does God listen to any prayer, big or small?

Give all your worries and cares to God,
for he cares about what happens to you.

1 Peter 5:7

God listens to all prayers. Nehemiah prayed that he would say the right words when he talked to the king (Nehemiah 1:11). Solomon prayed for wisdom (1 Kings 3:7-9). Hannah prayed for a child (1 Samuel 1:11-17). Each of these people prayed for something that mattered to him or her. It did not matter whether their prayer was big or small.

God wants you to bring your cares to him. What is important is what's on your mind, so tell God what you care about. He will listen.

ACTIVITY

One form of prayer called a "litany" is like a prayer list including things big and small. Litanies have a repeated line that gives the prayer rhythm. Write your own litany, and then read it to God. Here is an example:

For my friends at school.
 I pray to you, dear God.
For my grandpa's health.
 I pray to you, dear God.
For good weather for the picnic on Saturday.
 I pray to you, dear God.
For help on tomorrow's math test.
 I pray to you, dear God.
For your will to be done on earth.
 I pray to you, dear God, Lord of the universe. Amen.

September 8

Why do we pray for our enemies?

[Jesus is speaking:] "But I say, love your enemies! Pray for those who persecute you! In that way, you will be acting as true children of your Father in heaven. For he gives his sunlight to both the evil and the good, and he sends rain on the just and on the unjust, too."   Matthew 5:44-45

The main reason to pray for our enemies is because God tells us to. In fact, he tells us to love our enemies. Praying for enemies and loving them is God's way.

Another reason is because all people, especially bad people, need prayer. There is no better way to change them. If we want bad people to stop being bad, we need to ask God to do it. We need to pray for them so they will change.

Think about this: Jesus prayed for his enemies. And he had some pretty awful ones! Some of them were trying to kill him, and eventually they succeeded.

Jesus prayed for you. He did that because he loved you, even when you were his enemy. He still loves you, and he wants you to follow his example of love.

ACTIVITY

Today's verses come from some amazing teaching that Jesus gave, called the Sermon on the Mount because he preached it on a mountainside. Ask a parent if you can read aloud this passage (Matthew 5:38-48) at dinner. After you read it, talk together with your family about which of Jesus' statements in the passage is the most difficult for each of you to do and why.

Why do my parents want me to be involved in so many things?

You children must always obey your parents, for this is what pleases the Lord. Fathers, don't aggravate your children. If you do, they will become discouraged and quit trying.

Colossians 3:20-21

Your parents love you and want the best for you. They want you to have many experiences that will help you grow and be a more informed person. Because they don't know what you are going to be good at or what you're going to be interested in when you are older, they want you to try a lot of different activities now.

You can learn a lot through music lessons, church choir, sports, and other activities outside of school. Everything you learn will help you enjoy life more. Be thankful that God and your parents are trying to help you learn as much as you can.

ACTIVITY
On a piece of paper, write down the activities you're involved in outside of school. Count them. Now draw a circle, and divide it into the same number of pie pieces as your activities. Write in the name of an activity in each piece, and color the whole drawing. Put the picture up on your mirror or refrigerator as a reminder that you're growing up into an all-around neat person.

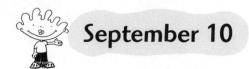

September 10

Why do teachers give so much homework?

If you stop listening to instruction, my child, you have turned your back on knowledge.

Proverbs 19:27

Teachers give homework because they are trying to be good teachers and they want to help you learn. Doing assignments at home will help you remember what the teacher said in class. The school system was designed to include homework. It's not a punishment—homework is an important part of learning.

The best way to get homework done is to start on it right away. Don't put off doing an assignment until the last minute. It's a good idea to do homework before watching TV, playing with friends, or talking on the phone. Even when you don't have assignments to do at home, you can review with your family what you learned that day.

ACTIVITY

A first step toward being a homework hero is being sure of the assignments. Buy a medium-sized spiral notebook. Decorate the cover with stickers or interesting designs if you wish, and write "Homework" on it. At the beginning of each school day, write down that day's date at the top of a page. When the teacher gives an assignment, write down the subject, the assignment, and when it's due. Don't forget a very important step: Before you leave school at the end of the day, check your notebook to be sure you're bringing home everything you'll need to do that day's homework.

One Year Book of Fun & Active Devotions for Kids

Why do people cheat?

[Jesus is speaking:] "Unless you are faithful in small matters, you won't be faithful in large ones. If you cheat even a little, you won't be honest with greater responsibilities."   Luke 16:10

I WOULDN'T RECOMMEND IT. I DIDN'T STUDY EITHER.

People cheat because they're lazy. They don't want to work hard to complete an assignment or do well on a test. Cheating is wrong because it's lying, and God tells us not to lie. People cheat in many areas, not just school. Some cheat in games—trying to win without following the rules. Some cheat with money, and others cheat by not being honest with their friends. People who cheat fall into a pattern of cheating and find it hard to stop.

If you cheat in school you'll keep yourself from learning. Then you'll have to cheat again. After a while, you'll lose confidence in yourself and your ability to learn anything. Don't be a cheat— God knows that you will only cheat yourself.

ACTIVITY

Do you know someone who has a problem with cheating? Perhaps a kid in your class or you yourself? Write down the name in your prayer journal, and ask God to help that person. Watch for God to work and help that kid become a better learner—and a better person!

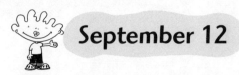

How can I do better in spelling?

Plans go wrong for lack of advice;
many counselors bring success.

Proverbs 15:22

The way to improve in any subject is to study and practice. You can become a better speller by reviewing the assigned words many times. Get someone to help you by testing you on those words. Your parents will be happy to help. Reading more will also help you improve your spelling because you will see words spelled correctly in the books.

Ask your parents to look over your papers before you turn them in. If you check your spelling every time you write something, you will improve. The world of words is part of God's world, too. He wants you to get as much as you can out of it.

ACTIVITY

The computer can be a helpful tool because writing programs have a spell-checker. But don't just automatically click the "Change" button. For example, computers may not recognize a name even though it is spelled correctly. It's a good idea to check a dictionary before having the computer make any change. Finally, you'll still need to read through your paper because spell-checkers can't catch mistakes when you typed in the wrong word. For fun, write a short story using the last names of real people. Then, each time the spell-checker suggests a change for a proper name, change it. You'll laugh at your silly-sounding story.

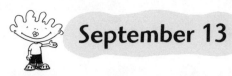

Why did Hannah leave her son at the church?

[Hannah is speaking:] "I asked the Lord to give me this child, and he has given me my request. Now I am giving him to the Lord, and he will belong to the Lord his whole life." And they worshiped the Lord there. 1 Samuel 1:27-28

For a long time, Hannah had been unable to have children. One day, while crying and praying to God, she promised that if God would give her a son, she would give the boy back to God to work for him. When Samuel was born, Hannah remembered her promise to God. A few years later Hannah brought Samuel to the tabernacle (the tent where God's people worshiped). Leaving Samuel there was like leaving him at a boarding school, with people who would love him, care for him, and teach him God's ways. Hannah knew that her son was in good hands. Samuel grew up to be a leader of Israel and a spokesperson for God. He was the last of the judges.

Like Hannah, you make vows (or promises). Perhaps you are in Scouts or say the Pledge of Allegiance in school. These are like vows. Do you keep your promises and vows? It is especially important to keep your promises to God.

ACTIVITY

The Israelites had a vow called the "Shema" that they would say twice a day. Some of the words from the Shema are in Deuteronomy 6:4-5. Try to memorize these Bible verses because they are very important to know. Then practice saying them every day, just like the Israelites did.

September 14

Why do some kids act tough?

Live in harmony with each other. Don't try to act important, but enjoy the company of ordinary people. And don't think you know it all! Romans 12:16

Usually kids who act cool or tough are trying hard to feel good about themselves. They want everyone to look up to them the way people look up to entertainment or sports celebrities. Tough kids might be nice if they would just start being themselves. And kids who act important would have a lot more friends if they didn't pretend to be better than everyone else. The best person to be is yourself. Then when people like you, you'll know that they like you for who you are and not for a pretend image that you are trying to have.

ACTIVITY

Draw a series of faces on a piece of paper. Each face should represent a kind of "self" that you are tempted to pretend to be (like putting on a mask). Then, on a Post-it note, write out "Be Yourself." Find a spot for the note that you will see today at school: in your lunch box, an assignment notebook, or a pocket of your backpack. During the day, let the note remind you that today's "you" is the best person for you to be.

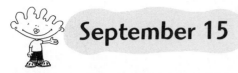

September 15

What if I don't have enough money to pay my bills?

The next year they came again and said, "Our money is gone, and our livestock are yours. We have nothing left but our bodies and land. Why should we die before your very eyes? Buy us and our land in exchange for food; we will then become servants to Pharaoh."   Genesis 47:18-19

EMERGENCY PLAN D:
DIVE FOR SUNKEN TREASURE

PIRATE'S BAYOU

Sunken
Galleon

It is very important to pay your bills. Paying what you owe is part of being honest and trustworthy. If for some reason you lose your money or run out of money, you need to work out a plan for paying what you owe. Your plan should involve getting more money and spending less. You may have to sell some of what you own. Part of the plan should involve talking to the people to whom you owe money and seeing if they will let you pay little by little. See if you can work out a way to pay them each a small amount every week or month until the bills are all paid off.

This is not a good situation to be in. If you learn to budget, save, tithe, and spend wisely, you may never have to go through it. That is why it is important to follow God's guidelines. God knows how things work best, and his way is always best.

ACTIVITY
Today's Bible verse is taken from the story of Joseph when he was a leader in Egypt. Read the whole story, found in Genesis 47:13-21. What happened to Egyptians who couldn't pay their bills?

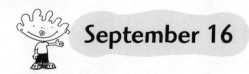

September 16

Does Jesus live with God in heaven or does he live by himself?

[Jesus is speaking:] "Now I am departing the world; I am leaving them behind and coming to you. Holy Father, keep them and care for them—all those you have given me—so that they will be united just as we are."

John 17:11

When Jesus left the earth, he went to heaven to live with God the Father. That's where he is right now, in his new, glorified physical body. He sits at the Father's right hand, the place of highest honor.

You have probably seen photos or movies of fancy palaces or huge royal events. The people of royalty—queen, king, princess, prince, and other titles—are held in great honor, aren't they? But in heaven, God the Father and Jesus the Son are held in even greater honor. Your God and his Son, your Savior, are truly awesome!

ACTIVITY
With some soft clay or Play-Doh, sculpt a throne—a fancy chair for a queen or a king. Imagine God the Father on it, with Jesus sitting to his right.

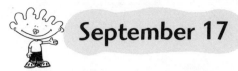
Are all people nice in heaven?

*Don't you know that those who do
wrong will have no share in the
Kingdom of God? Don't fool
yourselves.* 1 Corinthians 6:9

All the people in heaven are nice because everyone there loves
God and loves one another. No one will hurt anyone or be
mean to anyone in heaven. There will be no crying or pain caused
by bullies. There will be no pushing or shoving or name-calling in
heaven. The Bible says that in heaven we will know God like he
knows us. When we know and understand God and his love, we
won't want to hurt anyone ever again.

Do you believe that Jesus is God's Son and that he died on the
cross to take the blame for your sins? And have you asked him to
forgive you for your sins and to be your Savior? Then you'll live in
heaven someday. There you will be able to see family members
and other Christians who have died. You will always be safe and
feel loved.

ACTIVITY

Write a letter to God in your prayer journal. Tell him what you're
looking forward to about heaven. Describe the special people
you're looking forward to seeing again. Thank him for making
heaven so wonderful. Then leave some space at the end of your
letter so you can add to it when you think of something else.

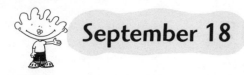

September 18

How does God concentrate on millions of people all praying at once?

[David is speaking:] What mighty praise, O God, belongs to you in Zion. We will fulfill our vows to you, for you answer our prayers, and to you all people will come.

Psalm 65:1-2

G od is unlimited and all-powerful. He has no trouble hearing everyone's prayers all at once. Even human beings can do two things at once. People can ride a bike and notice things in the neighborhood at the same time. God, who is far, far greater than we are, can easily do a million things at once. Also, he is everywhere at all times, and he knows everything. He knows what we think as well as what we say.

God made you to be in one place at a time. He made you to think about one thing at a time. God is not limited in those ways. He can concentrate on everyone's prayers—and that includes each of your prayers.

ACTIVITY

Try a concentration experiment. Have someone in your family read from a newspaper or magazine in a normal voice. Now put on a music CD or cassette, preferably an instrumental (no singing). You can probably follow both pretty well, right? Now turn on the TV or a radio talk show. Getting more difficult to concentrate? What if your brother or sister starts asking you a question? Just about anybody would give up and not be able to follow any of the messages when there are that many sounds. Praise God for being very different from you in this way!

One Year Book of Fun & Active Devotions for Kids

Why do you have to be good and obey in school?

Oh, why didn't I listen to my teachers? Why didn't I pay attention to those who gave me instruction? Proverbs 5:13

Principals, other school leaders, and teachers have rules for how students should act in school so that the school will be safe and students will be able to learn. Just think of the confusion if all the kids did whatever they wanted whenever they wanted. No one would learn anything, except how to be rowdy. In class, for example, if everyone talked at the same time, no one would hear the teacher. And if kids were allowed to run, push, and shove in the hall, people would get hurt.

God wants you to learn and be safe in school. The rules and the grown-ups who enforce the rules there are his ways of helping you.

ACTIVITY

Write down the word *PRINCIPAL* on a piece of paper. What word do the last three letters spell? Let the word *pal* remind you that the principal and other school leaders are God's friends and helpers so that you can learn and have fun in school. This will also help you learn how to spell the word. (Note: A "principal" is different than a "principle." Look up both words in a dictionary.)

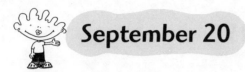

September 20

Why is it so hard to find things in my desk?

*Commit your work to the Lord,
and then your plans will succeed.*
Proverbs 16:3

If your desk is jammed with a lot of stuff, it certainly will be hard to find things. It's a good idea to go through your desk and take out all the notes, wrappers, old papers, stale food, broken pencils, and other extra materials that you don't need for your classes. Next, make sure that everything you do need is in there. Then organize everything; that is, put each item in a certain place so you know where it is and can find it when you need it. Try straightening out your desk at the beginning or end of each day. That will keep you from filling it with junk.

Keeping your desk neat will not make you a good person. And God will not stop loving you if your desk gets messy again. But he does want you to get everything you can out of every day at school and not waste time looking for things. He made your mind and wants you to keep learning.

ACTIVITY
Bring a bag to school and spend time at a break or after school cleaning and organizing your desk. Ask your teacher for help. Throw away the junk and take home what belongs there.

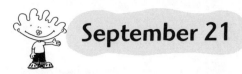

September 21

Why do movie companies make scary movies if they know people will have nightmares?

[David is speaking:] I will lie down in peace and sleep, for you alone, O Lord, will keep me safe.

Psalm 4:8

Many people want to see scary movies and will pay money to see them. The companies that make these movies don't care about whether or not they are scary or bad. They just want to make the money. Also, many scary movies are not made for children.

God doesn't want you to be afraid of monsters, demons, ghosts, or prowlers. He wants you to think good thoughts and be confident in his care for you, because he loves you and created you to enjoy life. So if something that you are watching scares you, stop watching it. And if you see something that bothers you, talk to your parents about it and pray together that God will protect you and give you good dreams. God does not want you to have nightmares.

ACTIVITY

The next time you have a dream, try to remember it the next morning. Write down the dream, and tell your mom or dad about it. Sometimes dreams tell us what's on our minds. Most of the time, they're pretty funny when we remember them the next day.

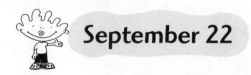

Why does God let animals suffer from dangers in nature?

You send the darkness, and it becomes night, when all the forest animals prowl about. Then the young lions roar for their food, but they are dependent on God.

Psalm 104:20-21

When sin entered the world, all of creation was damaged. Ever since that time, pain and suffering have been a part of life. People and animals suffer—no one escapes.

Probably the greatest danger to animals is that other animals attack and kill them for food. Animals eat each other because they are part of the food chain. While some animals eat only plants, many need to eat other animals to survive. For example, dragonflies eat mosquitoes, birds eat worms and other insects, cats eat mice and birds, and some big fish eat baby ducks. Some animals, called scavengers, eat dead animals that they find in the woods or along the highway. God created animals that way. If all the animals continued to live, soon the world would be filled up with them.

Learn all you can about animals and how God made them. Thank your Creator God for his great love and plan for all of his world.

ACTIVITY

A zoo is a great place to learn about things like the food chain and how God made animals to live together. If there is no zoo near you, or you won't be visiting one soon, check out the interesting Web sites for the San Diego Zoo, Brookfield Zoo, and the National Zoo (part of the Smithsonian Institution).

Do we have to give money to poor people?

[God is speaking:] "If any of your Israelite relatives fall into poverty and cannot support themselves, support them as you would a resident foreigner and allow them to live with you."

Leviticus 25:35

Christians have the responsibility to help people who have needs, including poor people. One reason for this is that God cares about people in need, and we should all try to be like God. God is kind to his people, so we should be kind to others. Another reason we should give is that God wants to work through us to show his love. Because Jesus doesn't live on earth now, God has chosen to show his love through Jesus' followers.

Remember, everything you have came from God because of his goodness and kindness to you. He wants you to treat others the way he treats you.

ACTIVITY
Talk to your family about taking food this weekend to a community food pantry that helps poor people. (Your church might have a collection box for this food.)

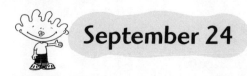

September 24

Why do some people believe that humans came from monkeys?

God created people in his own image; God patterned them after himself; male and female he created them. Genesis 1:27

Many people today believe that human beings descended from ape-like creatures millions of years ago. In other words, they believe that way, way back in time, certain animals changed so that eventually they became human. This is known as the theory of evolution. There are three main reasons that people believe this: (1) They prefer not to believe that God created Adam and Eve and that all people descended from those two people, so they need another explanation. (2) Many scientists say that the theory of evolution explains the fossil record; therefore, it seems reasonable to them. (3) So many other people believe the theory of evolution that they assume it must be true.

The Bible teaches, however, that God created human beings at a certain time and that he created them "in his own image" (Genesis 1:27). This means that humans are not just smart animals. Every human being—including you—is a special creation of God.

ACTIVITY

Write a thank-you letter to your Creator. And be creative with your words! You can do this because you were made to be like your creative Creator God in many ways. Draw a picture of yourself also, if you wish.

268

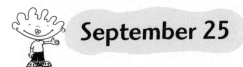

Why doesn't God want us to have fun?

[Jesus is speaking:] "I have told you this so that you will be filled with my joy. Yes, your joy will overflow!" John 15:11

If people think or say that God doesn't want anyone to have fun, they don't know the truth about God. He wants people to enjoy life. Jesus was happy, and he told people that they would find joy by following him. Also, God tells in the Bible that heaven is a place of nonstop joy.

Doing what is wrong (sinning) can be fun, but it doesn't last, and it leads to bad consequences. It's like eating something that tastes good but makes you sick later. The main reason that you shouldn't sin is because God tells you not to, and you need to trust him. God knows you better than anyone else does. His fun and joy and happiness are the greatest. And they last forever!

ACTIVITY
At dinner tonight, talk about the most fun times your family has had. Find out what each person has enjoyed the most—a visit to a water park, a vacation trip, a birthday party, or whatever! You may be surprised at some of the answers. Then thank God for all of these fun times.

September 26

If we've prayed all through the day, do we still need to pray at night?

Keep on praying.   1 Thessalonians 5:17

We should try not to think of prayer as a requirement that we have to meet. Remember that prayer is an opportunity to talk to God, who loves us. If we know God, we will pray often simply because we love him. But we will not worry about whether we have prayed enough.

Bedtime is a good time to pray because you can think through the day and pray about the next day. But please don't think of bedtime prayer as a chore to do. If you have already spoken with God about your concerns, just thank him for taking care of you as you drift off to sleep.

ACTIVITY

Ask your mom if you can decorate a pillowcase to remind you to say good-night to God. If she says yes, ask for a white or light-colored pillowcase. Decorate it with permanent fabric markers (not fabric paint, which could be uncomfortable against your face). Place a big piece of cardboard inside the pillowcase while you draw. Put whatever words or pictures you like on it, such as "Good night, God" or "Thank you for today." Ask a grown-up to help you follow any directions for the fabric markers—perhaps ironing the finished piece to set the colors or drying the pillow-case overnight before you sleep on it.

270

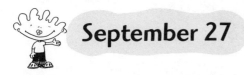

September 27

Are your daytime prayers as effective as your night ones?

Night and day we pray earnestly
for you, asking God to let us see
you again to fill up anything that
may still be missing in your faith.

1 Thessalonians 3:10

Any time can be prayer time. But some people find it easier to pray at night than during the day. Perhaps they become distracted during the day, thinking about all the things they have to do. Others find it easier to pray during the day because they become drowsy at night and fall asleep.

God does not care what time of day you choose to pray. What God cares about is your sincerity. He wants you to say what is on your mind. Whether nighttime or daytime, God always loves to hear from you.

ACTIVITY

Draw a line down a piece of writing paper to make two columns. Label the first column "Time of Day" and the second column "How I Feel." In the first column, list morning, after school, and bedtime. In the second column, next to each time of day, write down what you're like. Do you wake up easily and feel lively right away, or are you slow to wake up? Do you start to yawn as soon as you get your pajamas on at night and fall asleep as soon as your head touches the pillow? Ask God to show you what would be a good time of day to pray. He made you, and he knows when you two could have the best talk.

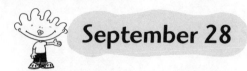

September 28

What did Goliath eat that made him so big?

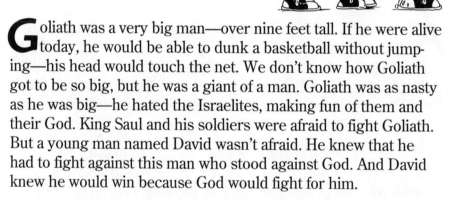

Goliath, a Philistine champion from Gath, came out of the Philistine ranks to face the forces of Israel. He was a giant of a man, measuring over nine feet tall!

1 Samuel 17:4

Goliath was a very big man—over nine feet tall. If he were alive today, he would be able to dunk a basketball without jumping—his head would touch the net. We don't know how Goliath got to be so big, but he was a giant of a man. Goliath was as nasty as he was big—he hated the Israelites, making fun of them and their God. King Saul and his soldiers were afraid to fight Goliath. But a young man named David wasn't afraid. He knew that he had to fight against this man who stood against God. And David knew he would win because God would fight for him.

The same God who fought for David is your God! Even when things seem hopeless, you can trust him, no matter how big your problems or enemies.

ACTIVITY

God has made people in amazing ways. Want to make your arms do something all by themselves? Stand in a doorway; bend your arms, and place the backs of your hands against the door frame. (If you can't reach both sides, do this with just one arm.) Do it as long as you can—try for a full minute. Now relax your arms and let them fall gently to your sides. They'll soon start floating up by themselves.

272

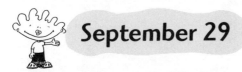

How did David fight Goliath if he was so small?

David shouted in reply, "You come to me with sword, spear, and javelin, but I come to you in the name of the Lord Almighty— the God of the armies of Israel, whom you have defied."

1 Samuel 17:45

Although David wasn't a big man or a soldier, he wasn't afraid to fight the giant Goliath. David trusted in God, not in his own strength or in a soldier's weapons and armor. (In fact, he wouldn't wear the king's armor.) David remembered that he had defeated lions and bears while protecting his father's sheep. David was about sixteen, much younger and smaller than Goliath. But David trusted God to help him. Goliath was mocking the armies of Israel and God, so it was more than just a fight between David and Goliath.

David knew that he had to do what was right, and he believed that God would help him win the battle. He did win, and we can learn from David's faith and courage how God wants us to live today.

ACTIVITY

Get your Bible and read 1 Samuel 17:40 to find out how David armed himself for the big battle against Goliath. Then go outside and see if you can find the same weapon. Use a little pouch to put your stones in, and carry them with you for a day. Whenever you think of something big that seems as though it will beat you, reach into your bag. Remind yourself that God's power is great enough to defeat a mean, nine-foot giant, and he will help you.

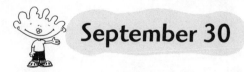

September 30

When will the world end?

[Jesus is speaking:] "Heaven and earth will disappear, but my words will remain forever. However, no one knows the day or hour when these things will happen, not even the angels in heaven or the Son himself. Only the Father knows."

Mark 13:31-32

JASON'S PRAYER
Lord, please come quickly To end all sin and hurt. But if you're coming today PLEASE, after dessert.

The world will end when God lets it happen, and not before. It will be when God is ready to take all believers home to heaven. It will happen when God decides that it is the right time. And no one knows when that time will come. Only God knows.

Do you trust in God? If so, you don't have to be afraid about the world coming to an end. When God sent his Son, Jesus, to die on the cross, he provided the perfect way to rescue you from trouble and pain.

ACTIVITY

Do a crossword puzzle today. (Many kids' magazines have one. If you don't subscribe, find one geared to your age at the library and photocopy that page.) There's only one solution, only one perfect way to complete the puzzle. Just like God has the perfect plan in mind to care for you.

If Jesus has already won, why is everyone still fighting?

What is causing the quarrels and fights among you? Isn't it the whole army of evil desires at war within you? James 4:1

J esus won over sin and death when he rose from the dead. But some people still sin and fight because they don't love or follow Jesus. Jesus is waiting for them to change their mind and follow him. As Jesus waits, they do what their sinful desires tell them to—they sin and fight. Satan has not surrendered, and he still tries to trick people. Jesus hasn't come back yet because he loves us all and wants many more people to trust in him as Savior so they can be saved from hell and go to heaven.

Jesus has won over sin and death, but he won't make you live at peace with other people. The more you love him, the more you'll want to live at peace and not fight.

ACTIVITY

Get out your prayer journal. In the column labeled "Prayers," write down the names of people with whom you sometimes fight or argue. Pray for each person. Pray that God will help you get along with all of those people better. Then, over the days and weeks, watch God answer your prayers! Be sure to write down what happens in the column "God's Answers."

What are politics?

[The apostles are speaking:] "Now look around among yourselves, friends, and select seven men who are well respected and are full of the Holy Spirit and wisdom. We will put them in charge of this business." Acts 6:3

Politics is the word we use to describe governing or ruling. Politics is when people deal with one another in government. It includes trying to persuade someone else to vote your way. One part of politics involves electing government leaders. The political activities leading up to an election are called a "campaign." In a political campaign, the people who want to be elected try to persuade voters to vote for them. The candidates do this through speeches, advertisements, debates, and so forth.

Governments are an important part of God's design for the world. God wants all rulers to obey him, and he expects citizens to obey the government's laws (as long as they don't contradict the laws of God himself). That is why voters should think carefully and pray often about whom to vote for. We want to pick the best rulers—the ones who will create and enforce laws that are just and pleasing to God.

ACTIVITY

Ask your mom or dad what the next big local or national election will be. Find out who the candidates are and what their platforms say—what do they believe and what do they plan to do if they are elected? Pray that the best person for the job will win.

October 3

Why do governments do wrong things?

I also noticed that throughout the world there is evil in the courtroom. Yes, even the courts of law are corrupt! I said to myself, "In due season God will judge everyone, both good and bad, for all their deeds."   Ecclesiastes 3:16-17

Governments do wrong things for the same reason that individual persons do wrong things—sin. Every person is sinful. That means that people are naturally self-centered and try to live their lives without God. Some people are more sinful than others. That is, they work very hard to cheat, lie, and steal. Governments are made up of people, so they will sometimes do wrong things unless someone stops them. This is why many governments are organized with "checks and balances," which lets one branch of government stop the actions of another. It is also why democratic governments hold elections every few years. That gives the people the chance to get rid of bad leaders.

God does not ignore the deeds of leaders. He watches over those who hold authority in government. Pray that God will make your country's leaders just and wise. And be certain that God is looking out for you and all the people in your country.

ACTIVITY
With the help of an encyclopedia or a history textbook, read about one of the following: Teapot Dome, Tammany Hall, Jim Crow laws, or Watergate. How did one part of the government put a stop to the wrongdoing? How do these events illustrate the "checks and balances" discussed in the answer above?

October 4

Does God have things to do at night time?

[God] will not let you stumble and fall; the one who watches over you will not sleep. Indeed, he who watches over Israel never tires and never sleeps.

Psalm 121:3-4

...PLEASE HELP US NOT HAVE TO WAKE UP AT NIGHT, AND DON'T LET LOUD NOISES HAPPEN, AND HELP THE CAT CATCH ALL THE MICE, AND DON'T LET MY DAD SNORE SO LOUD THAT HE WAKES UP MY MOM, AND HELP OUR BRAINS TO KEEP ON WORKING EVEN THOUGH WE HAVE THEM TURNED OFF, AND...

God does not have a body like ours, so he does not need to sleep. And because God is everywhere and lives in eternity, there's no night or day to him. (Besides, when it's night here, it's day somewhere else.) So God is always working, even when we are sleeping.

When you go to sleep, you can be sure that God is awake, watching over you and taking care of you. He wants to take care of you. And he's able to take care of you.

ACTIVITY

Make a nighttime picture. Here is one way to do it. Draw a big window on a piece of drawing paper. Put curtains by the window and make a wallpaper pattern all around it. In the window, draw a moon and add sticker stars. Across the top or bottom of your picture, write: "The one who watches over you will not sleep" (Psalm 121:3). When you go to bed tonight, thank God for his watchful care and protection. He will help you fall asleep and protect you through the night even if you have a nightmare or get sick.

If someone isn't popular, how come others think less of him or her as a person?

Why do you condemn another Christian? Why do you look down on another Christian? Remember, each of us will stand personally before the judgment seat of God.

Romans 14:10

Popular kids aren't better than others just because of their popularity, especially if they are popular for the wrong reasons. Each person, including you, is a valuable creation of God. Looking down on others is never right, for the Bible teaches that all people are important to God and valuable in his sight. God wants us to treat everyone well and with respect.

While you're wondering why more popular kids don't pay more attention to you, be careful that you aren't busy ignoring kids who seem even less popular. Go out of your way to make others feel good and respected, no matter how popular they are.

ACTIVITY

The next time you're with a group of kids, go on a kid hunt. All during the day, look for kids who seem to be lonely or very unpopular. Make a list of them. Then, over the next day or two, try to be friendly to all the kids on your list. See how much they appreciate your attention.

October 6

Why do some kids dress so weird?

[Jesus is speaking:] "Everything [the Pharisees] do is for show. On their arms they wear extra wide prayer boxes with Scripture verses inside, and they wear extra long tassels on their robes. They enjoy the attention they get on the streets." Matthew 23:5, 7

Some kids may like to dress weird. Actually, their clothes may seem weird to you but not to them. Of course, some kids wear loud and different clothes to be noticed. They want to get a reaction, to get attention. Some kids whose clothes seem weird may be copying musicians or other celebrities who they think are cool. Others may look different just because they don't have enough money to dress in style.

Clothes don't help you to know the real person. Remember not to judge people by the way they dress. God cares about what's on the inside . . . of them and of you.

ACTIVITY
Put on a fashion show for your family. Wear your clothes in different ways that are like certain groups of kids at school or in the community. See if your family can guess which groups you are depicting. Then talk about what these kids are like and why they dress the way they do.

280

How do you get someone to like you if you aren't as popular as everyone else?

Obviously, I'm not trying to be a people pleaser! No, I am trying to please God. If I were still trying to please people, I would not be Christ's servant. Galatians 1:10

BE RIGHT WITH YOU MAX, MY MAN. JUST NEED TO ORDER A DOUBLE DE-CAF LATTE, AND TALK TO THE PRESIDENT OF MY FAN CLUB!

You can't force people to like you, and you can't talk them into it. And you shouldn't do whatever they say just so they will be your friends. When you live for Jesus and let the Holy Spirit control your actions, people will like you for who you are. So the idea is to help people get to know the real you. You can be liked, even if you're not voted Most Popular.

Outgoing, likable people are often very popular, but you can be likable even if you're quiet. God made each person special and unique, so you should value all people (yourself included) no matter how popular they are.

ACTIVITY

Make a special frame for your school photo (or any other recent photo of yourself). Ask your mom for a plastic lid from a margarine tub or a container she got at the deli. Cut out a circle of construction paper the size of the lid. In the center, cut an opening just a little smaller than your photo and tape the picture in place. Then glue the frame and photo to the lid. Around the edge of the frame, use some stick-on letters to spell *UNIQUELY ME*. Enjoy the fact that God made you and loves you. If you like the way God made you, others will like you, too!

October 8

Should I hang out with popular people to become popular?

Oh, that my actions would consistently reflect your principles!   Psalm 119:5

This may seem like the way to be popular, but that kind of popularity is pretty shallow and won't last very long. Instead, be the right kind of person—the kind that others will want to hang with. Be confident in the fact that God loves you, and let popularity take care of itself. It's OK to want to be friends with the popular kids, but it's not OK to do whatever they say to be accepted by them.

The Bible teaches that you should think about the needs of others and not just your own. Spend some time and attention on kids whom others think are not very popular. Help them feel good about themselves. You'll be amazed at how good *you* feel when you make *others* feel good.

ACTIVITY

Take a popularity survey—ask a parent, a high school student, a neighbor, and another adult at church (possibly a youth leader or Sunday school teacher) what some students do or did to become popular at their schools. Make a list and see what the top three or four actions are. Decide which of these are good things to do and which are not.

October 9

How can I get better at art?

[Jesus is speaking:] "To those who use well what they are given, even more will be given, and they will have an abundance. But from those who are unfaithful, even what little they have will be taken away." Matthew 25:29

If you have talent in art, you will get better at it in the same way you get better at anything else—by practice. To get better at art, you need to do a variety of art projects. Ask your parents if you can get some art supplies for your birthday or Christmas. Then find creative ways to use things your parents are throwing out, such as old magazines and cardboard boxes. Get some scrap paper and spend time drawing or designing. You might ask your Sunday school teacher to help you find an adult at church who is artistic and would be willing to give you lessons.

You don't have to be a great artist all at once to enjoy art and get better at it. God, who is creative, made you to be creative, too. You and God are fellow artists!

ACTIVITY
Begin a secret art project. Draw or paint a picture or make a collage of your family. You can do this with photographs and other mementos of family members who have enjoyed special times together. Then present it to the family. If you wish, give this gift to your parents on their wedding anniversary.

Why didn't God give us money right away when my dad lost his job?

Trust me in your times of trouble,
and I will rescue you, and you
will give me glory. Psalm 50:15

Answer Booth

The opinions of this child do not reflect the views of this household

We don't always know why God does what he does. But we know that he loves us and has a plan for us, even for the tough times. Sometimes God is working out something that we don't know about yet. Maybe it's even better than what we wanted or had before. God can use times like this to teach us to trust him more. As we trust him more, he can trust us with more.

Losing a job can be very painful and difficult. The person without a job wonders what he or she will do and where the money will come from. If your dad has lost his job, pitch in with any money you can. Say encouraging words to him. Donate your allowance. Do odd jobs for neighbors to earn more money if you can. Ask God to provide what you need—and trust him to do so, just as he has done for many, many other families.

ACTIVITY

Has your family ever listened to the Christian singer Twila Paris? She has a song titled "God Is in Control." If you have her music or can borrow it from someone, listen to that song. Or make up your own poem or song about trusting God to care for you because you know he is in control.

Why does God sometimes wait until the last minute to supply our needs?

[God is speaking:] "For forty years I led you through the wilderness, yet your clothes and sandals did not wear out. You had no bread or wine or other strong drink, but he gave you food so you would know that he is the Lord your God."

Deuteronomy 29:5-6

It may seem as though God waits until the last minute to supply your needs, but remember that God has a timetable that you can't see. He has a plan for you. Nothing can stop that plan, not even a shortage of money. God may wait because he wants you to trust him more. God always remembers you and hears your prayers. And he never runs out of anything.

Do you wait till the last minute to pray? Instead, pray to God all the time about your needs. You can trust him to take care of you.

ACTIVITY

Do you wear a watch? Draw a picture of one. Make it fancy or plain, Mickey Mouse face or digital. It doesn't matter. Then draw a red circle around it with a diagonal line through it (like the no-turn signs you see on roads). Write underneath the picture "God's time is not our time." Put it up on your bulletin board or mirror as a reminder that God's timing is good, perfect, and not like your own ideas about time.

October 12

Do you need to learn math only if you want to be a pilot or a construction worker?

LET'S SEE, IF I DOUBLE THIS PIE RECIPE FOR 17 PEOPLE AND CUT THE SUGAR BY A THIRD, THAT WOULD WORK OUT TO...

MOM, JUST MULTIPLY THE RECIPE BY PIE SQUARED!

Intelligent people are always open to new ideas. In fact, they look for them. Proverbs 18:15

You'd be surprised how math is used in life. People in all kinds of jobs, not just pilots and construction workers, use math every day. Engineers, writers, homemakers, musicians, doctors, managers, and even professional athletes use math. Go figure. Even if you just wanted to paint a room in your house, you'd use math to figure out how much paint to buy.

Almost everything you learn now will help you understand the things you need to know later, whatever you end up doing. God made the world work in amazing ways, and he wants you to have fun figuring things out. Working with numbers is part of that.

ACTIVITY
Go on a math treasure hunt. Take a pad of paper and go around your house, trying to find all the things that use numbers—don't overlook all the ways you and your family count, measure, and in other ways work with numbers. Remember that all these things use math. Practice measuring by using a tape measure or yardstick to measure one or more of the rooms in your house. Why might you need to know the size of a room?

One Year Book of Fun & Active Devotions for Kids

October 13

Why do people believe that trees and plants and animals have spirits?

Let the fields and their crops burst forth with joy! Let the trees of the forest rustle with praise.

Psalm 96:12

Some people believe that trees, plants, and animals have spirits. Plants and animals don't have spirits, but many false religions teach that they do. Only people have eternal souls.

At the same time, God does want us to respect the world he created. God created all living things, including plants and animals. The Bible says that all of nature groans under the weight of our sin. And some of the Psalms in the Bible say, as a figure of speech, that the trees and the fields will "clap their hands" in praise of God. But plants and animals don't have spirits. And it's important to worship only our Creator God, not anyone or anything he has created.

ACTIVITY

Collect several leaves that have turned colors. Pick those that are not too dry or crunched at the edges but very colorful. With a grown-up's help, place a piece of waxed paper on an ironing board. Put the leaves on top of it, then put another piece of waxed paper on that. Place a thin cloth on top and iron it on low heat. The waxed paper will seal the leaves and keep them beautiful for a long time. But remember that leaves don't have spirits, so they won't last forever.

October 14

What will I do in heaven with no friends?

[Jesus is speaking:] "There are many rooms in my Father's home, and I am going to prepare a place for you. If this were not so, I would tell you plainly. When everything is ready, I will come and get you, so that you will always be with me where I am."

John 14:2-3

If your friends believe in Jesus, eventually they will be in heaven with you, and you will have a great time together. Jesus is preparing a place for all who believe in him, and he won't keep believing friends apart from each other. You will make new friends in heaven, too. If you aren't sure whether your friends will go to heaven, tell them about Jesus. If they put their faith in Christ, then you will eventually all be in heaven together.

You don't have to worry—heaven won't be boring. Remember, God created butterflies, sunsets, electrical storms, mountains, the Grand Canyon, and all of nature. He will give us so much fun, beauty, and joy in heaven that there is no way we can imagine it now.

ACTIVITY

Make a list of your friends. Circle those who already know Jesus and who will eventually go to heaven. Pray that the others will believe in Jesus and trust in him as their Savior.

One Year Book of Fun & Active Devotions for Kids

October 15

Does God have friends or is he alone?

[Jesus is speaking to his disciples:]
"You are my friends if you obey
me. I no longer call you servants,
because a master doesn't confide
in his servants. Now you are my
friends, since I have told you every-
thing the Father told me."

John 15:14-15

God doesn't have other "gods" to be friends with. He is the only God there is. God doesn't *need* friends the way we do, but God *wants* to have friendship with *us!* In fact, God wants to be our closest friend. So he has done a lot to make friends with us and to have our friendship. That's why he created us, sent Jesus to save us, gave us the Bible, and gave us the church.

When God became a human being and lived on earth as Jesus, he had many friends. Twelve of his closest friends were called the disciples. He did not absolutely need to have friends, but he wanted to. He wants to be your close friend, too. Are you friends with God?

ACTIVITY
Write or tape record a family letter to God, just as you might send to a friend. Thank God for things he has done for you. Tell him about all the exciting things the people in your family are doing. Then read your letter or play your tape as a prayer to God.

October 16

Why do they put horoscopes in the newspaper?

Do not let your people practice fortune-telling or sorcery, or allow them to interpret omens, or engage in witchcraft, or cast spells, or function as mediums or psychics, or call forth the spirits of the dead.

Deuteronomy 18:10-11

Newspapers print horoscopes because many people read them, and people read horoscopes because they believe that major parts of life are controlled by outside forces beyond their control. They look to the horoscopes for guidance.

Believers should not look to horoscopes for guidance. Only God controls what happens, and only God knows the future. If you need advice, do three things: (1) read the Bible, (2) talk to wise people as Proverbs 13:20 says, and (3) ask God for wisdom, which is what James 1:5 tells us to do.

ACTIVITY
Philippians 4:6 is a great verse to memorize if you're wondering about your future. Write it out on an index card—don't forget the chapter and verse numbers—and work on learning it by heart. Put it in a coat pocket or your backpack so you can pull it out and read it any time.

October 17

Why do people commit crimes?

*When they refused to acknowledge
God, he abandoned them to their
evil minds and let them do things
that should never be done.*

Romans 1:28

The main reason that people commit crimes is that they are
selfish. They want what others have and take it by force.
Another big reason is anger. People lose their temper and do
things that they would not normally do. Both selfishness and
uncontrolled anger are sin. Crime happens when people are cut
off from God and his love. Some people do not know God at all.
Other people know him but lose touch with him, then fail to trust
and obey him.

God's way is for you to know him, to ask and trust him for the
things you need, and then to love and help others. If everyone did
things God's way all the time, crime would never happen. That is
why you need to trust God to provide for you instead of selfishly
trying to get what you want regardless of how it affects others.
Practice this way of thinking and living now. God will provide.
He does love you.

ACTIVITY

The book of Proverbs in the Bible has a lot of good advice about
selfishness and anger. Read Proverbs 12:15-20. Sing the verses
to the tune of "Twinkle, Twinkle, Little Star." (You'll need to go
through the tune twice to sing all six verses.) Or make up your
own tune.

October 18

Why did Jesus talk about money when he didn't have very much?

He took his twelve disciples with him, along with . . . Mary Magdalene, from whom he had cast out seven demons; Joanna, the wife of Chuza, Herod's business manager; Susanna; and many others who were contributing from their own resources to support Jesus and his disciples. Luke 8:1-3

We don't know how much money Jesus had. We know that he didn't own a home and that he had few possessions. But we also know that he had everything he needed. The Bible doesn't say that Jesus or the disciples lived in poverty. Luke 8:3 says that the wives of some wealthy men gave money to support Jesus and his disciples. Judas was in charge of the money bag. Jesus talked about money because he wanted to teach us how to use it rightly.

Jesus, who was a human person as well as God, knew that people are tempted to be greedy and to love money. The love of money leads to all kinds of evil (1 Timothy 6:10). How you feel about money and how you use it matter a great deal. So you can count on God's help to keep from being greedy or in love with money.

ACTIVITY
Read more about Judas. Money became more and more important to him. In John 12:1-8, he complained about Mary wasting money when he really just wanted it for himself. Then, in Luke 22, you can find out how far his greediness took him. Judas lived a long time ago, but we can learn from his wrong ideas about money.

292

October 19

Does money make people bad?

The love of money is at the root of all kinds of evil. And some people, craving money, have wandered from the faith and pierced themselves with many sorrows.

1 Timothy 6:10

Money itself isn't bad, and money doesn't make people bad. But the *love* of money does. When people love money, they become greedy, doing all sorts of bad things to get and keep money. God wants us to use money to help people who are hurting. When we turn things around and treat people badly to get money, we've got it wrong.

The way to deal with money problems is to use money wisely. You won't solve any money problems by getting rid of it all. Everybody needs money to live. Just be sure you use some money for the work of God's kingdom, which includes helping others.

ACTIVITY
Make a chart and give it the title "Ways to Use and Misuse Money." Divide it into two columns. Label the first column "Wise Uses for My Money" and write down all the good things you could do with your money, including saving, giving to church, and helping people who are in trouble. Put down specific things, such as "Buying macaroni for the food pantry." The second column is for "Dumb Uses for My Money." In that column, put down all the things that would be wrong, such as "Spending all my allowance on candy." God wants you to really think about how you spend and invest your money.

Why do people like different kinds of music?

[Elihu is speaking:] "Just as the mouth tastes good food, the ear tests the words it hears."

Job 34:3

People like different kinds of music because people have different tastes. Each person is different and special—a part of the variety in God's creation. It's the same with people's tastes in food. Everyone has favorite foods. We wouldn't expect everyone to eat and like all the same foods. Also, certain groups of people like certain kinds of music. People of one nationality may like one kind, and people from one area of the country may have their own musical likes and dislikes. Some people just listen to whatever is popular.

Choose music wisely, like other forms of entertainment, because it's something you put into your mind. God wants you to think about what is good.

ACTIVITY
Go to the library and check out a CD or cassette of music from another country. How is it different from what your family usually listens to?

October 21

Why are musicians treated like idols?

[Paul is speaking:] "Friends, why are you doing this? We are merely human beings like yourselves! We have come to bring you the Good News that you should turn from these worthless things to the living God, who made heaven and earth, the sea, and everything in them."   Acts 14:15

Everybody looks up to somebody. God made us this way so we could learn and grow into people who love and obey him. He gives us parents to start the process, and as we get older we choose others from whom to learn. Many people choose to idolize musicians because they appear in the spotlight a lot. They are featured in newspapers, magazines, and TV and are held up as heroes. Many people look up to them simply because of all the attention they get.

Others "worship" musicians because their music makes them feel something very deeply. That is the way art works—it touches people's emotions. Still others idolize musicians because they assume that they're rich and successful and, therefore, great.

Choose your heroes carefully, and be careful not to idolize them. Choose to look up to parents and others who love God, and try to do what is right. Learn from them. Also, realize that no one is perfect, not even great heroes.

ACTIVITY
Read the whole story about Paul and Barnabas in Acts 14:8-18. Paul and Barnabas could have let the crowd worship them as gods, but instead, they turned the glory to God. Identify some of your heroes, and talk with your family about appropriate ways to respond to them.

October 22

What should I do if other kids laugh at me for going to church?

[Jesus is speaking:] "God blesses you who are hated and excluded and mocked and cursed because you are identified with me, the Son of Man." Luke 6:22

HA HA, GOODY TWO SHOES IS GOING TO CHURCH.

You can ignore their laughter. If you get the chance, you can quietly explain that you go to church because you love God and because you enjoy church and want to be with your family and friends there. Someone who laughs at you for going to church may not know what church is, may have never been to church, and probably doesn't know what it means to love God and his Son, Jesus. That's someone for whom you can pray. You can even invite that person to go to church with you sometime, especially when your church has a fun night or other social activity.

Try not to get upset or take it personally when someone laughs about your going to church. God is happy that you go. You're getting to know him and his people better. And that lasts a lot longer than a few laughs by kids who don't understand.

ACTIVITY
Talk with your pastor or Sunday school teacher about having a Friends Day. Plan a party or other special event to which class members could invite other kids. Invite neighbors and others you know who might not feel comfortable going to a worship service for their very first church activity. Ask God to help you think of something fun.

How can I love my enemies?

[Jesus is speaking:] "Love your enemies!
Do good to them! Lend to them! And don't
be concerned that they might not repay.
Then your reward from heaven will be
very great, and you will truly be acting as
children of the Most High, for he is kind
to the unthankful and to those who are
wicked. You must be compassionate, just
as your Father is compassionate."

Luke 6:35-36

God wants you to do kind things for your enemies, such as wishing them well and praying for them. Loving enemies also means forgiving them and not condemning them. It means that rather than fighting back or trying to hurt those who mistreat you, you treat them like a friend. If that sounds difficult to do, you're right. Enemies don't like us and are out to hurt us. They may push us, hit us, call us names, and try to get us into trouble.

Even though you don't like what they do, with the help of God's Holy Spirit you can love your enemies. After all, God loved you before you became his friend. God can change people. Who knows—today's enemies may turn out to be tomorrow's friends. Wouldn't it be great to have a new surprise friend?

ACTIVITY

Get out your prayer journal. In the left-hand column, write down the names of any enemies you have. Promise God that you will pray for those people every day for the next week . . . and do it! God will answer your prayers, though it's up to him how he will do it.

October 24

Can an angel be a person to us like a real person?

Don't forget to show hospitality to strangers, for some who have done this have entertained angels without realizing it!

Hebrews 13:2

HERE YOU GO, ANGEL

Sometimes, angels have taken on human form and appeared to people. That's how they appeared to Abraham one day (Genesis 18:1-15). Abraham was sitting outside his tent when three men walked up and greeted him. As far as Abraham knew, they were men—perhaps travelers looking for a place to stay. But in fact, they were angels.

The Bible urges God's people to be kind and neighborly to visitors. You never know when a visitor might be an angel. It is possible that you have met an angel and did not know it. But don't go looking for angels. Angels almost always stay invisible.

ACTIVITY

Have you ever stayed overnight or had dinner in someone else's home? Write down a list of the ways your host or hostess was kind to you and your family—things such as offering you your favorite drink, putting a clean towel out for you to use, or sleeping on a couch so that you or your parents could sleep in a bed. Which of these things could you do the next time you have a guest? Mark these things with a star, and ask your mom or dad to put the list in a "hospitality place," such as taped to the inside of a linen closet where you keep extra towels and tablecloths.

One Year Book of Fun & Active Devotions for Kids

October 25

Why do we have to respect teachers?

The authorities do not frighten people who are doing right, but they frighten those who do wrong. So do what they say, and you will get along well. Romans 13:3

The he Bible says that God expects his people to respect those in authority over them. That includes teachers. Also, for teachers to do their best, they need the respect of their students. If you respect your teachers, you'll be polite and kind to them, listen to them, and do what they say.

Remember, the only one who benefits from your going to school and learning is you. If you don't cooperate, listen, and learn, you won't be hurting the teacher—you will be hurting yourself and your future. And that's not the kind of life your loving God wants for you.

ACTIVITY

It's time to pray for all those hard-working teachers and others at your school. Write down the names of your principal, all your teachers, the school librarian, and any other grown-ups at your school who help you learn. Ask God to help them in their work. You may want to write a thank-you note or draw a thank-you picture for one or more of these people.

October 26

Why was Saul jealous of David?

This made Saul very angry. "What's this?" he said. "They credit David with ten thousands and me with only thousands. Next they'll be making him their king!" So from that time on Saul kept a jealous eye on David.
1 Samuel 18:8-9

After David killed Goliath, people were singing, "Saul has killed his thousands, and David his ten thousands!" (1 Samuel 18:7). Saul was angry that David had become so popular with the people. Saul became very jealous, knowing that David was a better warrior than he was. This jealousy made Saul cruel and deceitful—he tried for years to kill David. Eventually, God told Saul he couldn't be king anymore. Then, after Saul died, David became king.

We must be careful to be content with the abilities God has given us.

If you look around at other people, you will see great variety. Some are smart. Some are funny. Some are good at sports. Some have beautiful singing voices. But you are you. No one else has your exact combination of brain, body, and spirit. God made you!

ACTIVITY
Start an "I'm Special" scrapbook." You can add to it over the months and even years ahead. Write the date on a corner of the page whenever you add something: photos of a special day with your friends or family, tickets from a fun event, a poem, drawings, magazine pictures, and so forth. Make it a book that tells how special you are and reminds you that there's no reason to be jealous of anyone else. You may also want to start another scrapbook titled "My Friends Are Special."

October 27

Is it OK to use Canadian coins in U. S. vending machines?

The Lord despises double standards of every kind.
Proverbs 20:10

Many vending machines have a sign that says, "No foreign coins." Money from other countries may get jammed in the machine. But even if the coins work, they may not be worth the same amount. So putting foreign coins in the machine would cheat the owner of the machine. That would be wrong.

Do not look for ways to "save money" by being dishonest. Instead, be honest all the time and trust God to take care of you. God owns everything. He can help you with the extra few cents you think you would gain from cheating the vending machine.

ACTIVITY

Instead of using foreign coins to cheat, start a collection of money from other countries. Find a nice box to save both paper money and coins. What pictures and words are there? What is the money called in that country? Some other countries have "dollars," but most call their currency other names. Reference books, including many dictionaries, will help you find out the names of money in other countries.

October 28

Why does God kill nature with forest fires?

God said, "Let the land burst forth with
every sort of grass and seed-bearing plant.
And let there be trees that grow seed-
bearing fruit. The seeds will then produce
the kinds of plants and trees from which
they came." And so it was. The land was
filled with seed-bearing plants and trees,
and their seeds produced plants and trees
of like kind. And God saw that it was
good.   Genesis 1:11-12

Forest fires don't kill nature. They are part of the life cycle that
God built into our world. Raging forest fires can destroy many
thousands of trees and wildlife. But forest fires also help life continue. For example, they burn away dead growth and open seed
pods, such as those of Jack Pines, that can't be opened any other
way. Forest fires are a little like lightning—they may be danger-
ous, but they do important work.

Some forest fires start naturally, and some are started by people.
You should not try to start forest fires just to destroy property.
And you should try to keep fires from damaging property or
endangering people's lives. But some fires start naturally, and
you know now that they are necessary. This is just part of God's
plan for his world.

ACTIVITY
Read Psalm 148, a song to the glory of God and his hand in
nature. Choose one or several verses to illustrate. You may want
to draw one big picture or a number of little pictures.

October 29

When kids tease me, should I tease them back?

Don't repay evil for evil. Don't retaliate when people say unkind things about you. Instead, pay them back with a blessing. That is what God wants you to do, and he will bless you for it. 1 Peter 3:9

MAN! WHERE DID YOU GET SUCH WEIRD HAIR?

STOMP!

There's a difference between fun teasing and mean teasing. Sometimes kids say nonsense things about each other, not meaning to hurt anyone's feelings. That's OK. When kids tease you in a mean way, however, don't tease them back. Try to ignore them if possible. Just stay quiet.

This won't be easy because it's natural to want to say something back to hurt them. If you can, be kind to them. Jesus calls this "turning the other cheek." If a certain group of kids seems to tease you all the time, don't go near those kids. If they call you names, remind yourself that the names do not describe the real you. God knows you, and he says you're special.

ACTIVITY

In today's verse, the apostle Peter told believers to repay unkind things with a blessing. What does it mean to give a blessing or to bless someone? Look up the word *bless* in a dictionary. What blessing could you say quietly to God the next time kids tease you?

October 30

How come some people are asking for sunshine while other people are asking for rain?

Our God is in the heavens, and he
does as he wishes.   Psalm 115:3

People ask God for different things because they have different needs and different concerns. A baseball player might ask God for sunshine so she can play her game. At the same time, a farmer nearby might ask God for rain to grow his crops. Fortunately, God sees everything and knows what is best. And he can work out all things everywhere for everyone's best because he is all-knowing and all-powerful.

You can be thankful that God is wiser than you or any other person. He sees the whole picture! He sees what's best for you and for all of his creation.

ACTIVITY
Look at a weather map. You can find them on a weather channel on TV, in a daily newspaper, and on the Internet. What kind of weather do you get in your area? What good comes from each kind of weather? Thank God that he is Lord over all of nature.

304

October 31

Why are there spooky things like skeletons and monsters?

[Moses is speaking to Joshua:]
"Be strong and courageous! Do not be afraid of them! The Lord your God will go ahead of you. He will neither fail you nor forsake you."

Deuteronomy 31:6

Some people like to be frightened by funny skeletons and make-believe monsters. And they like scaring others, especially at Halloween. Many Christians have parties and other activities at Halloween that do not glorify bad things and monsters. It can be fun to dress up and play make-believe.

But you don't have to be afraid of ghosts and goblins—they aren't real. Besides, God is with you and will take care of you. Keep trusting in him to protect you.

ACTIVITY
You'll probably see lots of wild things today. Maybe you'll even wear a fun type of costume yourself! Every time you see a scary mask or costume, let it remind you of God's protection. Say to yourself each time you see something scary, "God is real. That costume is not."

November 1

Does God know about people who are hungry?

He is the one who made heaven and earth, the sea, and everything in them. He is the one who keeps every promise forever, who gives justice to the oppressed and food to the hungry. The Lord frees the prisoners. Psalm 146:6-7

God knows everything. He even knows how many hairs you have on your head. God knows about all the hungry people in the world, and it makes him sad. Many, many children will go to bed hungry tonight because their parents don't have enough money to buy all the food their families need.

Remember, God put *us* in charge of the world. He wants us to care about people and help those who need it. This includes helping to feed those who are hungry. What is being done to help feed the hungry people in your community?

ACTIVITY
Perhaps in the last couple of months you have followed the suggestions to take some food to a food pantry, where people can get food at low cost or even free. Ask one of your parents if you can go there again and take some canned goods.

November 2

Why did the people (of Israel) want to have a king?

[God is speaking to Samuel:] "Do as they say," the Lord replied, "for it is me they are rejecting, not you. They don't want me to be their king any longer."

1 Samuel 8:7

...and I'll focus on your kids'education, more instruction time, more discipline, more homework...

POLITICAL CAMPAIGN

The people of Israel were dissatisfied with God as their king and wanted to be like all the other nations—to have a human king who would lead them in battle. Times were tough, and Samuel's sons were turning out to be bad judges—they were accepting bribes and making wrong decisions. Samuel knew that God wanted the people to trust in God and not in a king. But God told Samuel to give them one anyway, warning him that a king would bring many problems. The man chosen to be Israel's first king was Saul.

Your town, your state, your country, and the whole world have many leaders. These men and women have much power—but their power is nothing compared to God's power. He is the true king and leader. Make sure to honor and obey God's rules for living.

ACTIVITY

In your prayer journal, write down the names of your mayor, the governor of your state, the president (or the top leader in your country if you live outside the United States), and other important political leaders. When you see photos of these leaders in the newspaper, cut the pictures out and place them in your journal. Pray for these men and women. Praise God that he is our true king and top leader.

November 3

Why do some kids always try to be first?

[Jesus is speaking:] "Many who are first now will be last then; and those who are last now will be first then." Matthew 20:16

Some kids are selfish. By the way, that's part of the sinful, human nature—all people tend to be selfish. God will help us be unselfish and think of others, but we have to depend on him. Kids who always try to be first may be trying to feel better about themselves. They may feel that they are important and valuable because they won the game or are first in line.

But God says that each person is valuable and important to him, even those who come in last. When you know how much God loves and cares for you, you can let others go first.

ACTIVITY
Where do you need to get in line? At school when it's time for recess? At the checkout counter in the grocery store? At a drinking fountain? At the ticket counter when you want to see a movie? Decide right now that the next time you need to get in a line you won't try to get ahead of everyone else. You'll let others get in line ahead of you without getting mad about it. It's good practice for growing up—there are a lot of lines in life!

Why does God let us get sick?

Are any among you sick? They should call for the elders of the church and have them pray over them, anointing them with oil in the name of the Lord. And their prayer offered in faith will heal the sick, and the Lord will make them well. And anyone who has committed sins will be forgiven.
James 5:14-15

Sometimes sickness is the body's way of telling people that they should stop living a certain way. Perhaps they ate too much (or something bad). Maybe they didn't get enough sleep or exercise. Sickness and disease are problems that came into the world with sin. All kinds of people get sick: good and bad, rich and poor, old and young.

God wants us to take care of ourselves and be healthy so we can live for him. And when we are sick, we can pray to God and ask him to help us. He really cares.

ACTIVITY
When you get sick, you feel bad, don't you? You may even feel a little sad and lonely because you can't see your friends. Do you know anybody who is sick now? Perhaps your neighbor down the street, or a teacher at your school, or another child at church. Make a get-well card for that person. Really take your time and do a nice job. Then mail it or take it to the person. You can be a messenger of good wishes, telling the sick person that you and God care.

November 5

How does medicine make someone better?

Then Isaiah said to Hezekiah's servants, "Make an ointment from figs and spread it over the boil." They did this, and Hezekiah recovered!   2 Kings 20:7

Medicine helps your body heal itself. Some medicines do this by killing germs; antibiotics work that way. Some medicines help the body do better what it already does; diuretics, which take out extra fluids, work that way. Some medicines stop the body from doing what it should not do; some asthma medicines work that way. Doctors know what medicines to give for each sickness. The purpose of medicine is to help your body do the healing work.

The one thing medicine cannot do is heal your attitude. You can be cured of an illness but remain angry, selfish, and bitter. Or you might not be cured and yet be thankful and peaceful, trusting God to do what's best. It is important to place your hope and trust in God no matter how sick you may be. And remember, you can choose your attitude. That is what Job did when he had many problems, including bad health. In the end, it is God who heals people. God has given you your body and has created the ingredients used to make medicines.

ACTIVITY
What medicines have the people in your family taken in the last few months? Have each person identify a medicine, tell why he or she took it, and describe how it helped. For example: You took amoxicillin (an antibiotic) because you had a bad earache; it cleared up your ear infection.

November 6

Why do doctors and nurses give some shots that are long and some that are short?

Wounds from a friend are better than many kisses from an enemy.

Proverbs 27:6

Doctors and nurses give different kinds of shots for different reasons. If the doctor uses a long needle, it is because he or she needs to get the medicine deep into your body so it can do its work. Doctors are trained to know what kind of shots to give. It's a matter of using the treatment that fits what the patient needs. God gives doctors the wisdom and the training they need to treat their patients with skill.

Of course, doctors don't know everything, but God does. You can ask him to give your doctor wisdom and to help him or her to do an even better job. One of the big ways that God shows his care for you is by giving you good doctors.

ACTIVITY

Get out your prayer journal again. It's time to pray for your doctors and nurses! In the left column, write the names of all your doctors. Don't forget your regular doctor (often called a pediatrician) and the nurses there, dentist, orthodontist, eye doctor, and any other doctor you may visit. Now pray for God's help as these special people do their work.

November 7

If I die when I'm a kid, will I miss out on doing fun things on earth?

I'm torn between two desires: Sometimes I want to live, and sometimes I long to go and be with Christ. That would be far better for me, but it is better for you that I live.

Philippians 1:23-24

JASON'S IMAGINATION

When a person dies, that person's life on earth ends. That's true no matter how young or old a person is when he or she dies. But do these people miss their "fun" on earth? Are they up in heaven being sad about all the fun things they didn't get to do? Not at all! Living in the presence of God is the most enjoyable thing a person can do. It is what we were created for.

Don't worry—God has a wonderful plan for your life here on earth. Enjoy the life God has given you. You won't be sorry you went to heaven when the time comes for you to go!

ACTIVITY

Did you ever think of dance or creative movement as a way to praise and thank God? That's what Miriam, David, and others in the Bible did. With a couple of friends, make up a dance routine together. Think of ways to stretch and jump to communicate— through your creative movements—how much you love God.

November 8

Why did Elijah go up to heaven before dying?

As [Elijah and Elisha] were walking along and talking, suddenly a chariot of fire appeared, drawn by horses of fire. It drove between them, separating them, and Elijah was carried by a whirlwind into heaven. 2 Kings 2:11

Elijah was a famous prophet who had spent most of his life telling others about God. He is one of only two people mentioned in the Bible who didn't die before going to heaven. Instead, God took them. (Enoch is the other one—see Genesis 5:21-24.) Elijah's departure took place in a whirlwind. The whirlwind and fire didn't kill Elijah or burn him. Instead, the chariot and horses separated Elijah from his good friend and student, Elisha. Then the whirlwind carried Elijah to heaven. This showed that God approved of Elijah and that Elijah was a good man who loved God. When God took Elijah to heaven, it was just the right time, not early. We don't know how old Elijah was when God took him—he may have been an old man.

God is all-powerful—more powerful than death or anything else. He also is all-wise—more wise than anyone about the right timing for the events in Elijah's life and in your life.

ACTIVITY

Make a cartoon strip of the story of Elijah being taken up to heaven. Divide your paper into several squares and tell the story, complete with the chariot of fire and the whirlwind.

November 9

Do you pray in heaven or just talk to God face-to-face?

Now we see things imperfectly as in a poor mirror, but then we will see everything with perfect clarity. All that I know now is partial and incomplete, but then I will know everything completely, just as God knows me now.

1 Corinthians 13:12

W̲e will be able to talk to God face-to-face. (Moses talked with God face-to-face on earth, but that was unusual.) Remember, God wants to be our friend. Right now we are separated a little, and we have to pray to talk to God.

Your relationship with God will be made perfect in heaven. Finally, you will be able to go right up to God and talk to him, just as you have always wanted to do. In heaven, you will see God just as he is. Won't that be amazing?

ACTIVITY

Make a piece of artwork that you can't see clearly for a while—but then something beautiful shines through. You'll need to work on a table covered with newspapers, and get permission from your parents. On a large, plain white index card or piece of light cardboard, draw heavy bands of color with several different crayons. Cover the whole card. Now paint over the crayon with a mixture that is half black poster paint and half India ink. Let it dry completely. With an unbent paper clip, scrape a picture or design into the paint. This will reveal a beautiful design. Your picture can remind you that you will see everything clearly someday in heaven.

How can we think of something good to pray about if we've had a bad day?

Always give thanks for everything to God the Father in the name of our Lord Jesus Christ.

Ephesians 5:20

E ven when we have had a terrible day, we have good things to pray about. For example, we can thank God for being good, for being in control, and for caring about us. We can tell God how upset we are about our bad day. Then we can ask him to help us with our bad situation. Also, we can tell God that we trust him to help us. We can say that we are glad he is with us.

God knows when you have had a bad day. He has been right there with you through it all. Praying and praising God is a good way to take your mind off your troubles.

ACTIVITY

The very next time you have a bad day, try this: At bedtime, kneel next to your bed. Tell God that the day was hard for you, but then ask him to remind you of three things you can be thankful for. He might help you think about a nice sunset, your favorite food, a phone conversation with your grandparents, or something good that happened to someone in your family. God wants to know how you felt about the bad things, but he also likes to hear that you're thankful for the good things he does for you.

November 11

Why do countries have armies, navies, and air forces?

The authorities are sent by God to help you. But if you are doing something wrong, of course you should be afraid, for you will be punished. The authorities are established by God for that very purpose, to punish those who do wrong.　　　Romans 13:4

A few countries build up their armies, navies, and air forces mainly so they can attack others. But most countries have armed forces only as a defense against invasion. Their forces protect the country from other nations that might want to go to war against them.

Armed forces can also help in peacetime. The soldiers keep order inside the country during protests and riots. They also rescue and help people during natural disasters like floods and hurricanes.

It is important to honor those who have risked their lives to protect us. Most countries do this by setting aside a Memorial Day, Remembrance Day, Veterans' Day, or another holiday for remembering the people in the armed forces. Remember to show your appreciation to these authorities "sent by God to help you."

ACTIVITY

Today is the traditional Veterans' Day in the United States, a day to honor those who have fought in wars. Do you know someone who fought in a war? Perhaps a relative or an older friend at church? Ask if you can interview this person to find out about his or her war experience. The following questions could get you started: Which war did you fight in? What years did you serve, and how old were you? What part of the armed forces were you in? Why did you serve?

Why are nuclear weapons even around?

A gentle answer turns away wrath, but harsh words stir up anger.   Proverbs 15:1

N uclear weapons were invented during World War II. The United States government hired scientists to build a bomb so powerful that the Japanese would have to surrender. We have had these terrible weapons ever since. Because nuclear weapons can kill thousands of people at once, people all over the world have been working to get rid of them. They feel that we will only destroy ourselves if we use them. Others know that these weapons make their country powerful, so they work to keep the ones they have, or they make new ones.

God commands us to be kind, to forgive, and to return cruelty with kindness. God's way is best. He wants us to overlook offenses and go on with life instead of looking for ways to hurt others.

ACTIVITY

Think about the different rooms of your home. Where do you seem to have the most arguments? At the kitchen table? Pounding on the bathroom door to make your sister hurry up? In your bedroom after your mom asks you to clean it up? Write out Proverbs 15:1 neatly on an index card. Draw a wavy border around the words to remind you about a "gentle answer." Display the card in the room where you have the most arguments.

 **November 13**

Why does God let wars happen?

What is causing the quarrels and fights among you? Isn't it the whole army of evil desires at war within you? You want what you don't have, so you scheme and kill to get it. You are jealous for what others have, and you can't possess it, so you fight and quarrel to take it away from them. And yet the reason you don't have what you want is that you don't ask God for it.   James 4:1-2

W ars are a result of sin in the world. Because people aren't perfect, sometimes they get angry and fight. When leaders of countries do this, wars start. Wars are like fights between people—only much, much bigger. If all people followed God's instructions for living, there would be no wars. God doesn't want people to fight and kill each other. But if we ignore God and break his rules, we suffer. God could stop all wars and fights in the world, but he wants human beings to choose to trust him, to listen to him, to obey him, and to live in peace with each other.

Think of the little "wars" in your home or at your school. How do they usually start? What could you do to bring peace instead of fighting?

ACTIVITY

Look at a globe with an adult. (If you don't have a globe at home, you can find one at most libraries.) Have the adult point out the places in the world where wars are being fought right now. Think about the people in those countries, especially the children. Pray for peace in those places.

 318

Why did people used to have so many kids?

God blessed them and told them, "Multiply and fill the earth and subdue it. Be masters over the fish and birds and all the animals."

Genesis 1:28

One reason is that before modern medicine, more children died young (from disease and other problems) than die today. Parents could not be sure that their children would live. Another reason families of the past had a lot of children is that they needed many family members to help with the family work—around the house, on the farm, and so forth. Also, people long ago did not have modern medicine, which some couples use today to prevent pregnancy.

Some families still have a lot of children. But it is not as common as it used to be. God loves families of all shapes and sizes. He loves your family just as it is.

ACTIVITY

Get a long piece of paper and make a timeline of your family. The left edge of the paper is the earliest time, and the right edge is today. Include your grandparents (or even great-grandparents) and other relatives. Ask a grown-up to help you figure out when your relatives from long ago were born, when some special things happened to them, and when they died. Then make Play-Doh figures of your family, and thank God for each person.

November 15

Does God get angry when I spend my money foolishly?

Do not bring sorrow to God's Holy Spirit by the way you live. Remember, he is the one who has identified you as his own, guaranteeing that you will be saved on the day of redemption.

Ephesians 4:30

Does God rant and rave if we spend our money foolishly? No. But he does want us to be wise, and he's sad when we are foolish. He has given us a lot of good teaching about money in the Bible. We can also learn from the example of wise people, both today and throughout history.

Think of it this way: God is your biggest fan. More than anyone else, he wants you to win. That's why he cares about how you take care of your money. If you keep wasting it and ignoring wise advice from everybody all the time, of course he will be sad because things won't go well for you.

ACTIVITY

If you have access to a computer, check out the Money Matters for Kids website (at mmforkids.org). You'll find lots of fun, interesting money-related things on this site. If you don't have a computer at home, go onto the Internet on a computer at your public library.

Why can't I have all the things I want?

[Jesus] said, "Beware! Don't be greedy for what you don't have. Real life is not measured by how much we own." Luke 12:15

There are at least three reasons. First, you don't ask God for them. Two, you ask God for them but you want them only for yourself, so he says no. Three, they cost too much or are bad for you, so your parents say no. God wants you to love him, help others, give to his work, and be content. Money gets in the way of all that. You can't spend all day every day shopping and also love God, help others, give to his work, and be content. Sooner or later you have to stop being selfish.

You don't need all the things you want anyway. And think about this: If you got everything you wanted, what would you do with all that stuff? Remember: God loves you, knows what you need, and will take care of you.

ACTIVITY

Look up the word *greed* in a dictionary. What does it mean? Write down a definition in your own words, and then use it in a sentence. God thinks being greedy is very bad. We know this because Jesus spoke strongly against it.

November 17

How fast is technology changing?

People should eat and drink and enjoy the fruits of their labor, for these are gifts from God.   Ecclesiastes 3:13

"NEW COMPUTERS" & DAY-OLD COMPUTERS SOLD HERE

Technology is changing very fast. Just think of some of the things that people use every day:

- Television was invented in 1927.
- Penicillin was discovered in 1928.
- The microwave oven was invented in 1947.
- Cellular phones were invented in 1947 but didn't become popular with the public until the 1980s and 1990s.
- The minicomputer, which was invented in 1960, led to personal computers in the 1970s.
- The VCR was invented in 1969.
- The first browser for accessing what would become known as the World Wide Web was released in 1991.

These recent inventions have become very important to us. And right now, as you are reading this, people are inventing new machines, medicines, appliances, and computers. They are making technological discoveries that may be even more helpful than those we have now. People can do this because of the creativity God gave us. God has put you in a very exciting time and place to grow up!

ACTIVITY

Ask your mom and dad about other inventions that have become part of everyday life since they were kids. Ask them about household items, transportation, and medicine. (Be sure they don't forget about Velcro!) Thank God for the knowledge he has given scientists and other inventors.

322

How do people think of things like the Hubble telescope?

You made us only a little lower than God, and you crowned us with glory and honor. Psalm 8:5

People who invent marvelous instruments like the Hubble telescope are very talented and intelligent. God gave them the brains and ability to think of such things. God let them learn and develop the skills to make them. They read, investigated, learned, and studied hard for a long time. The skills and knowledge that those people use to create such amazing tools come from God, and those people have used their skills and knowledge well.

A beautiful part of human nature is to be able to create and invent things that are useful. It is a part of God's image in us. It is a part of God's image in you.

ACTIVITY
When inventors and designers are creating a new product, machine, or other invention, they often make clay models. What would you like to invent—a new kind of car or boat? an amazing appliance? a handy tool? a jazzy toy? Take some modeling clay and put some shape to your ideas. Who knows? Maybe someday you'll design the rest of it!

Why do people have to speak different languages?

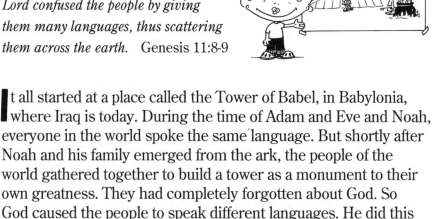

The Lord scattered them all over the earth; and that ended the building of the city. That is why the city was called Babel, because it was there that the Lord confused the people by giving them many languages, thus scattering them across the earth.   Genesis 11:8-9

It all started at a place called the Tower of Babel, in Babylonia, where Iraq is today. During the time of Adam and Eve and Noah, everyone in the world spoke the same language. But shortly after Noah and his family emerged from the ark, the people of the world gathered together to build a tower as a monument to their own greatness. They had completely forgotten about God. So God caused the people to speak different languages. He did this to confuse the people so they wouldn't finish building the tower. Groups of people who spoke the same language settled in different areas all over the world.

Ever since then, people have spoken different languages. But all people started out being able to communicate clearly. So look at what you have in common with different ethnic groups rather than looking at what is different. God is your heavenly Father . . . and theirs.

ACTIVITY

Languages came about because of people's disobedience, but languages are very interesting. Make a list of all the languages that are spoken in your country. Which ones are especially common in your state or area? What words do you know in other languages? Can you learn to say "Jesus loves you" in another language?

November 20

How do I become even closer to God than I am now?

Draw close to God, and God will draw close to you.   James 4:8

Walk closer to God!
stilts $10.00

Think of God as someone who wants to be your very close friend. For that to happen, you will need to spend time together. You can do that by reading God's Word, the Bible. Also, you can talk with God about your fears and hopes. Thank him for loving you. Tell him that you are sorry for disobeying him, and ask him to help you get closer to him and do what he says. You also can ask him to help other people.

Another way to get closer to God is through worship. That's why churches have worship services. With other Christians you can sing praises to God, pray, and learn from God's Word. You don't get closer to God just by doing a few "Christian" things, but by seeking a real friendship with him.

ACTIVITY
Remember that God will draw closer to you if you draw closer to him. This means seeking him. Tell God you want to get to know him better. Ask him to draw you closer to himself. Then, ask a parent or another adult Christian friend to recommend some chapters to read from the Bible that will help you know God better. Perhaps they can tell you their favorite psalms. Learn a praise song that you can sing every day also.

November 21

Why do we have to learn geography and history?

MOM! HOW COME THERE'S NO 'YOU ARE HERE' SIGN ON THIS GLOBE?

All these events happened to them as examples for us. They were written down to warn us, who live at the time when this age is drawing to a close.
1 Corinthians 10:11

Geography helps you learn about the world—about your own country as well as other countries and their citizens. One day you might be able to visit some of the countries that you have studied. Wouldn't *that* be exciting! History is also an important subject. When we read about mistakes people made in the past, we can learn not to repeat the same mistakes.

You are part of God's world. He wants to teach you about his world—both now and long ago. So let him.

ACTIVITY

Doing a craft from another country is one way to learn about that part of the world. The Huichol Indians of northwest Mexico are famous for yarn paintings, which they make by pressing yarn into beeswax warmed by the sun. You can make a yarn picture on cardboard with glue instead of beeswax. Take several colors of yarn. Squeeze out white glue into a design. The Huichol use the sun, people, birds, fish, and other animals, but you can make any design you wish. Take a long piece of yarn and press it into the glue. You can use a Popsicle stick to help press the yarn in place. Fill up the cardboard with different colors of yarn, using still a different color for the background. Let the picture dry well.

One Year Book of Fun & Active Devotions for Kids

November 22

Does Jesus come into your house in heaven for a visit?

[Jesus is speaking:] "Mark my words—I will not drink wine again until the day I drink it new with you in my Father's Kingdom." Matthew 26:29

Jesus always visits those who let him in. On earth, Jesus often visited his friends Mary, Martha, and Lazarus (see John 12:1-7). In his early ministry he went to a friend's wedding (see John 2:1-11). And just before Jesus went to the cross, he told his disciples that he would eat and drink with them in heaven.

Jesus will visit all of his friends in heaven, including you. Just think—you will finally get to see him face-to-face!

ACTIVITY
Imagine what it might have been like for Mary, Martha, and Lazarus to see Jesus again in heaven. Write a script that tells what they might have said to one another. Or speak the words into a cassette tape recorder. Or act out the scene on a videotape.

November 23

Why did God send the Jews to Babylon?

King Nebuchadnezzar took ten thousand captives from Jerusalem, including all the princes and the best of the soldiers, craftsmen, and smiths. So only the poorest people were left in the land.   2 Kings 24:14

The people of Judah (the Jews) turned away from God, worshiped idols, and mistreated the poor. So God allowed a wicked nation, Babylon, and a wicked king, Nebuchadnezzar, to capture their cities and take many of the people to Babylon. When the Babylonians conquered a nation, they often took the best young people to Babylon and trained them in Babylonian ways. That's what happened to the Jewish people, who had to spend seventy years in Babylon. God had sent Jeremiah and other prophets to warn the people, but they didn't listen.

God wants to warn you about bad things, too. His warnings are for your good. When you ignore them again and again, you end up being hurt, just like the people of Judah were hurt.

ACTIVITY

God sent the Jews to Babylon so that they would learn the importance of obeying him. But what happened after that? Did the Jews stay in Babylon? Are they still there? On a piece of paper, number from one to four. Then look up the following verses in the Bible to figure out where the Jews went: 2 Kings 24:14-16; Isaiah 14:1; Ezra 1:3; Luke 2:4-7.

When you finish your Time Line, you will know where many Jews live now—and where Jesus was born.

328

November 24

How does God feel when we pray?

The Lord hates the sacrifice of the wicked, but he delights in the prayers of the upright.

Proverbs 15:8

God is very happy when we pray. The Bible makes it clear that God is glad to hear from us and rejoices over us. He loves us and wants us to love him. So God is delighted when we come before him, just as a loving father is happy when his children come to him. The father welcomes his children with open arms and listens carefully to everything they say because he loves them so much.

You can make your heavenly Father happy by praying to him every day with an open heart. When you pray, think of him smiling at you.

ACTIVITY

Make a collage by cutting out words and pictures and colors that come to your mind when you think of happiness. Paste these onto a piece of poster board or construction paper. Label your collage: God is happy when I pray! Then let God know how happy you are that prayer makes him happy.

November 25

Can Christians hear God talking to them?

Long ago God spoke many times and in many ways to our ancestors through the prophets. But now in these final days, he has spoken to us through his Son. God promised everything to the Son as an inheritance, and through the Son he made the universe and everything in it.

Hebrews 1:1-2

In Bible times, some people heard God's voice. Today, the main way that God speaks to us is through the Bible. That's why it's called "God's Word"—the Bible is God's message. God may also speak to us through people and circumstances and in other ways. The Bible itself tells us about people hearing from God through dreams, like Joseph and Peter. God even communicated to one man (Balaam) through his donkey!

If you ever wonder whether or not God is speaking to you through a person or a situation, remember that God will never tell us to do something that goes against what he says in the Bible. You can always ask him to make clear to you what it is he wants you to do, for God is with you all the time.

ACTIVITY

You probably learned the song "Jesus Loves Me" when you were very young. But it's not just a song for preschoolers. Read through the words, like a poem. Remember that all people—even grown-ups—are "little ones" compared to God. Thank God that he speaks to us through the Bible about Jesus' love for us.

Jesus loves me, this I know; for the Bible tells me so.
Little ones to him belong; they are weak but he is strong.
Yes, Jesus loves me. Yes, Jesus loves me.
Yes, Jesus loves me. The Bible tells me so.

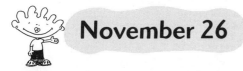

Why do we have to give thanks for things we don't like?

No matter what happens, always be thankful, for this is God's will for you who belong to Christ Jesus.
1 Thessalonians 5:18

DON'T FORGET TO THANK GOD FOR THAT ADORABLE OUTFIT AUNTIE GERTRUDE GOT FOR YOU.

God tells us to be thankful "no matter what happens." This means thanking him in all circumstances, not for everything that happens. When something bad happens, we should thank God for being there with us through those bad times. This helps us remember that God is in control, still loves us, and has a plan for us no matter what happens. We do not have to thank God for bad events. If a pet or a relative dies, for example, it's OK to cry about it.

Some of the things you do not like may actually be good for you. Sometimes God has a plan that you cannot see. If you trust in God's goodness, you'll be able to thank him in all things.

ACTIVITY
Write the letters for the word *THANKS* down the left side of a piece of paper. After each letter, write something that begins with that letter for which you can thank God. For example, for *T* you could write "Time" or "Toys" and after *H* you could write "Holidays" or "Heaven." Put one item after each letter. Then add another item for each one. See if, eventually, you can get five for each letter. Then thank God for giving you so much and for always being with you.

Why do we have to thank God at every meal when he already knows we're thankful?

Whatever you do or say, let it be as a representative of the Lord Jesus, all the while giving thanks through him to God the Father.

Colossians 3:17

DITTO FROM THE PRAYER I PRAYED AT BREAKFAST.

JASON'S LUNCH

Thanking God for food is a good habit to form because it reminds us to be thankful for all that God gives us. Sometimes we think we are thankful when we really aren't. Pausing to say thank you helps us renew our thankfulness. If we just sit down and eat without thanking God every time we eat, we can easily and quickly forget to be thankful. We can forget that our food came from God.

Praying before we eat is also a nice thing to do. After all, God is a person. You should say thank you to God because God, your friend, has done something kind for you. Don't you like it when your friends say thank you to you?

ACTIVITY

In your family, do you take turns giving thanks before meals? Or does your mom or dad always pray? At your next family dinner, try something new to call attention to being thankful. Make your table grace like a circle prayer, with each person thanking God for something different. Include all the foods you will be eating, the dishes and silverware, and the people around your table to share it with.

November 28

Why do we call it "saying grace"?

Let us come boldly to the throne of our gracious God. There we will receive his mercy, and we will find grace to help us when we need it. Hebrews 4:16

LET'S SAY GRACE.

GRACE.

The word *grace* means "thanks to God." It can also be used to mean "I ask for God's favor." The apostle Paul used the word *grace* to close some of his letters, such as Galatians, 1 Timothy, and Philemon. When we pray before meals, we are thanking God for the food and asking for his blessing on that time of eating. So this prayer is called "grace."

Praying before meals is a way of showing our dependence on God. It can be a strong reminder that all we have comes from God. This is an important part of prayer—thanking God for life and everything else he gives to us.

ACTIVITY

Start a "grace collection." Many people have traditional table graces or prayers that their families have said and shared for years. Some graces are common to certain areas of the world or to a particular church group. In a small spiral-bound notebook, write down the blessings different people say before meals. Ask your parents, grandparents, friends, and people in your church for contributions. Your family may want to use some of these prayers from time to time.

November 29

Can we ask God to give us whatever we want for Christmas?

God said to Solomon, "Because your greatest desire is to help your people, and you did not ask for personal wealth and honor or the death of your enemies or even a long life, but rather you asked for wisdom and knowledge to properly govern my people, I will certainly give you the wisdom and knowledge you requested. And I will also give you riches, wealth, and honor!" 2 Chronicles 1:11-12

It is all right to ask God for fun things. But God may not give us something because it is not good for us. Or he may have another reason for not letting us have something.

The Bible warns us not to be selfish. God promised to give Solomon whatever he asked for. Solomon decided to ask for wisdom. God was very pleased with this. He said Solomon made the right choice because he did not ask for great wealth or power. Then God rewarded Solomon for his selflessness by making him rich and powerful.

Try to ask for things that help others. God wants you to be selfless and to trust him to meet your needs. He will deliver!

ACTIVITY

Christmas is coming in a few weeks, so perhaps you've been thinking about making a Christmas list. Why don't you start a different kind of Christmas list today? Write down the names of your family, relatives, and friends. Be sure to pray for them every day, and ask God to help you think of Christmas gifts to give them—both presents and extra-nice things you could do for them in the next few weeks.

What are morals?

Don't you know that those who do wrong will have no share in the Kingdom of God? Don't fool yourselves. 1 Corinthians 6:9

Morals are standards for right and wrong living. A person's morals are the rules that he or she follows for doing one thing and not another. People live by many different moral rules—what they think is best or fair or right. But only God, who created everyone, can tell us what is right for all people everywhere all the time.

God has only one set of moral rules that he wants you to follow. If you live by God's moral standards, you will not steal because that's one of God's standards. The reason stealing is wrong is because it goes against who God is and how he made life to work. It also causes hurt. It's not wrong just because *you* think it's the wrong thing to do. As you grow up, God will make his rules clear to you because he loves you that much.

ACTIVITY
Flip through some newspapers and magazines. Look for photos or drawings of people who help others obey rules and laws. (Hint: Such people would include parents, principals, teachers, police officers, umpires, and referees.)

December 1

Did people in the Bible have Christmas?

Jesus was born in the town of Bethlehem in Judea, during the reign of King Herod.

Matthew 2:1

No, because Christmas is a celebration of the birth of Christ. Many years after Jesus was born, Christians decided to celebrate his birth. They chose December 25 as the day to observe it. December 25 is probably not the exact day Jesus was born, but that's not important.

What is important is that you remember that Christmas is a special time to celebrate the birth of Jesus, our Savior. It's not just a time to get presents, vacation days from school, and a lot of cookies and candy. When you think about your gift list of toys you want, be sure to think also about God's special gift of his Son Jesus—a gift for you and for everyone!

ACTIVITY

Choose a simple song—like "Mary Had a Little Lamb," "Row, Row, Row Your Boat," or "The Wheels on the Bus." Change the words to tell about Jesus' birthday. Later, teach the song to your family.

Or you can have a dinner-table talk about Christmas traditions with your family. What things do you do every year? Which decorations have special stories behind them? Decide together to have at least two evenings between now and Christmas Day to sing carols.

Will God give children toys if they ask him for them?

We can be confident that he will listen to us whenever we ask him for anything in line with his will.
1 John 5:14

God cares for you, and you can talk to him about anything. Yes, you can ask him for toys, but you shouldn't focus on getting things. Some people think God is there to give them toys and other things they want. But God doesn't just hand out stuff to people. His purpose is to make people become like Jesus, his Son.

God really cares about us, and he knows what we need. Although toys seem important sometimes, there are other things that we need more. God also doesn't want us to get our happiness from toys, but from him and from other people. Make it a habit to ask God to give you everything you need and to thank him for all his good gifts.

ACTIVITY
Make a list of about fifty items that God has given you. Include people on this list, as well as food, clothes, and housing. Don't forget his special gifts of the Bible, church, and other spiritual resources. Oh, and it's OK to put toys on the list, too. Keep the list near this book, and add to it when you think of new things. This will help you remember to thank God.

December 3

If God gives us everything we ask for, then how come we don't have everything?

And even when you do ask, you don't get it because your whole motive is wrong—you want only what will give you pleasure.

James 4:3

God doesn't give us everything we ask for. He gives us everything we need at the time when we need it. Sometimes we ask God to give us things that could hurt us. This is like when a baby wants to play in the fire. A good parent wouldn't say, "Oh, let the baby play in the fire. See how happy it makes her!" Instead, the parent would do everything to keep the baby away from the fire.

God knows what can hurt us, so he doesn't give us those things because he loves us. God wants to give us what is good for us. What things have you asked God to give you? Thank him for his loving protection.

ACTIVITY
Ask a parent to tell you an example of when God answered his or her prayer. Then ask for an example of when God said no and later your parent realized that it was good that God had said no. You might have fun going around the table at dinner time and naming silly things you *won't* ask God to give you because you know it wouldn't be right to ask.

How come Zacharias couldn't talk until his son was born?

When he finally did come out, he couldn't speak to them. Then they realized from his gestures that he must have seen a vision in the Temple sanctuary. Luke 1:22

Zacharias was a priest who served in the temple. One day he entered an area of the temple where only the priest could go. There the angel Gabriel appeared to him and announced that Zacharias's wife Elizabeth would have a son. Zacharias doubted the angel's promise. Because of Zacharias's unbelief, God made him unable to speak until the birth of the baby. This was a sign to the people that Zacharias had met with God. When his son was born, Zacharias wrote, "He shall be called John," the name Gabriel had said to give his son. Then Zacharias was able to talk again. The baby grew up to be John the Baptist.

Zacharias had many months to think about God's message and the importance of words. What would your life be like if you couldn't talk? Thank God for the gift of speech.

ACTIVITY

Play "Charades" with your family or friends. Act out a book title, TV show, movie, or song. (If you don't know the symbols for these categories, a grown-up or older brother or sister can probably tell you.) It's fun but sometimes frustrating, isn't it? How hard is it not to say something when the other people don't understand what you're trying to act out?

December 5

Is it OK to lie, knowing you will tell the truth later?

Just as damaging as a mad man shooting a lethal weapon is someone who lies to a friend and then says, "I was only joking."

Proverbs 26:18-19

One of the most common excuses for lying is, "I was going to tell the truth later." That may sound all right, but usually it is just another lie. This often happens when people are joking around. They make up a story to make their listeners laugh. It's OK to joke and to kid around, but it's not OK to lie.

Be careful not to make an excuse for lying by saying, "It was just a joke," or "I was going to tell the truth later." If you do, after a while people won't know when you're telling the truth and when you're not, and they could stop trusting you. Next to our friendship with God, the second most important part of living is our relationship with other people. And one of the most important parts of good relationships is trust. No joke is that important.

ACTIVITY

Have you ever heard the story "The Boy Who Cried Wolf"? That boy sure learned the danger of lying. Try to find his story, either in a storybook at home or at the library. If you can't find it, ask an adult to tell you the story. Then make up a modern version that could take place in your neighborhood.

December 6

Why do people do wrong when they know that it's wrong?

When Adam sinned, sin entered the entire human race. Adam's sin brought death, so death spread to everyone, for everyone sinned.

Romans 5:12

When God created the first man and woman, Adam and Eve, the world was perfect, with no sin, evil, or wrongdoing. But when Adam and Eve disobeyed God, sin entered the world. Ever since then everyone has been born with a sinful nature. This means that people find it natural or easy to do what is wrong

Do you sometimes do what you know is wrong and will hurt someone? You might be afraid to do the right thing. You might feel pressured by your friends. You might have a bad habit. It's easy to make the wrong choices, isn't it? You still have the same choice today as Adam and Eve had. You can trust God and follow his way or do things your own way, the wrong way. Your heavenly Father wants to help you make the right choices—let him!

ACTIVITY

Take a square piece of yellow construction paper. You're going to make a road sign for today! Make a right-turn sign by drawing a thick black arrow that curves to the right. Then draw a cross at the right so that the arrow points to it. Let the road sign remind you to make good choices in life, "right turns" that lead to Jesus, who died on a cross for your sins.

Why did John the Baptist live in the desert?

In those days John the Baptist began preaching in the Judean wilderness. His message was, "Turn from your sins and turn to God, because the Kingdom of Heaven is near."

Matthew 3:1-2

John the Baptist was a prophet who gave God's messages to people. John was also Jesus' cousin, and they were about the same age. God had given John the important job of preparing the way for Jesus. John wanted to preach away from where people were living, so everyone had to go out to hear him. Living in the desert also kept him from having arguments with religious leaders who didn't like what he was saying. And by living in the desert, John showed that he was serious about his message and that a person's relationship with God is more important than having a comfortable life.

John the Baptist is one of the most interesting and important people in the Gospel books. But he knew that Jesus was the really important one. You can learn from John's life and example how pointing people to Jesus is what really counts.

ACTIVITY

Read more about John the Baptist in Luke 3:1-18. When you finish, read one more verse, Mark 1:6, to find out just how strange John the Baptist was. Offer to make your family a "John the Baptist" meal. For each person, pour some honey into the bottom of a bowl. Then throw in some dry cereal. Delicious—a desert man's delight!

December 8

Why did the Holy Spirit come down on Jesus like a dove?

The Holy Spirit descended on him in the form of a dove. And a voice from heaven said, "You are my beloved Son, and I am fully pleased with you."   Luke 3:22

When Jesus was thirty years old, John the Baptist baptized him. As Jesus was praying, the Holy Spirit came down on him in the form of a dove. The Holy Spirit is a spirit and doesn't have a body, so he took a form that people could see. A dove was a great form to take because when people saw doves, they thought of peace and purity—that's exactly what the Holy Spirit brings to people.

After Jesus left the earth, he sent the Holy Spirit to live here in his place. But now, instead of taking a special form, the Holy Spirit can live inside you. He does that when you trust in Christ as Savior.

ACTIVITY

Do you know the song that begins, "On the wings of a snow-white dove"? If no one in your family knows it, perhaps your church has a hymnal or songbook that includes the music. Check out other songs under the topic "God, the Holy Spirit," and read the words to remind you of the Holy Spirit's coming to Jesus and to us.

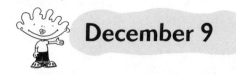

Is it OK to listen to bad music groups if you only listen to the music?

*Whatever you eat or drink or
whatever you do, you must do
all for the glory of God.*
1 Corinthians 10:31

Trying to listen to bad songs without hearing the words would be like trying to watch a video with your eyes closed. It can't be done. Even if you aren't concentrating on the words, you still hear them, and they affect your thoughts. Also, imagine what others would think of you if they saw and heard you listening to music that is bad. They probably would wonder what kind of a Christian you were. Also, buying and listening to music supports the musicians who perform it, and you don't want to support the bad groups.

Of course, not all music is bad. Many songs are fun to listen to, and they have good words. Fill your mind with what is good— do everything to the glory of God. Trust that the things God approves are the best for you—and fun. He loves you!

ACTIVITY
Ask your parents, minister, or Sunday school teacher for suggestions about good contemporary Christian singers. Go to a store to listen to some of them if you don't have any of their CDs or cassettes. Put one on your Christmas or birthday-present list.

If I see someone who is poor, do I have to give that person money?

[God is speaking:] "There will always be some among you who are poor. That is why I am commanding you to share your resources freely with the poor and with other Israelites in need."

Deuteronomy 15:11

There are a lot of poor people in the world. Obviously, we can't give money to every poor person. If we did that, we would run out of money very soon and be poor ourselves. But we can and should help poor people. We can help people in the neighborhood by working around their homes and giving them food. We can give money to our churches and Christian organizations to help poor people in our community and around the world. We can give our time at a local mission.

God wants you to be loving and kind to people. He wants you to show his love to widows, prisoners, the poor, and the hungry. When you help poor people, you are acting like Christ. Besides, God has promised to bless those who give to the poor. If you help poor people, you can be sure that God sees, notices, and will take care of you.

ACTIVITY

Talk with your parents about how your family can help poor people. Here are some ideas to get you started: (1) Set aside some of your allowance money to give to your church or a Christian organization to help poor people in your community and around the world. (2) Give time at a local mission. (3) Pray for poor people.

December 11

Is it OK for Mom and Dad to lie to me about my Christmas presents?

Most of all, dear brothers and sisters, never take an oath, by heaven or earth or anything else. Just say a simple yes or no, so that you will not sin and be condemned for it. James 5:12

God wants us always to be truthful. But that doesn't mean that we have to answer every question that people ask us. Nor does it mean that we have to tell them everything we know. Let's say you ask your parents, "What did you get me for Christmas?" or "Did you get me a bike for Christmas?" They might say something like: "I'm not going to tell you because I want you to be surprised."

Be careful not to make excuses for lying. Don't lie and then make up a reason for doing it. When it comes to giving gifts, there are ways to surprise people and make them feel special without lying to them. Giving good surprises is a special way to show God's love.

ACTIVITY

Think of someone who needs a special surprise gift. Perhaps a grandparent, a neighbor, someone who is sick or lonely, someone at church, or a friend. Make a present for that person and surprise him or her with it. It might be a Christmas ornament, a plate of decorated cookies, or a framed index card that says: "You are special to God and to me."

One Year Book of Fun & Active Devotions for Kids

December 12

Is it wrong to stop telling my friends about Jesus even when they won't listen?

[Jesus is speaking:] "Don't hide your light under a basket! Instead, put it on a stand and let it shine for all. In the same way, let your good deeds shine out for all to see, so that everyone will praise your heavenly Father."   Matthew 5:15-16

It is good that you want to tell your friends about Jesus, but it is also good to respect them as people. Sometimes your friends won't seem interested. And sometimes they may tell you that they don't want to talk about it anymore. When that happens, respect their wishes.

This doesn't mean that they won't learn about Jesus from you. You can always tell what God is doing in your life. And, most important, you can live like a Christian. Your friends will see Jesus in you. The good news about Jesus will reach them someday, somehow. And you will have played a part in that!

ACTIVITY

Make a candleholder to represent the light Jesus brought into the world. Take a short, clear glass jar and soak off the label. From an old Christmas card, cut out a picture that will fit on the side of the jar. Cover the back of the picture with glue, and glue it on the jar. Put a couple of rubber bands around the jar to hold the picture in place until the glue dries. Then use a paintbrush to cover the outside of the jar and the picture with glue. Sprinkle salt over it to make the jar sparkle. Tie curling ribbon around the rim of the jar and curl the ends. Put a small candle inside.

December 13

Why are some people rich?

Riches and honor come from you alone, for you rule over everything. Power and might are in your hand, and it is at your discretion that people are made great and given strength.

1 Chronicles 29:12

Polite, young handsome boy seeks rich parents to pay his allowance

People become rich for different reasons. Some people are rich because they were born into rich families. Others become rich by working hard, saving, and investing wisely. A few get their money as gifts or by winning contests. Some people get their money illegally—they cheat others and commit crimes. Also, some people who seem rich have lots of nice things but no money. They're so far in debt that they may never get out.

Remember that "rich" and "poor" are just labels. Many people who live in poor countries would say that everyone in North America is rich. They would say you are rich. Why? Because compared to them, you are. You have a lot more than they have.

You are truly rich only when you are content with what you have. If you have enough for your needs and enough to give, and if you're glad just to love and serve God, you'll be the richest person in town.

ACTIVITY

Watch the movie *It's a Wonderful Life.* There's a lot in the movie about being rich and being poor. Who are the rich people? How did they make a lot of money? How does the main character, George Bailey, become rich at the end? What does his brother say about him?

December 14

Why do some people find a subject hard, and others find it easy?

God gave [Daniel, Shadrach, Meshach, and Abednego] an unusual aptitude for learning the literature and science of the time. And God gave Daniel special ability in understanding the meanings of visions and dreams.

Daniel 1:17

Some people do better in math. Others do better in reading and writing. Still others do better because they work harder than most students. They listen in class, ask questions, and do their homework. Some people may learn a subject right away because God gave them the ability to do so.

God could have made each person's mind the same, but he didn't. Each mind is unique. People are good at different things. Isn't that great?

ACTIVITY

Look at photos of your friends and yourself, thinking about what each kid is good at doing. What's special about each friend and about you? Thank God for different subjects and different things you and your friends enjoy learning.

December 15

How do you get permission to go to heaven?

*[Jesus is speaking:] "God so loved
the world that he gave his only
Son, so that everyone who believes
in him will not perish but have
eternal life."* John 3:16

Only people who trust in Jesus go to heaven. We can place
our trust in Jesus by telling God that:

- We are sorry for our sins—for disobeying him and living only
  for ourselves.
- We believe that Jesus, his only Son, came to earth and died
  on the cross to take the punishment for our sin, and that he
  rose from the dead.
- We want his Holy Spirit to live inside us and guide us.

The Bible says that whoever does this becomes a new person,
a child of God. And all of God's children go to be with him in
heaven when they die. You, too, can become a child of God.
These promises are meant for you!

ACTIVITY
John 3:16 is one of the most important verses in the Bible. Learn
it by heart. If you have already memorized it, teach it to a younger
brother, sister, or friend. If you wish, print the words on poster
board, using pictures for some of the words, such as a heart for
loved, a globe for *world,* a picture of Jesus for *Son* and for *him.*
Add a photo of yourself and pictures of people of all ages and
races for *everyone.* Hang your poster up on a bedroom wall.

What do we need to pray for?

[Jesus] said, "This is how you should pray: Father, may your name be honored. May your Kingdom come soon. Give us our food day by day. And forgive us our sins—just as we forgive those who have sinned against us. And don't let us yield to temptation."   Luke 11:2-4

DEAR GOD, I DON'T FEEL LIKE PRAYING FOR ALL THE USUAL STUFF TODAY. CAN WE JUST TALK?

We need to pray for three things: (1) our needs, (2) the needs of others, and (3) God's will to be done. For example, we need food, clothing, and shelter. So do other people. And we need help resisting temptation, doing good, and becoming what God wants us to be. So do other people.

Jesus also taught us to pray, "May your will be done here on earth, just as it is in heaven" (Matthew 6:10). This is one reason the Bible tells us to pray for leaders. We can affect world events by praying for leaders to do God's will.

You don't have to limit your prayers to needs. You can pray for anything that is important to you. God is your friend. He wants to hear from you. So if something concerns you, it concerns him. What concerns do you want to take to him right now?

ACTIVITY
On a piece of notebook paper, draw lines to make three columns. Label the first column "My needs," the second column "The needs of others," and the third column "Places where God's will needs to be done." Then write things in each column. Ask your family for ideas to add to the second and third columns, and use the chart to guide your prayers this week.

December 17

Why did Jesus pray?

*While Jesus was here on earth,
he offered prayers and pleadings,
with a loud cry and tears, to the
one who could deliver him out of
death. And God heard his prayers
because of his reverence for God.*
Hebrews 5:7

J esus is the God-man. That is, he is totally God and totally man. Because Jesus lived on earth as a man, he had human needs. It made sense for God the Son to pray to God the Father just as it makes sense for us to pray. Jesus depended on his Father in heaven for all his needs. He also loved his Father and enjoyed being with him, so he wanted to spend time talking with him. Jesus was perfect. He did everything that God wanted. God told his people to pray, so Jesus obeyed his Father and prayed.

In other words, Jesus prayed for the same reasons you do—he needed God, he loved God, and he wanted to please God. If Jesus needed to pray, just think how much *we* need to pray! Be like Jesus and make prayer an important part of your daily schedule.

ACTIVITY

The New Testament of the Bible gives us a look at some of the times Jesus prayed. Here are some verses that tell about a few of these times. Read the verses and make a list of things we know Jesus prayed about.

- Matthew 14:13-21 (especially verse 19)
- Luke 6:12-16
- Luke 22:39-46
- John 17:1, 9-24

December 18

Would God make a friendly ghost like Casper?

[Jesus is speaking:] "When the Father sends the Counselor as my representative—and by the Counselor I mean the Holy Spirit—he will teach you everything and will remind you of everything I myself have told you." John 14:26

No. Some people in the Bible thought they saw a ghost (a spirit) at times. When the disciples saw Jesus walking on the water they thought he was a ghost (Matthew 14:25-27). When an angel freed Peter from prison and his friend Rhoda saw him, the people she told thought she had seen "his angel" (Acts 12:13-15). When Jesus appeared to his disciples after he rose from the dead, he said he was not a ghost (Luke 24:37-41). And some Bible translations use the word *ghost* to mean "spirit." But the Bible does not teach that spirits fly around visiting people. Many people have believed that after death, people come back as ghosts. But that's not taught in the Bible at all.

The person that some people call the Holy Ghost is the Holy Spirit. When Jesus, God the Son, left the earth, he sent God the Holy Spirit to live within us. He is the one who comforts, guides, and protects you.

ACTIVITY
Look up the Bible references in the above answer and act out one of those stories. Be sure to show the emotions that the people must have felt when they lived through those actual events.

December 19

Why do people die?

The Lord God gave him this warning: "You may freely eat any fruit in the garden except fruit from the tree of the knowledge of good and evil. If you eat of its fruit, you will surely die."

Genesis 2:16-17

People die because of sin. When God created the first people, they weren't supposed to die. But when they disobeyed God, sin and death entered the world. From that point on, every person born has been born a sinner in a sinful world. With sin came death, so plants, animals, and people started to die. Every person has to die. But people can live eternally in heaven with God if they trust in Christ and ask God to forgive their sins. In heaven, there isn't any more sickness or pain or dying.

One of the great things about heaven is that you will see your Christian relatives from long ago. And think about all the famous Bible people who will be there. What a family reunion that will be!

ACTIVITY

Ask your mom for an apple. Take out one of the seeds and look at it carefully. Can you believe that something this tiny, when buried in the ground, can grow into something as big and beautiful as an apple tree? Amazing, isn't it? But it's true. It's just as true that when people die, God can raise them up again with perfect, new bodies (1 Corinthians 15:42-44). Now that's something to look forward to.

December 20

Will I go to heaven when I die?

[Jesus is speaking:] "This is the will of God, that I should not lose even one of all those he has given me, but that I should raise them to eternal life at the last day. For it is my Father's will that all who see his Son and believe in him should have eternal life—that I should raise them at the last day."

John 6:39-40

Every person who trusts in Jesus gets to go to heaven. That's God's promise. And nothing can take away God's promise of heaven.

If you have asked Jesus to take away your sins, then God's promise of heaven applies to you. When you die as a Christian, you go straight to live with God—you don't need to be afraid of death.

ACTIVITY
Sunflower seeds look rather dead, don't they? But they have much life in them and grow quickly. Put some dirt in a paper cup and bury a sunflower seed about halfway down. Cover it up with dirt and add a little water. Put it in a sunny window. In a few short days you'll see how God raises it up with new life.

December 21

Would it be right to keep the money if someone paid too much?

A person who gets ahead by oppressing the poor or by showering gifts on the rich will end in poverty. Proverbs 22:16

Suppose you sold something to a friend, and the friend paid you too much by mistake. You should give back the extra. That's just being honest and fair. And isn't that the way you would want to be treated? You should be truthful and honest with people—just the way you want them to be truthful and honest with you.

Also, you shouldn't cheat people by charging them too much for something. God told his people not to take advantage of each other, and he had harsh words for people who broke this rule. Some people say, "If the person doesn't notice, then it's her own fault." But that's not God's way. God wants us to look out for each other. If we are dishonest or mean, people soon find out and then won't want to be with us or do business with us. Doing things God's way is always best.

ACTIVITY
Make a watercolor sign. It's best to paint with watercolor paints on thick paper—thicker than regular drawing paper, for example. Spread some newspapers on your work surface. Paint a reminder such as "Be Honest" or "The Golden Rule is Golden." Plan ahead so all the words fit on the sign. Hang the sign (when it's dry) on your bedroom door.

December 22

Whose hand made the writing on the wall?

At that very moment they saw the fingers of a human hand writing on the plaster wall of the king's palace, near the lampstand. The king himself saw the hand as it wrote, and his face turned pale with fear.
Daniel 5:5-6

It was a miracle of God, performed to announce judgment on the king of Babylon for his pride. Belshazzar was holding a great feast. During the eating and drinking, he sent for the gold and silver cups that had been taken from the temple in Jerusalem. As Belshazzar used these cups to drink a toast to idols of wood and stone, a human hand began writing on the wall. The frightened king called for Daniel (one of God's prophets) to interpret the writing. It contained this message: The king had been evil and proud, and soon his enemies would defeat him (which they did). God used the hand and the writing to get the king's attention, and it worked! This is how the saying "the handwriting on the wall" got started.

God usually doesn't use such dramatic methods to give messages. The Bible tells us everything we need to know about believing in him and doing what he wants. Do you pay attention to God's messages? Are you thinking, not just blinking?

ACTIVITY
Cut a lemon in half and squeeze the juice into a bowl. Now dip a cotton swab into the juice and write with it on a piece of paper. After it dries, have a grown-up press the paper with a hot iron to make the words appear.

December 23

How did Daniel sleep with the lions without being afraid?

[Daniel is speaking:] "My God sent his angel to shut the lions' mouths so that they would not hurt me, for I have been found innocent in his sight. And I have not wronged you, Your Majesty."　　Daniel 6:22

Daniel was a young man when he was captured and taken to Babylon. He lived the rest of his life there, serving several kings. When he was old, the last of these kings, Darius, signed a law that no one could pray to anyone except him, the king. Because Daniel continued to pray to God, the king had to punish him by putting him into a den of lions. Daniel spent all night with the lions but wasn't hurt.

The Bible doesn't say that Daniel wasn't afraid. But it clearly shows that Daniel was willing to face the lions because he trusted in God. Daniel believed that obeying God was right, even if it meant being in danger.

Everybody is afraid sometimes. But, like Daniel, we shouldn't let our fears keep us from doing what God wants. God knows your fears, and he is able to protect you. He wants you to be confident in him, just like Daniel was.

ACTIVITY

Talk with your mom or dad about scary things that you have gone through. Find out what was scary to your parent when he or she was a child. What might make you afraid now? Think about how God helped you with past scary things, and pray for his help with the new things. He will protect you again.

Why was Jesus born in a stinky stable?

*While they were there, the time came
for her baby to be born. She gave birth
to her first child, a son. She wrapped him
snugly in strips of cloth and laid him in
a manger, because there was no room for
them in the village inn.* Luke 2:6-7

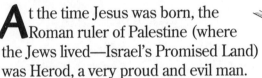

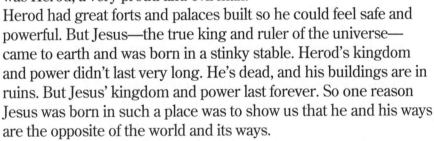

At the time Jesus was born, the
Roman ruler of Palestine (where
the Jews lived—Israel's Promised Land)
was Herod, a very proud and evil man.
Herod had great forts and palaces built so he could feel safe and
powerful. But Jesus—the true king and ruler of the universe—
came to earth and was born in a stinky stable. Herod's kingdom
and power didn't last very long. He's dead, and his buildings are in
ruins. But Jesus' kingdom and power last forever. So one reason
Jesus was born in such a place was to show us that he and his ways
are the opposite of the world and its ways.

Jesus' kingdom doesn't come by force but by God working in
each individual person, including you. Jesus' birth in a stable
where farmers and shepherds keep their animals also lets us
know that he came for all kinds of people, not just the rich and
famous.

ACTIVITY

Ask your mom or dad to take you to a zoo, a petting zoo, or a
farm sometime soon. Be sure to get there at feeding time. Smell
the smells. Listen to the noise. And remember that God became
a baby, born in a stable and placed in an animals' feed box, so he
could truly be part of our everyday world.

December 25

Why do angels light up and get bright?

Suddenly, an angel of the Lord appeared among [the shepherds], and the radiance of the Lord's glory surrounded them. They were terribly frightened.   Luke 2:9

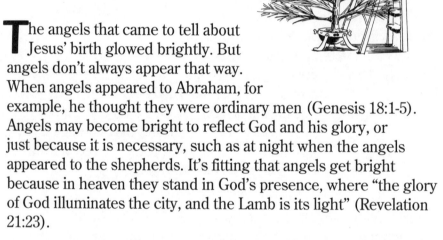

The angels that came to tell about Jesus' birth glowed brightly. But angels don't always appear that way. When angels appeared to Abraham, for example, he thought they were ordinary men (Genesis 18:1-5). Angels may become bright to reflect God and his glory, or just because it is necessary, such as at night when the angels appeared to the shepherds. It's fitting that angels get bright because in heaven they stand in God's presence, where "the glory of God illuminates the city, and the Lamb is its light" (Revelation 21:23).

Just think of how glorious and bright heaven is. Won't it be great to live there in the presence of God and his angels?

ACTIVITY

Make a cover for a flashlight and think about the ways God shows his light to us. Use a hole punch to make many holes in the top two-thirds of a piece of construction paper. Form a cylinder with the paper and slide the bottom third over the top of a flashlight. Trim the paper so that only about an inch overlaps, then tape it closed. Cut another piece of construction paper big enough to cover the open top of the cylinder. Tape it in place. Then turn on the flashlight, turn off all the lights in the room, and let the light shine around.

December 26

Did Jesus ever do anything bad when he was little?

This suffering is all part of what God has called you to. Christ, who suffered for you, is your example. Follow in his steps. He never sinned, and he never deceived anyone. He did not retaliate when he was insulted. When he suffered, he did not threaten to get even. 1 Peter 2:21-23

Jesus was born as a baby, grew up as a little boy, and became a young man. When he was a child, Jesus had to learn many things, like how to hold a cup, how to talk, and how to count. He learned from his parents and went to school to learn, too. Although Jesus was a real human being, he never did anything wrong—he never sinned—like stealing, lying, disobeying his parents, or saying bad words. Sometimes Jesus did things that others said were bad—like helping bad people and speaking out against wrong. But Jesus always did what was right—he always obeyed God.

Because Jesus was perfect, he is the perfect example for how to live. In every situation, you can ask, "What would Jesus do?"

ACTIVITY

On an index card, write the letters *WWJD*. That stands for "What Would Jesus Do?" Tuck the card into the corner of a bathroom mirror where you can see it every day. It will remind you to try to be like Jesus in all you do.

December 27

Why do some kids get huge allowances and others don't get any?

Stay away from the love of money;
be satisfied with what you have.

Hebrews 13:5

A llowances vary a lot among kids for many different reasons. Some families have lots of money and others have very little. Some parents have no money left after paying the bills, so their children get no allowance—the money just isn't there. Remember also that some parents give their children money in other ways besides allowances. They may give money for doing special work around the house. Or some parents may give their kids a large amount of money and let them buy all their own clothes.

Every family is different—different personalities and different situations. In fact, no other family is exactly like yours. Thank God for your family and make the most of it. God will always supply what you need.

ACTIVITY
Ask your parents if you can have a talk about your allowance. Write down exactly how much the allowance will be and for how long. (For example, many families increase the amount starting on the kids' birthdays.) Is it part of the deal that you'll do chores? Will there be penalties (money held back) when chores are not done? What things, such as clothes, are you expected to buy with your allowance?

Is it wrong to watch music videos?

Dear friends, let me say one more thing
as I close this letter. Fix your thoughts
on what is true and honorable and right.
Think about things that are pure and
lovely and admirable. Think about things
that are excellent and worthy of praise.

Philippians 4:8

It's not wrong to watch television, listen to the radio, watch videos, or listen to music. But God wants us to be wise about what we put into our minds. A lot of the stuff on TV shows, movies, and videos is not good. In fact, often the people on them use bad language, do bad things, and make it look as though sinning is the right thing to do. That's a lie. We know that God wants us to do what is right, not wrong.

So be very careful about what you watch and listen to. Seeing and hearing the bad videos is like eating garbage. It's bad for you, won't help you grow, and will make you sick. Instead, fill your mind with pictures, words, and thoughts that honor God.

ACTIVITY
Go on a "Good Stuff Hunt" in your home and yard. Find something good for each category in Philippians 4:8: true, honorable, right, pure, lovely, admirable, excellent, worthy of praise. Look for things like flower petals (but don't pick them without asking permission first), magazine pictures, and Bible verses. You'll find lots of things once you start looking. Put them in a collection by gluing them on a piece of construction paper. Label them with the positive words from the verse.

Why didn't an angel take Jesus off the cross?

[Jesus is speaking:] "Don't you realize that I could ask my Father for thousands of angels to protect us, and he would send them instantly? But if I did, how would the Scriptures be fulfilled that describe what must happen now?"

Matthew 26:53-54

It was God's will for Jesus to die on the cross. Jesus could have called on thousands of angels to rescue him, but he did not do that because he was dying for his people, taking the punishment for their sins. If angels had stepped in and rescued Jesus, he would not have died for us, and then we could not be forgiven. Peter, one of Jesus' disciples, tried to stop Jesus from being arrested, but Jesus told him not to do that because it was God's plan for him to die.

Just before Jesus died he cried out, "My God, my God, why have you forsaken me?" (Matthew 27:46), meaning that God had left him totally alone. No one was there to help him or comfort him, not even the angels. This was part of his suffering for our sins.

Think about it—Jesus suffered in your place. He loves you that much!

ACTIVITY

Write a letter or poem of thanks to Jesus for taking your place on the cross. Tell him that you know he could have sent angels to rescue him. If you write a poem, you may want to turn it into a song by making a tune to go with the words.

If the Bible says we'll live for eternity, why is there an end on earth?

All creation is waiting eagerly for that future day when God will reveal who his children really are. . . . All creation anticipates the day when it will join God's children in glorious freedom from death and decay. Romans 8:19, 21

The earth was not made to last forever. Things last forever only if God wants them to. God has determined that the world the way it is now will be destroyed and made new again. God will give us a new heaven and a new earth to replace the old one. The new earth will be perfect in every way, as God intended it to be.

But people *will* last forever. When Jesus returns to make the world new, he will judge every person who ever lived. Those who have received his forgiveness will be welcomed into his home, to live with him forever. And those who have refused God's forgiveness will be thrown into the lake of fire. That is why Jesus came, "so that everyone who believes in him will not perish but have eternal life" (John 3:16). This promise is for you, too!

ACTIVITY
On a clear night this week, after it's dark and the stars are out, go for a walk with a grown-up! Walk slowly around your neighborhood and try to get away from trees and streetlights if possible. Are many stars out? Try to imagine all the skies and the heavens waiting for God's new creation. We have a wonderful eternity to look forward to!

When will Jesus come back?

[Jesus is speaking:] "No one knows the day or the hour when these things will happen, not even the angels in heaven or the Son himself. Only the Father knows."

Matthew 24:36

No one knows when Jesus will come back, not even the angels. God has chosen not to tell us. God has also warned us not to listen to people who say that they know when Jesus will return. When Christ returns, he will come "like a thief in the night" (1 Thessalonians 5:2), when no one is expecting it. People who say they know the date of Christ's return are wrong or are just trying to trick you.

You don't have to worry about missing Christ when he returns. When Jesus comes back, it will be obvious to everyone. All people all over the world will know. Trust in Jesus and don't worry about God's schedule.

ACTIVITY

Draw a line down a piece of paper to make two columns. Label one column "Things People Decide" and the other column "Things Only God Can Control." The first column should include stuff like attending events at school, whether to do your chores, and what to serve for dinner. But look at the second column! God controls really big things: the weather, the day you were born, sending Jesus to earth. (You can think of many more items for both columns.) Be glad that God is so powerful!

INDEX OF SCRIPTURE VERSES

Matthew 17:20 (July 29)
Matthew 18:8 (June 2)
Matthew 18:10 (Feb. 2, Aug. 14)
Matthew 19:5 (June 1)
Matthew 19:8-9 (Apr. 21)
Matthew 19:14 (Mar. 5)
Matthew 20:16 (Nov. 3)
Matthew 23:5, 7 (Oct. 6)
Matthew 24:36 (July 16, Dec. 31)
Matthew 24:36, 42 (Mar. 12)
Matthew 25:29 (Oct. 9)
Matthew 26:14-15 (Apr. 12)
Matthew 26:29 (Nov. 22)
Matthew 26:53-54 (Dec. 29)
Matthew 28:2 (June 18)
Matthew 28:19 (Aug. 4)
Matthew 28:19-20 (Feb. 26)
Matthew 28:20 (June 24)

Mark 4:33 (May 31)
Mark 9:2 (July 12)
Mark 10:34 (Apr. 15)
Mark 13:31-32 (Sept. 30)
Mark 13:32-33 (Apr. 17)
Mark 15:16-19 (Apr. 13)
Mark 15:29-30 (Apr. 14)

Luke 1:22 (Dec. 4)
Luke 2:6-7 (Dec. 24)
Luke 2:9 (Dec. 25)
Luke 3:22 (Dec. 8)
Luke 6:22 (Oct. 22)
Luke 6:31 (June 13)
Luke 6:35-36 (Oct. 23)
Luke 8:1-3 (Oct. 18)
Luke 10:18 (Jan. 11)
Luke 11:2-4 (Dec. 16)
Luke 12:15 (Nov. 16)
Luke 14:28 (June 29)
Luke 16:10 (Mar. 27, Sept. 11)
Luke 18:13-14 (Aug. 19)
Luke 22:41-42 (Feb. 21)

John 1:1-3 (Mar. 24, Aug. 3)
John 3:16 (Dec. 15)
John 4:9 (Aug. 24)

John 4:11 (Feb. 9)
John 4:21-24 (Jan. 26)
John 6:12 (Apr. 23)
John 6:28-29 (Apr. 2)
John 6:39-40 (Dec. 20)
John 8:44 (Mar. 16, Aug. 6)
John 9:2-3 (July 24)
John 11:35 (Jan. 18)
John 14:1 (Mar. 21)
John 14:2 (May 22)
John 14:2-3 (Jan. 24, Apr. 16,
    May 1, Oct. 14)
John 14:6 (May 2)
John 14:26 (Dec. 18)
John 15:11 (Sept. 25)
John 15:14-15 (Oct. 15)
John 16:7 (May 5)
John 16:24 (Feb. 1)
John 17:11 (Sept. 16)

Acts 5:29 (July 3)
Acts 6:3 (Oct. 2)
Acts 9:3-4 (June 22)
Acts 10:28 (Aug. 25)
Acts 12:6-7 (May 18)
Acts 14:15 (Oct. 21)
Acts 24:16 (Mar. 10)

Romans 1:21-23 (May 28)
Romans 1:28 (Oct. 17)
Romans 2:11 (Jan. 16)
Romans 3:23 (May 9)
Romans 3:23-25 (Apr. 18)
Romans 3:27-28 (June 27)
Romans 5:6 (Feb. 8)
Romans 5:8 (Apr. 1)
Romans 5:12 (Dec. 6)
Romans 5:19 (Feb. 17)
Romans 7:15-17 (Jan. 22)
Romans 8:19, 21 (Dec. 30)
Romans 10:9-10 (May 11)
Romans 12:3-5 (Jan. 27)
Romans 12:4-5 (May 16)
Romans 12:10 (Jan. 4)
Romans 12:16 (Sept. 14)
Romans 12:17 (Jan. 17)

Romans 12:20 (May 15)
Romans 13:3 (Oct. 25)
Romans 13:4 (Nov. 11)
Romans 14:10 (Oct. 5)

1 Corinthians 6:9 (Sept. 17,
    Nov. 30)
1 Corinthians 6:19 (Feb. 23,
    June 15)
1 Corinthians 9:14 (July 14)
1 Corinthians 10:11 (Jan. 28,
    Apr. 9, Nov. 21)
1 Corinthians 10:31 (May 8,
    Dec. 9)
1 Corinthians 13:4 (Mar. 6)
1 Corinthians 13:12 (Nov. 9)
1 Corinthians 15:43 (Jan. 7)

2 Corinthians 5:1 (Apr. 24)
2 Corinthians 7:8-10 (Mar. 28)
2 Corinthians 8:3 (July 13)
2 Corinthians 9:7 (May 17)
2 Corinthians 9:11 (Aug. 13)

Galatians 1:10 (Oct. 7)
Galatians 3:23 (Mar. 17)
Galatians 3:28 (Apr. 26)

Ephesians 1:4-5 (Feb. 16)
Ephesians 2:8-9 (Aug. 31)
Ephesians 2:10 (July 21)
Ephesians 4:15 (Feb. 19, Aug. 2)
Ephesians 4:17-19 (Aug. 30)
Ephesians 4:25 (Mar. 15, June 30)
Ephesians 4:26 (Mar. 29)
Ephesians 4:28 (Aug. 9)
Ephesians 4:29 (Mar. 3)
Ephesians 4:30 (July 22, Nov. 15)
Ephesians 5:4 (Mar. 20)
Ephesians 5:11 (Apr. 27)
Ephesians 5:18 (Mar. 1)
Ephesians 5:20 (Nov. 10)
Ephesians 6:1 (June 3)
Ephesians 6:1-3 (Feb. 11)
Ephesians 6:11-12 (Aug. 7)
Ephesians 6:18 (Apr. 25)

Philippians 1:21-23 (July 15)
Philippians 1:23-24 (Nov. 7)
Philippians 2:3 (July 30)
Philippians 2:14 (April 6)
Philippians 4:6-7 (Mar. 18)
Philippians 4:8 (Dec. 28)
Philippians 4:19 (Aug. 22)

Colossians 3:11 (Jan. 15)
Colossians 3:17 (Nov. 27)
Colossians 3:20-21 (Sept. 9)
Colossians 3:23-24 (Sept. 4)

1 Thessalonians 3:10 (Sept. 27)
1 Thessalonians 5:17 (Sept. 26)
1 Thessalonians 5:18 (Nov. 26)
1 Thessalonians 5:22 (Jan. 10)

2 Thessalonians 1:9 (May 19)
2 Thessalonians 3:16 (July 8)

1 Timothy 2:1 (Feb. 18)
1 Timothy 4:8 (Jan. 19)
1 Timothy 6:10 (Oct. 19)
1 Timothy 4:12 (Feb. 12)

2 Timothy 1:3 (Aug. 27)
2 Timothy 2:15 (Feb. 27, Sept. 5)
2 Timothy 3:16-17 (Mar. 9)

Titus 3:2 (Aug. 20)

Hebrews 1:1-2 (Nov. 25)
Hebrews 4:12 (Jan. 12)
Hebrews 4:16 (Nov. 28)
Hebrews 5:7 (Dec. 17)
Hebrews 10:12 (Sept. 2)
Hebrews 10:25 (Mar. 31)
Hebrews 11:3 (July 19)
Hebrews 13:2 (Oct. 24)
Hebrews 13:5 (Dec. 27)

James 1:5 (Feb. 24, July 17)
James 4:1 (Oct. 1)
James 4:1-2 (May 29, Nov. 13)
James 4:3 (Apr. 8, Dec. 3)

James 4:8 (Nov. 20)
James 5:12 (Dec. 11)
James 5:14-15 (Nov. 4)
James 5:16 (Apr. 19)

1 Peter 2:13 (July 4)
1 Peter 2:21-23 (Dec. 26)
1 Peter 3:9 (Oct. 29)
1 Peter 3:14-15 (June 19)
1 Peter 5:7 (Sept. 7)
1 Peter 5:8 (June 20)

1 John 1:9 (June 5, July 23)
1 John 3:12 (Sept. 3)
1 John 5:14 (Dec. 2)

Jude 1:6 (June 21)

Revelation 4:1-3 (Jan. 25)
Revelation 21:1 (June 25)
Revelation 21:3 (June 7)
Revelation 22:12 (Aug. 28)
Revelation 22:18 (May 26)